ROBERT CAPA
American
photographer
(1913-1954) and
co-founder of
the Magnum Agency.
On 6 June he landed
on Omaha Beach
with the first assault
wave. His work bore
witness to the human
distress and the
horrors of war.
He was later killed
during the conflict
in Indo-China.

American troops embarking at Weymouth, England, the day before D-Day.

American soldiers pinned down by enemy fire on Omaha Beach.

General view of Omaha Beach
(Saint-Laurent-sur-Mer).

GIs from the 4th US Infantry Division,
part of the Third Army, advancing
through the Normandy *Bocage*.

American troops being welcomed by the inhabitants of Notre-Dame-de-Cenilly.

THE BATTLE OF NORMANDY OPEN AIR MUSEUM

The Battle of Normandy Open Air Museum represents a permanent place
of memory and culture and presents a new view of the events that took place in 1944.
By emphasizing the importance of the historical heritage
of the area and presenting it in the form of coherant and chronological routes
which integrates the major sites memorials and museums,
it offers an examplary historic experience.

ACKNOWLEDGEMENTS

We would particularly like to thank the General Council of the Calvados,
of the Channel, and the Orne, the regional Council of Normandy,
the association for sites and museum of the Battle of Normandy Open Air Museum,
the Touristic and Leisures Studies Society (SETEL) and also:
Jean-Pierre Bénamou, O.B.E.,
curator of the Memorial Museum of the Battle of Normandy of Bayeux;
Gilles Henry,
genealogist and writer, author of many biographies and «literary walks»;
Anthony Kemp, M.A., Ph.D.,
one time lecturer in History at Southampton University.
Several books on the Battle of Normandy published.

GALLIMARD GUIDES
DIRECTION:
Pierre Marchand
Assisted by: Hedwige Pasquet, Philippe Rossat

EDITORIAL DIRECTOR:
Nicole Jusserand

ART DIRECTOR:
Élisabeth Cohat

RESPONSIBLE EDITORS:
ARCHITECTURE: Bruno Lenormand
NATURE: Frédéric Bony
PICTURES: Éric Guillemot, Patrick Léger
UPDATING: Anne-Josyanne Magniant

FABRICATION:
Catherine Bourrabier

PARTNERSHIP:
Philippe Rossat

MARKETING:
Jean-Paul Lacombe

PRESS AND PROMOTION:
Manuèle Destors

BATTLE OF NORMANDY:
FRENCH EDITION: Patrick Jézéquel,
Philippe Gallois, Édouard de Pazzis
ENGLISH EDITION: Antoine Prévost,
Nicole Hinrichs
PRACTICAL INFORMATION: Odile George,
Vincent Brochier, Stéphane Grand-Chavin
DESIGN: Olivier Brunot,
Béatrice Desrousseaux, Carole Gaborit,
Isabelle Roller
PICTURE RESEARCH: Isabelle Volf-de Latour
UPDATING: Samuel Péron,
assisted by: France Bourboulon

KEYS TO UNDERSTANDING:
HISTORY: Anthony Kemp
NATURE: René Chaboud, Anthony Kemp,
Franck Levoy
MILITARY ART, ARCHITECTURE: Anthony Kemp
CINEMA AND DOCUMENTARIES: François Joseph
GRAPHICS AND PAINTINGS: Odile George

ITINERARIES:
Jean-Pierre Bénamou (Overlord, the assault),
Gilles Henry (Caen), Anthony Kemp

TRANSLATOR:
Anthony Kemp

ILLUSTRATIONS:
John Batchelor, Philippe Biard,
Jean-Philippe Chabot, Di Marco,
Donald Grant, Jean-Marie Guillou,
Gilbert Houbre, Olivier Hubert,
Maurice Pommier, Jame's Prunier,
Michel Sinier, Jean Torton, Nicolas Wintz

MAPS:
Stéphane Girel
COLOURING:
Christine Adam, Caroline Picard,
Catherine Totems

PUBLICITY AGENT FOR GALLIMARD GUIDES
Bilobas Média
86, boulevard Malesherbes 75008 Paris
Tél. 01 53 96 06 81
Fax 01 53 96 06 82
e-mail : bilobas@pratique.fr

FRANCE

BATTLE OF
NORMANDY

GALLIMARD GUIDES

CONTENTS
BACKGROUND INFORMATION

ITINERARIES
OPEN-AIR MUSEUM OF THE BATTLE OF NORMANDY

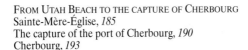

▲ THE BATTLE OF NORMANDY
EIGHT HISTORIC ROUTES

CHERBOURG

QUINÉVILLE

GÉNÉRAL
LAWTON COLLINS

SAINTE-MÈRE-
ÉGLISE •

POINTE DU HOC

SAINTE-MARIE-DU-MONT

6 June

6 June

COLL
SUR

MONT CASTRE

BAYEU

30 June

GÉNÉRAL
GEORGE S. PATTON

SAINT-LÔ

GÉNÉRAL
SIR BERNARD LA
MONTGOMERY

• COUTANCES

1 August

• GRANVILLE

VIRE

1 August

GÉNÉRAL
OMAR BRADLEY

AVRANCHES

• MONT
SAINT-MICHEL

• PONTAUBAULT

MORTAIN

1. Overlord, the assault
2. D-Day, the shock
3. Objective, a harbour
4. The confrontation
5. Cobra, the breakthrough
6. The counter-attack
7. The encirclement
8. The final phase

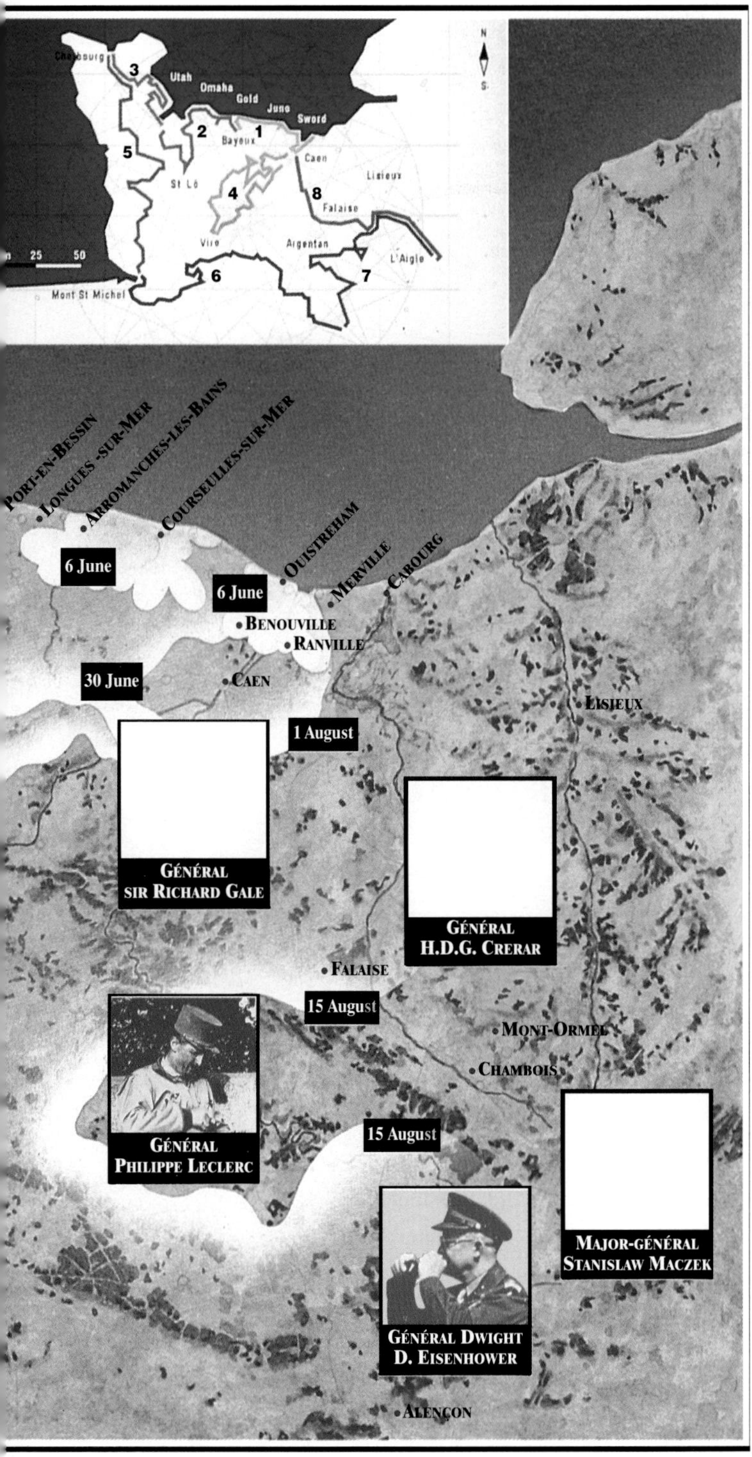

N
S
3
Utah
Omaha
Gold
Juno
Sword
2
1
Bayeux
5
Caen
Lisieux
8
St Lô
4
Falaise
Vire
Argentan
L'Aigle
25
50
6
7
Mont St Michel
Port-en-Bessin
Longues-sur-Mer
Arromanches-les-Bains
Courseulles-sur-Mer
6 June
Ouistreham
6 June
Merville
Cabourg
Benouville
Ranville
30 June
Caen
Lisieux
1 August
Général sir Richard Gale
Général H.D.G. Crerar
Falaise
15 August
Mont-Ormel
Chambois
Général Philippe Leclerc
15 August
Major-général Stanislaw Maczek
Général Dwight D. Eisenhower
Alençon

HOW TO USE THIS GUIDE

The symbols at the top of each page refer to the different parts of the guide.
■ NATURAL ENVIRONMENT
● KEYS TO UNDERSTANDING
▲ ITINERARIES

The colour of the seagulls correspond to the eight itineraries proposed by the Battle of Normandy Open-Air Museum, which are posted in French along the Norman routes.
The French names are indicated under the title of each itinerary.
◆ PRACTICAL INFORMATION

The symbols alongside a title or within the text itself provide cross-references to a theme or place dealt with elsewhere in the guide.

The itinerary map indicates the main points of interest along the way and is intended to help you find your bearings on a road map.

▲ COBRA, THE BREAKTHROUGH
CHERBOURG TO AVRANCHES

BRADLEY;
IN THE COTENTIN BOCAGE

The territory covered in this itinerary illustrates several important phases of the Battle of Normandy as far as the American forces were concerned. First, the westward move to cut off the Cotentin peninsula in mid-June, second the southward attacks towards Saint-Lô and Périers through the Bocage. Last, the events of Operation Cobra ● 276 that finally broke through the crust of the German defence and initiated

The mini-map locates the particular itinerary within the wider area covered by the guide.

At the beginning of each itinerary, the suggested means of transport to be used and the time it will take to cover the area are indicated:
🚗 By car
🕐 Duration
The indicated mileage does not take into account suggested detours.

The graphic maps relate the historical events of the area covered by the itinerary.

♥ The heart symbol signifies that a particular site has been singled out by the publishers for its special historical or cultural interest
* The asterix indicates a site not signposted by the Battle of Normandy Open-Air Museum.

HISTORY

● Chronology

The heads of State at the signing of the Treaty of Versailles in 1919.

Adolf Hitler, the charismatic orator.

THE ORIGINS OF THE WAR

THE MAGINOT LINE
Built between 1927 and 1936 on the French north-east frontier. It was outflanked by the Germans who marched through Belgium.

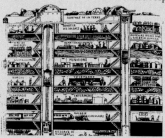

THE HUMILIATION OF GERMANY. The sanctions imposed by the Treaty of Versailles on defeated Germany in 1919 provoked widespread resentment among all sections of the population.
THE NAZI RISE TO POWER. Ten years after the failure of the Munich putsch in 1923, Hitler won an election and became Chancellor of the Reich. Abrogating the restrictions imposed by the Versailles Treaty, he rebuilt his army and marched it into the Rhineland in 1936. France responded by strengthening the Maginot Line fortifications along her frontier with Germany.
THE MUNICH AGREEMENT. In March 1938 Hitler annexed Austria. In September he marched into the Sudetenland after the Czech people had been abandoned by the allied powers who had signed the Munich agreement with Hitler. Great-Britain began a crash programme of rearmament. In March 1939, Hitler annexed the remaining Czech provinces of Bohemia and Moravia.

THE START OF THE CONFLICT

1939
1 September. Invasion of Poland.
3 September. Britain and France declare war on Germany.

1940
10 May. German offensive in the West.
20 May. Churchill becomes Prime Minister.
June. The remaining British troops are evacuated from France.

Chamberlain, Churchill and Daladier at the Allied Conference in Paris in February 1940.

THE NAZI-SOVIET PACT. In order to have their hands free in the West, the Germans signed a non-aggression pact with the Soviet Union on 23 August. On 1 September the Nazis invaded Poland.
THE DECLARATION OF WAR. In return, Britain and France declared war on Germany on 3 September, which did not deter Hitler and Stalin from carving up Poland between themselves with impunity.
"THE PHONEY WAR".
The French sat in the Maginot Line and British forces dug in along the Belgian border. For eight months both sides stared at each other.
THE ARMISTICE.
At dawn on 10 May, German armies invaded the Netherlands, Belgium and France.

BOMBERS.
German
Messerschmitt
and an American-
made Douglas.

Crossing the Meuse at Sedan, Guderian's tanks
roared towards the coast separating the bulk of
the French forces from the British
Expeditionary Force. As a result, the latter,
together with a considerable number of French troops, were
compelled to retreat to Dunkirk from where they were
evacuated to England. An armistice was signed by the
government of Marshal Pétain, while General de Gaulle
escaped to London where he launched his appeal to continue
the fight and founded the Free-French organisation.

*18 June. General
de Gaulle's appeal.
22 June. France
signed the armistice
with Germany.
23 June. First British
commando raid
on Boulogne.*

THE ALLIED REACTION

THE BATTLE OF BRITAIN. Prior to an invasion of Britain,
Hitler had to ensure the destruction of the Royal Air Force.
Throughout the summer the Battle of Britain was fought in
the clear skies. But, at the point of victory the Luftwaffe
stopped bombing the airfields and instead concentrated on
the systematic destruction of towns and cities. To carry the
war onto the continent, Churchill decided to create the
Special Operations Executive (SOE). Its mission was "to set
Europe ablaze" by arming and training resistance movements
in the occupied countries. To carry out raids, a new command
known as Combined Operations was set up.

THE WAR IN THE MEDITERRANEAN.
In North Africa, Italian troops fighting to
defend their colonies suffered a severe
defeat at the hands of the British Eighth
Army. To strengthen his ally, Hitler sent
the Afrikakorps which was commanded
by General Rommel. In Greece the
British suffered a crushing defeat. Having
removed a large part of the army from
North Africa for the campaign in the
Balkans, the British were pushed to retreat
by Rommel in June.

THE CAMPAIGN IN RUSSIA. Renouncing
his idea of invading Britain, Hitler turned
to the conquest of the Soviet Union. His
offensive into the Balkans, however, forced a postponement
until June, and the onset of an early winter brought his armies
to a halt at the gates of Moscow and Leningrad.

*13 August. Start of
the Battle of Britain.
27 September. Axis
Pact between
Germany, Italy
and Japan.*

*1941
8 March. Lend-lease
Act passed.
6 April. Hitler invades
Yugoslavia and Greece.*

*Rommel and one
of his officers.*

*22 June. Germany
declares war on the
USSR.
19 August. Signature
of the Atlantic Charter.*

THE ENTRY OF THE USA INTO THE WAR

LEND-LEASE. Although officially neutral
until December 1942, the United States
supported Britain in the
struggle against the Nazis.
The Lend-lease Act
enabled certain
armaments to be
"loaned" to
Britain.

**PEARL HARBOR AND THE
PACIFIC WAR.** At the end of
1941 Japan entered the fray and
launched an unprovoked air attack

*7 December. Japanese
aircraft attacked Pearl
Harbor.*

Dieppe beach after the defeat of the Canadian landing in 1942.

The Russians at Stalingrad (1942).

An Afrikakorps soldier observing enemy positions.

1942
7 February. The British victory at Bir Hakeim.
19 August. Anglo-Canadian raid on Dieppe.

on the Pearl Harbor naval base which caused the United States to declare war. The Japanese also eliminated the weak garrisons of the British colonies in the Far East. Japanese expansion was stopped at the Battle of Midway on 4 June 1942.

THE EARLY INVASION PLANS. The Americans, pressed by Stalin to open a second front to relieve German pressure on his armies, decided to produce a plan for an invasion of France in 1942. This operation was codenamed Sledgehammer. The British General Staff vetoed the idea as being unrealistic as the menace of German submarines in the Atlantic still remained very effective. That same year a large-scale raid, codenamed Jubilee, was carried out. In August a strong Canadian force, supported by two Commando units, attempted to operate a landing at the port of Dieppe, but suffered a severe defeat. On the Eastern front the Red Army retreated but managed to inflict heavy losses on the Germans. In North Africa Rommel advanced as far as the Egyptian frontier. After having sacked most of the generals in the Middle East, Churchill insisted that the British regain the initiative. To do so he decided to appoint a little-known general, Bernard Law Montgomery, to command the Eighth Army.

THE TURNING-POINT OF THE WAR

8 November.
Operation Torch.
13 November. Start of the Battle of El Alamein.
Mid-November. German Sixth Army surrounded in Stalingrad.

Hitler and Mussolini on an inspection of the Eastern front.

THE BATTLE OF EL ALAMEIN.
In November the success of the Allied landings in Algeria and Morocco, Operation Torch, altered the balance of power in the Mediterranean. At the same time, Montgomery inflicted a heavy defeat on the troops of Rommel's Afrikakorps at El Alamein.

The Canadian General Simonds in Sicily on 10 July 1943.

THE EASTERN FRONT. In the USSR, Marshal Zhukov surrounded the Sixth German Army at Stalingrad, forcing it to surrender at the end of January 1943. In spite of a brilliant counter-attack led by Field Marshal von Manstein, the Germans were forced onto the defensive. After the German defeat at Kursk in July, the greatest tank battle in history, the Red Army attacked all along the Eastern front.

THE DEFEAT OF ITALY. The remaining German forces in North Africa surrendered on 12 March 1943. On 10 July the Allies invaded Sicily. In September, Mussolini's Fascist government collapsed. His successor, Marshal Badoglio, entered into negotiations with the Allies who had gained a foothold on the mainland after crossing the Straits of Messina and landing at Salerno.

PREPARATIONS FOR D-DAY

THE CASABLANCA CONFERENCE. At the beginning of 1943 the Allied heads of state gathered at Casablanca to plan a large-scale landing of troops in France in the summer of 1944, a decision that was confirmed at the Teheran Conference. To carry this out a special staff was formed: COSSAC (*Chief of Staff to the Supreme Allied Commander*). In the Atlantic the submarine menace had diminished, opening the way for convoys of American arms. In the Pacific the war had turned in the favour of the Allies where the Americans were recapturing one by one the islands occupied by the Japanese.

THE ARRIVAL OF MONTGOMERY. At the beginning of 1944 the assembly of men and material gathered momentum. By that time the entire south coast of England was transformed into a vast military camp. Montgomery, appointed to command the ground forces, arrived in England. At the same time, his old adversary, Rommel, took command of German forces along the Normandy coast.

THE OTHER FRONTS. In Italy, an Allied landing took place at Anzio near Rome, which nearly became a disaster with the arrival of German reinforcements. Overall, though, being paralysed by Hitler's obsession with holding onto every inch of ground, the Germans were on the defensive. In the Dodecanese, British and Greek special forces harassed the enemy garrisons on the islands, and in Yugoslavia, Tito and his partisans forced Hitler to tie down twelve divisions to contain them. In spite of the daily bombardment of its big cities and industrial capacity, Germany was still able to resist.

OPERATION OVERLORD. On 15 May the final Overlord plan was unveiled to the Allied high command, in the presence of the King and the Prime Minister. The initial assault divisions began to move down to the coast into sealed camps where the men would receive their orders. Because of poor weather conditions Eisenhower had to postpone the invasion for 24 hours, but at dawn on the morning of 6 June, the invasion fleet was in sight of the Normandy coast.

1943
January. The Casablanca Conference.
10 July. Allied landings in Sicily.
8 September. Armistice with Italy signed.
28 November. Teheran Conference.
24 December. Eisenhower appointed Supreme Allied Commander.

1944
1 January. Field Marshal Rommel appointed commander of Army Group B.
15 May. Montgomery presented the final invasion plan.
6 June. D-Day for Operation Overlord.

Roosevelt and Churchill at the Quebec Conference where they decided to mount a second landing in Provence.

Chrismas card "To Victory".

THE LIBERATION OF FRANCE

Bradley (1893-1981)

25-28 July. Operation Cobra which launched the American breakthrough.
30 July. American armour entered Avranches.
6-8 August. German counter-attack at Mortain.

CAEN, THE ANVIL. Montgomery's plan envisaged the fall of Caen on the first day, but the Germans resisted stoutly. The difficulties encountered at Omaha Beach, in the east of the Cotentin, hindered the junction of the British and American beach heads, and although taken by surprise, the Germans reacted swiftly. A few days later a violent storm wrecked one of the artificial Mulberry harbours and severely damaged the other. Cherbourg fell at the end of June but the garrison had time to demolish the harbour installations, which were not serviceable again until 14 August.

STALEMATE. With the British bogged down around Caen, the Americans were forced to battle their way south for themselves, fighting for possession of each hedgerow in the Normandy *Bocage* country, while the poor weather hindered air support. In the meantime, public opinion both in Britain and America questioned the slowness of the campaign. The final capture of Caen and Saint-Lô tipped

the scales in favour of the Allies, however, enabling the Americans to position themselves for a breakthrough from the constrictions of the *Bocage*. To divert the German armour from the American front, Montgomery decided to launch three of his own armoured divisions down a narrow corridor out of the bridgehead which was captured

Churchill, Dempsey and Montgomery.

12 August. Argentan liberated by the Americans and Alençon by the French 2nd Armoured Division.

General von Schlieben, garrison commander of Cherbourg, who surrendered on 26 June.

by the airborne troops east of the Orne. The operation known as Goodwood was brought to a halt by the enemy anti-tank guns placed along the Bourgébus Ridge.

THE BREAKTHROUGH AT AVRANCHES. A few days later than planned, on account of poor weather conditions, Bradley launched Operation Cobra. Between 25 and 28 July the Americans broke the German defence in the *Bocage* south of Saint-Lô and found themselves behind the enemy forces at last. Patton's armoured columns raced for Avranches fanning out into Brittany and towards Le Mans. At that time, the Germans attempted a weak counter-attack in the area around Mortain but were unable to contain the American penetration, thus sealing their own fate.

FINALE IN NORMANDY. By mid-August the German Seventh Army was caught in the grip of a vice between the Anglo-Canadian and American forces in the Falaise pocket. Many enemy troops were unable to escape the tightening noose. On 19 August the first of Patton's tanks crossed the Seine at Mantes-Gassicourt and the battle on Mont-Ormel sealed the Allied victory in Normandy.

THE LANDING IN PROVENCE. On 15 August an Allied Army Group consisting of an American and a French army landed on the coast of the Riviera and a month later effected a junction with the units which had landed in Normandy, greatly assisted by French resistance groups known as the "FFI" (*Forces françaises de l'intérieur*).

THE LIBERATION OF PARIS. At the head of the French Second Armoured Division, General Leclerc entered Paris on 25 August. The Committee of Liberation founded by de Gaulle formed a provisional government, supplanting the Vichy administration. The Allies did not recognize the new government until October.

THE PROGRESS IN THE LANDS. In September Belgium was freed. In mid-November it was the liberation of Metz, Mulhouse and Strasbourg. In December, however, a German counter-offensive in the Ardennes checked Allied progress and a further three months of bitter fighting ensued before the Rhine was crossed.

Crowds celebrating the liberation of Paris on 25 August 1944.

On 15 August, Allied troops landed near Sainte-Maxime in Provence.

THE END OF THE WAR

THE DEFEAT OF GERMANY. On the Eastern front after the Battle of Kursk, the Soviet armies won a series of stirring victories in a bitterly-fought campaign. On 12 April they entered Austria and finally crossed the Oder-Neisse Line. Zhukov's entry into Berlin on 22 April marked the end for the Nazi regime.

THE AMERICAN DEFENSIVE ASSAULT. Between the end of 1943 and the end of 1944, the Americans cleared the route to the Philippines and in April 1945 they gained a toehold at Okinawa on the southern tip of the Japanese home islands.

THE END IN JAPAN. In the Pacific the war still raged as the British advanced into Burma. The American commanders General MacArthur and Admiral Nimitz were convinced that the Japanese on their own territory would resist to the last man, and were unwilling to risk heavy casualties. The USSR declared war on Japan on 8 August and the allies summoned the Emperor to capitulate. The final decision to drop atomic bombs on Hiroshima and Nagasaki signified a dramatic end to the conflict.

The island of Okinawa under bombardment by the American fleet in April 1945.

1945
22 April. Zhukov entered Berlin.
8 May. The surrender of Germany.
6 August. Hiroshima.
9 August. Nagasaki.
2 September. Emperor Hirohito capitulated.

21

● D-DAY
HOUR BY HOUR

00.10. Lieutenant Poole was the first Allied soldier to touch the soil of France.

00.20. Six gliders commanded by Major Howard crash-landed near Pegasus Bridge.

01.11. Reports of the first American parachute drops reached the headquarters of the German LXXXIV Corps at Saint-Lô.

01.30. The US 101st and 82nd Airborne Divisions started dropping inland from Utah Beach.

01.50. Start of the main British parachute drop east of the Orne.

02.30. Heavy bombers started to attack the coast defences.

02.45. The Omaha Beach assault force transferred into their landing craft.

03.00. All the warships took up their planned positions.

03.25. The German naval staff located the presence of warships along the coast.

03.50. British parachutists entered the village of Ranville.

04.30. The Stars and stripes were hoisted at Sainte-Mère-Église. The Americans occupied the Saint-Marcouf islands off Utah Beach.

04.45. Two miniature submarines surfaced off the beaches where the British troops were due to land, and activated their beacons to guide in the landing craft. The Merville Battery was captured.

05.30. The Allied warships opened fire on the coast defences.

06.00. Sunrise. Medium bombers attacked the defences on Omaha and Utah Beaches.

06.30. H-Hour for Utah and Omaha Beaches.

06.40. US Rangers landed at the foot of the Pointe du Hoc.

06.52. Admiral Ramsay received the first news of the landings.

07.00. German radio broadcast the news of the landings.

07.25. H-Hour for Gold and Sword beach.

07.35. H-Hour for Juno Beach.

09.00. General Eisenhower authorized the release of a commmuniqué to the press, announcing the landings.

09.13. General Bradley, in the belief that he might have to abandon Omaha, demanded reinforcements.

09.30. The casino building at Riva-Bella cleared by Free French commandos led by Commandant Kieffer. The first small parties managed to scale the cliffs behind Omaha Beach. At the same time, Hermanville, inland from Sword Beach was liberated.

09.45. Utah Beach cleared of enemy troops.

12.00. Winston Churchill made a statement in the House of Commons.

13.00. Troops from Utah met up with airborne troops landed in the interior.

13.30. Troops landed at Omaha beach began to progress inland. Lord Lovat's commandos reached Pegasus Bridge which was then held by the parachutists.

14.30. Ranville finally cleared of enemy. 21st Panzer Division began to move towards the coast, halting at Ryes.

15.00. 12th SS Panzer began to move towards Caen.

16.00. The first British tanks entered Arromanches.

18.00. Saint-Laurent, inland from Omaha was captured.

20.00. Six light tanks of the 21st Panzerdivision reached the coast at Luc-sur-Mer between the Sword and Juno bridge-heads. In the meanwhile, the first British patrols reached Bayeux.

21.00. Gliders bringing in reinforcements for the 6th Airborne Division landed in the Orne bridge-head. Vierville, a strongpoint menacing Omaha Beach was finally cleared.

22.00. Rommel arrived back at his HQ after a few days leave in Germany. The British advance towards Caen was stopped at the Bois de Lebisay.

22.07. Sunset.

S W O R D

7.25

J U N

7.

**RESCUE
AT OMAHA BEACH**
Some GIs saved
from drowning by their
buddies. The line of cliffs
and the fortifications behind
the beach made it particularly
difficult for the Americans
to get off the beach. It took
several hours of bitter combat
before the German resistance
was finally broken.

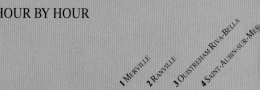

. 35

6.30

GOLD

OMAHA

etween Juno
nd Omaha, the XXX
ritish Corps attacked onto
beach that stretches for six kilometres.
he surface between Ver-sur-Mer and
rromanches is sandy, interrupted at Saint-Côme
y a cliff which was topped by a radar station. A dense
efensive system was based on sea walls flanked by casemates
72. Inland, an extensive area of inundations ran as far as
he coast road after which the ground rose towards the spires
f Bayeux Cathedral, ten kilometres to the south.

6.30

OMAH

Pointe du He

**THE BRITISH
ON SWORD BEACH**
41 Royal Marine
Commando preparing to
enter Lion-sur-Mer after
having landed on Sword.

A

c

6.30
U T A H

THE WAVES ROSE COLD AND UNFRIENDLY LIKE,
AND ALONG THE COAST OUR BURSTING BOMBS AND SHELLS THREW
UP A CRIMSON CURTAIN."

A CANADIAN PADRE

6 JUNE 1944

S H A

Eisenhower. After the attack on Pearl Harbor "Ike" was posted to the plans division at the Pentagon and in 1942 was appointed Commander of US troops in Britain. In August he was made Supreme Allied Commander for the Torch landings in North Africa. He continued to conduct the Allied war effort until May 1945, and in 1952 was elected President of the United States.

Tedder. At the beginning of the war he was attached to the Ministry of Aircraft Production and in 1942 was named as Allied Air Commander in the Mediterranean. He headed the combined air forces for the Torch landings and those in Sicily. He was Ike's assistant on D-Day. After the war he became Chief of Air Staff.

Bedell-Smith. At the time of Pearl Harbor he was a colonel in the Plans Division in Washington.. Appointed as Chief of Staff to Eisenhower he joined him in London in 1942.

GENERAL DWIGHT D. EISENHOWER
● 37, 104, ▲ 241, 245 (1890-1969)
Supreme Commander of the Allied Expeditionary Force

ADMIRAL SIR BERTRAM H. RAMSAY
● 37, 60 (1883-1945)
C-in-C Allied Naval Forces

AIR MARSHAL SIR TRAFFORD LEIGH-MALLORY
● 37 (1892-1944)
C-in-C Allied Air Forces

AIR MARSHAL SIR ARTHUR CONINGHAM
(1895-1948)
C-in-C 2nd Tactical Air Force (RAF)

GENERAL LEWIS BRERETON
(1890-1967)
C-in-C 9th US Air Force

REAR-ADMIRAL ALAN G. KIRK USN
▲ 171 (1888-1963)
Commander Western Naval Task Force

REAR-ADMIRAL SIR PHILIP L. VIAN
(1894-1968)
Commander Eastern Naval Task Force

1 AUGUST 1944

GENERAL DWIGHT D. EISENHOWER

GENERAL SIR BERNARD LAW MONTGOMERY C-in-C 21st Army Group (British)

GENERAL SIR MILES DEMPSEY
● 52, ▲ 224
C-in-C Second British Army

GENERAL HARRY D. CRERAR
▲ 251 (1888-1968)
C-in-C First Canadian Army

VIII British Corps
XXX British Corps
XII British Corps

II Canadian Corps
I British Corps

E F

AIR MARSHAL SIR ARTHUR TEDDER
● *37* (1890-1967)
Deputy Supreme Commander

**LIEUTENANT-GENERAL
WALTER BEDELL-SMITH**
● *37* (1895-1961)
Chief of Staff to Supreme Commander

GENERAL SIR BERNARD LAW MONTGOMERY
● *20, 37, 52,* ▲ *137, 248* (1887-1976)
Commander-in-Chief 21st Army Group and of Allied ground forces

GENERAL SIR MILES DEMPSEY
(1896-1969)
C-in-C Second British Army

LIEUTENANT-GENERAL OMAR BRADLEY
● *102,* ▲ *171, 182, 216* (1893-1981)
C-in-C First US Army

**MAJOR-GENERAL
GERARD BUCKNALL**
(1894-1980)
Commander XXX
British Corps
GOLD

**MAJOR-GENERAL
J. T. CROCKER**
(1899-1963)
Commander I British
Corps
GOLD AND JUNO

**MAJOR-GENERAL
LEONARD T. GEROW**
(1888-1982)
Commander V US
Corps
OMAHA

**MAJOR-GENERAL
LAWTON COLLINS**
▲ *194*
(1905-1992)
Commander VII US
Corps
UTAH

S H A E F

GENERAL OMAR BRADLEY C-in-C 12th Army Group (US)

**LIEUTENANT-GENERAL COURTNEY HICKS
HODGES**
(1887-1966)
C-in-C First US Army

GENERAL GEORGE S. PATTON
▲ *216, 220, 222* (1885-1945)
C-in-C Third US Army

VII US Corps
XIX US Corps
V US Corps
VIII US Corps

XX US Corps
XV US Corps
XII US Corps

31

● THE GERMAN COMMANDERS

6 JUNE 1944

Rundstedt He was already a general when Hitler came to power and commanded army groups for the invasions of Poland, France and Russia. Sacked in December 1941 for disagreeing with Hitler's conduct of the war, he was recalled in March 1942 and appointed Supreme Commander West. He was again sacked on 6 July 1944 for daring to suggest to Hitler that he sue for peace.

ADOLF HITLER
● *16, 38* (1889-1945)
Commander-in-Chief

FIELD MARSHAL GERD VON RUNDSTEDT
● *39* (1875-1953)
Supreme Commander West

GENERAL KARL HEINRICH VON STULPNAGEL
(1886-1944)
Commander of German occupation forces, France

ADMIRAL THEODOR KRANKE
(1893-1973)
Commander-in-Chief Naval Group W

FIELD MARSHAL ERWIN ROMMEL
● *38, 72,* ▲ *173* (1891-1944)
Commander-in-Chief Army Group B

[Fifteenth Army]

COLONEL-GENERAL FRIEDRICH DOLLMANN
● *42* (1882-1944)
Commander, Seventh Army

XXV Corps

LXXIV Corps

GENERAL ERICH MARCKS
(1897-1944)
Commander LXXXIV Corps

32

"MANY LIKE HIM [LIEUTENANT HÖLLER], VETERAN OF THE AFRIKAKORPS WHO HAD SUCCEEDED IN ESCAPING CAPTIVITY IN TUNISIA, FOUND THEMSELVES BACK IN THE RANKS OF THE 21ST PANZER DIVISION. ONE ALSO FOUND THOSE WHO HAD FOUGHT ON THE RUSSIAN FRONT OR OLD LAGS FROM CRETE."

P. CARREL

He returned to favour in September 1944 when reappointed as Supreme Commander of the western front, which was, at that stage of the war, an honorific post. **Keitel** was appointed Chief of Staff of National Defence by Field Marshal Blomberg. Hitler sacked the latter so as to proclaim himself Commander-in-Chief. Keitel retained his position in what became the OKW, the Supreme Command of the Armed Forces, but was completely dominated by his chief. Always loyal to the Fuehrer, he was tried as a major war criminal at Nuremberg and subsequently hanged.

FIELD MARSHAL WILHELM KEITEL
(1882-1946)
Chief of Staff, Armed Forces

FIELD MARSHAL HUGO SPERRLE
(1885-1953)
Commander-in-Chief Air Fleet West

JOHANNES BLASKOWITZ
(1883-1948)
Commander-in-Chief Army Group G

GENERAL LEO GEYR VON SCHWEPPENBURG
▲ *232* (1886-1964)
Commander-in-Chief
Panzer Group West

South of Loire

3rd Armoured
Division
(in reserve)

Partial Commandment

GENERAL PAUL HAUSSER
(1880-1972)
Commander Seventh Army after
Dollmann's death

2nd Panzer division
116th Panzer division
21st Panzer division

1st S.S. Panzerdivision
12th S.S. Panzerdivision
17th S.S. Panzerdivision
Panzer Lehr Division

4 infantry divisions + 1 in reserve

33

Even while those British and French troops who had escaped from the trap at Dunkirk were arriving at Dover on board a motley collection of vessels, Churchill was planning to aid the Resistance and launch commando raids on the mainland. When America came into the war, differences of opinion between the Allies about the strategy to be adopted appeared. Finally, in early 1944, Montgomery was appointed to command all ground forces for the landings in Normandy, decided at the Casablanca Conference (January 1943).

ADMIRAL LORD LOUIS MOUNTBATTEN (1900-1979)

Mountbatten, a member of the royal family, served during the 1914-18 war as a midshipman and in 1941 was a captain, in command of the aircraft carrier *Illustrious*. In October he replaced Admiral Keyes as chief of Combined Operations. Although he had to bear a portion of the blame for the disaster at Dieppe, his original ideas played a large part in the success of D-Day. It was he who encouraged the development of artificial ports ● *76*, ▲ *141* and some of the special armour used. ● *64*.

THE DIEPPE RAID (19 AUGUST 1942)

After the defeat of the raid on Dieppe mounted by a Canadian division ● *52*, ▲ *250* and supported by commandos, those who survived left behind a beach littered with the dead, burnt-out hulls of tanks and wrecked landing crafts. German propaganda had a field-day, claiming that their troops had defeated a serious attempt to launch an invasion of France.

THE COMMANDOS

When Churchill ordered the formation of commando units in the summer of 1940, many soldiers, bored with inactivity guarding the coast, rushed to volunteer. They were the sort of men with independent characters who did not necessarily like military routine and were itching to get to grips with the enemy. Among the officers one found artists, writers and even members of the aristocracy who were accustomed to hunting game.

LE REVEIL DU NORD

NE ACTION DESESPÉRÉE SUR L'ORDRE DE MOSCOU

S LES ENVIRONS DE DIEPPE,

unde tentative de débarquement
méricaine est brisée en 10 heures

> "THINGS HAVE BEEN IN A PROPER MESS (...) OWING
> TO THE AMERICAN DESIRE TO DO SOMETHING
> QUICKLY WITHOUT KNOWING WHAT
> IS POSSIBLE TO DO."
>
> ADMIRAL RAMSAY. SUMMER 1942.

THE LOFOTEN RAID (APRIL 1941)

Apart from a few pin-pricks on the coasts of France and the Channel Islands, the first large-scale raid was mounted against the Norwegian Lofoten Islands, which were attacked by 3rd and 4th Commandos. They destroyed the fish-oil factories, much prized by the Germans, sank a number of ships and reembarked having suffered only minor casualties. Such raids did wonders for troop morale at a time when, in other theatres, British troops were fated to suffer one defeat after another.

CASABLANCA

Roosevelt and Churchill met there to define a common set of aims. As a result, a staff known as COSSAC was formed to coordinate preparations for Overlord. Apart from their differences over strategy, they had to sort out the divisions among the French factions. They engineered the escape from France of General Giraud who was not, however, supported by the authorities in Algeria who remained loyal to Vichy. De Gaulle and Giraud had to wait until June to create the National Liberation Committee in which the former rapidly asserted himself.

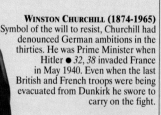

WINSTON CHURCHILL (1874-1965)

Symbol of the will to resist, Churchill had denounced German ambitions in the thirties. He was Prime Minister when Hitler ● *32, 38* invaded France in May 1940. Even when the last British and French troops were being evacuated from Dunkirk he swore to carry on the fight.

As American soldiers began to arrive on the south coast of England, large areas of land had to be cleared of inhabitants so to create vast training areas. Because of poor weather conditions, the date of the invasion, which was up to then planned for 5 June, was postponed for 24 hours. Eisenhower therefore ordered the Allied fleets supported by the air forces, to land on the French coast on the morning of 6 June.

TRAINING

Training for the invasion was carried out along the south coast of England. Using live ammunition, the assault divisions practised landing on beaches chosen for their similarity to those in Normandy. Owing to the lack of combat experience of the bulk of the US divisions, large areas of the countryside had to be converted into training areas. There they were

In the British harbours, the shortage of landing craft of all types, especially those for transporting tanks ● 62, 64, limited the number of troops that could be embarked. All over the country, garages and factories were used for building the smaller craft. But, by the beginning of April 1944, the harbours along the south coast began to fill to capacity with landing craft ready to sail for Normandy.

EXERCISE TIGER

One of the major training exercises for the landings, Exercise Tiger, carried out at the end of April, turned into a disaster. A flotilla of German E-boats based at Cherbourg ▲ 194 got in among one of the convoys and sunk two LSTs with the loss of more than 700 American soldiers. Above, a landingship tank ● 60 damaged during the incident.

taught cooperation with the Navy ● 56, 58 which would transport them, and the aircraft which would support them on D-Day.

SHAEF

Supreme Headquarters Allied Expeditionary Force. The commanders, from left to right. Bradley, Ramsay, Tedder, Eisenhower, Montgomery, Leigh-Mallory, Bedell-Smith ● *30*. During May the various headquarters moved to the south coast. Admiral Ramsay, commanding the naval forces engaged in Operation Neptune, set up in Southwick House near Portsmouth, with Eisenhower and Montgomery nearby in caravans. It was there that the postponement was decided.

Above, the commanders photographed at St. Paul's School, London. On the left a British officer briefs troops with the aid of a map.

MONTGOMERY WITH HIS STAFF
Final briefing before embarkation.

OPERATION FORTITUDE Prepared at the beginning of 1944, this was designed to persuade the Germans that the landings would be in the Pas-de-Calais. All over Kent, dummy tanks, landing craft and aeroplanes were placed to confuse German reconnaissance aircraft. Some, like the tank above, were inflatable, while others were made of plywood and canvas.

ARRIVAL OF THE GIS IN BRITAIN
A huge operation, code-named Bolero, brought more than a million young Americans across the Atlantic, most of whom had never been abroad before. Although resented by some Europeans, they were remembered for their chewing-gum, jazz music and warm friendliness.

EMBARKATION FOR NORMANDY
Two weeks before D-Day the men of the assault divisions moved into sealed camps near the embarkation points. Once inside, all contact with the outside world was suspended. Embarkation started on 1 June as interminable convoys of men and vehicles moved through towns and villages to take their places on board the ships.

THE GERMANS IN NORMANDY

Uncertain about Allied intentions, the Germans resorted to passive defence behind the Atlantic Wall. The senior officers were unable to agree on a common strategy of defense.

Von Rundstedt (left) preferred to await the enemy inland while Rommel busily reinforced the coast fortifications. The German general staff allowed themselves to be fooled by Allied deception measures and as a result the initial landings achieved total surprise.

MARK IV TANK OF THE 21ST PANZERDIVISION
The panzer divisions ▲ 230 were elite units of the Army and the SS. Although the German tanks had better guns and thicker armour than the Allies' Shermans, they were vulnerable to air attack. With total air superiority the Allies forced them to move only by night and hide by day.

GERMAN LAYING MINES
On Gold Beach alone those responsible for clearance counted 100,000 mines. ● 72.

HITLER THE AUTOCRAT
Having no confidence in his generals, Hitler ● 16, 32, from his distant headquarters in East Prussia, intervened by giving orders to formations direct. Officers had to report their positions directly to him at all times and were ordered to hold onto territory regardless of cost.

COASTAL DEFENCE The fortifications that had been built along the Normandy coast were reinforced following the arrival of Rommel in January. He calculated that building obstacles would force the Allies to land at high tide, right in front of the fortifications. In fact, the landings were carried out at low tide. To hinder the landing of gliders, tall stakes ("Rommel's asparagus") were planted in likely fields.

ERWIN ROMMEL ● 32, ▲ 173
Rommel who had fought courageously with the infantry in the Great War, was given command of a Panzerdivision in France and then of the Afrikakorps in North Africa, where he fought against Montgomery ● 31 who defeated him at El Alamein. Implicated in the plot to kill Hitler (20 July 1944) he was forced to commit suicide.

GERD VON RUNDSTEDT ● *32*
The most senior field marshal in the army, he was 69 on 6 June. Placed in command of an army group in 1940 he served on the Eastern Front. As Supreme Commander West he led a comfortable life at his HQ in the château at Saint-Germain-en-Laye. In private he referred to Hitler as the "Bohemian Corporal".

SURVEILLANCE OF THE LITTORAL
The Germans knew that there would be an invasion in the summer of 1944 but did not know where. For the soldiers the waiting period meant hours of staring out to sea. At dawn on the 6 June wave after wave of bombers dropped their loads on the coast defences before being relieved by the naval artillery massed offshore.

FOREIGN UNITS
Muslim workers from North Africa were conscripted to take part in the Org Todt for the constuction of the Atlantic Wall (Above, at La Pallice), as well as the "volunteers" from among the Russian prisoners – Cossacks, Uzbeks and Tartars – who preferred wearing German uniforms to starving in the camps. They all put up little resistance to the invaders and by 25th August, 25,000 had been taken prisoner.

THE ATLANTIC WALL
All sorts of camouflage were used to conceal the bunkers (right). The most powerful elements of the Atlantic Wall ● *72, 74, ▲ 144* were built in the Pas-de-Calais where the Germans were convinced that the landings would take place. In Normandy the defences did not prove an insurmountable obstacle for the Allies because the system did not extend in depth and the artillery was insufficient. The casemates were designed to pour flanking fire along the beaches but were inefficient against an enemy out at sea.

● THE ROLE OF THE RESISTANCE

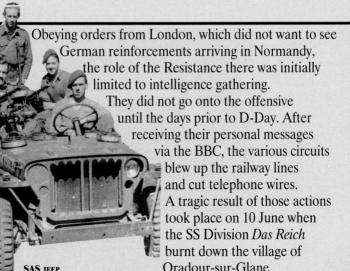

Obeying orders from London, which did not want to see German reinforcements arriving in Normandy, the role of the Resistance there was initially limited to intelligence gathering. They did not go onto the offensive until the days prior to D-Day. After receiving their personal messages via the BBC, the various circuits blew up the railway lines and cut telephone wires. A tragic result of those actions took place on 10 June when the SS Division *Das Reich* burnt down the village of Oradour-sur-Glane.

SAS JEEP
A jeep crew from the Special Air Service Regiment parachuted into France in June 1944. The small missions were sent in to arm and train the Maquis as well as to help them in attacking the enemy lines of communication. Such activities tied down many German units which might otherwise have fought in Normandy.

RESISTANCE POSTER
In spite of active patrolling along the lines by German guard units, sabotage by the Resistance hindered the moves and arrival of reinforcements ▲ *232*, especially tanks ● *62* which had to be brought close to the front lines by train.

BRITISH SUITCASE RADIO
Liaison between agents on the ground and London was by radio. Several types were used including the one below disguised as a suitcase.

LOCOMOTIVE DESTROYED BY SABOTAGE While one or two men kept a lookout, the sabotage teams crept down to the rails to place their charges of plastic explosive wired to a detonator activated by the weight of an engine. Various memorials honour the heroism of the Resistance ▲ *244*.

SOUVIENS-TOI D'ORADOUR SUR GLANE REMEMBER

NAZI BARBARITY
The ruins of Oradour-sur-Glane, near Limoges, which have been left as they were after the German attack, bear witness to the price paid by the civilian population. Irritated by constant partisan attacks against their columns heading for Normandy, a unit of the 2nd SS Panzer- division, *Das Reich* ● *54*, ▲ *230*, invaded the village one morning, shot the men and then assembled the women and the children in the church which they set alight.

PARACHUTE DROPS
On clear moonlit nights small groups assembled all over France, listening for the noise of aircraft engines ● *56, 58*. When the planes approached, the torches were lit and down fluttered the ghostly silhouettes of the parachutes bearing arms, ammunition and sometimes men. Everything was quickly recovered and hidden away before the men dispersed into the night. There was always the worry that the Germans would hear the noise of the low-flying aircraft.

THE RADIO AND THE STEN
The greatest danger to the radio operators came from the detection system used by the Germans to locate clandestine transmitters within a matter of minutes ● *68*. Among the many weapons supplied to the Resistance, the British Sten sub-machine-gun was one of the most popular. Simply constructed and excellent for close-quarter battle, it was fitted with a weak cocking device: a simple blow could trigger a hail of bullets.

● THE MAIN EVENTS OF THE BATTLE OF NORMANDY DAY BY DAY

The Battle of Normandy started the day after the landings. The primary mission was for the Allied troops commanded by Generals Montgomery and Bradley to break through the German line and destroy their armoured divisions which were assembling around Caen. Their spirited resistance and Montgomery's need to limit their offensive capability resulted in the destruction of many Norman towns.
But at the end of the bitter eleven-week campaign the Allied armies were in the open. In three days they were in Paris and in three months in Strasbourg.

7 JUNE
Bayeux liberated by the British.

12 JUNE Carentan cleared, which permitted the joining of the two American bridgeheads. An army corps advanced on Cherbourg but the British were pinned down at Caen.

19-22 JUNE
A violent storm hit the Mulberry harbours. The battle was overshadowed by supply problems as the Allies had to concentrate men and material faster than German reinforcements could arrive.

26-30 JUNE
Operation Epsom was launched by the British to the west of Caen to establish a bridgehead over the Odon. The attack petered out and the British were unable to outflank the city, which resulted in a stalemate.
On their front the Americans attempted to

force a route through the *bocage*, but bad weather hindered close air support. In the background, public opinion both in Britain and the USA criticized the slowness of the campaign. Montgomery, however, stuck to his strategy of pinning down the German armour around Caen to enable the Americans to break out to the south.

27 JUNE
Cherbourg was captured, although the destruction of the harbour installations rendered it unusable until mid-August.

28 JUNE
Death of General Dollmann, commander of the German Seventh Army.

2 JULY
Field Marshal von Rundstedt was replaced as Supreme Commander West by Field Marshal von Kluge.

7-8 JULY
Operation Charnwood. The British cleared the northern half of Caen. At that stage of the battle most German divisions had suffered severe casualties and were reduced to the size of regiments. They were still willing to fight, however, and the British attacks ground to a halt.

17 JULY
Rommel, wounded in a fighter attack, was relieved of his command.

18-20 JULY
Operation Goodwood, launched by the British east of Caen, was defeated by the enemy anti-tank guns on Bourguébus Ridge.

19 JULY Capture of Saint-Lô after fifteen days of bitter fighting.

20 JULY Failed attempt to kill Hitler.

23 JULY
The First Canadian Army became operational.

24-28 JULY
Operation Cobra, heralded the start of the American breakthrough.

30 JULY
Patton's tanks took Avranches and began to fan out into Brittany. Others

drove west towards Le Mans and the Loire. At the same time, to disguise his real intentions, Montgomery launched Operation Goodwood on both sides of the river Orne, in the east of Caen.

6-8 AUGUST
A counter-attack by German armour at Mortain was defeated by American power.

8 AUGUST
The Canadians started Operation Totalize down the Caen to Falaise road, beginning the encirclement of the remaining Germans.

12 AUGUST
Argentan liberated by American troops.

15 AUGUST
Operation Anvil: Allied landings in Provence.

16 AUGUST
The Canadians entered Falaise.

18 AUGUST
Von Kluge committed suicide and was replaced by Field Marshal Model.

19 AUGUST
The first Americans crossed the Seine at Mantes.

18-22 AUGUST
The closing of the Falaise pocket.

25 AUGUST
The liberation of Paris by the Allied troops.

NATURE

RENÉ CHABOUD,
FRANK LEVOY,
ANTHONY KEMP

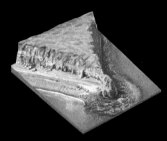

Landing-Craft Assault.
It requires 20 men and
their equipment.

The beaches on which the Allies landed comprise very different
environments of which one can find three main types
of shoreline: sandy coasts such as Utah beach, coasts backed
by vertical chalk cliffs or rock falls like the cliffs at the Pointe
du Hoc, and finally, the more sheltered places such as the
Veys Bay. The composition of the beaches is determined by
the daily action of the tides, the strong currents caused
by tidal action, as well as the frequent storms at all times
of the year.

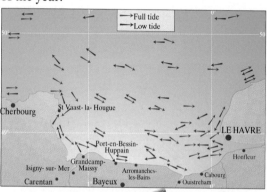

THE CURRENTS

All along the coast
the tidal currents
are relatively strong,
reaching 0.7 metre
per second.
Running parallel
to the shore they set
eastwards on a rising
tide and westwards
on a falling tide.
During storms
these currents are
modified by the
action of the swell.

Cut from the Jurassic chalk rock
of the Bessin region, the
vertical cliff appears
very fissured.

THE POINTE DU HOC

Situated on the west coast of the Calvados
region, it consists of a strong rocky spur
pushing out into the Channel which
is battered by the waves of the open
sea. The numerous overhangs are
the cause of frequent rock falls
which pile up on the beach
below.

The sand is mixed with
pitch which gives it a
muddy consistency.

The Veys Bay
forms the
estuary of
the principal rivers
draining the interior.
Grass is progressively
becoming established on
this sheltered coastal region.

The area of uncovered
rock is a way to measure
the amplitude of
the tide.

THE SANDS

They mainly consist of fragments of quartz originating from the break-up of the ancient substrata, chalk debris from the erosion of the cliffs and shells present at low water. The granulation of the sandy beaches generally increases gradually, from the low water mark of the shoreline to the upper part.

A FROGMAN
In January 1944, frogmen swam ashore from an X-class miniature submarine to analyse the quality of the sand. On their belts they carried cords for measuring and condoms to bring back samples.

The combat swimmers paid two clandestine visits to the landing beaches to gather intelligence about the precise nature of the surface, so as to be sure it was sufficiently solid to bear the weight of tanks.

THE TIDE ALONG THE COAST
Twice a day the landing beaches experience the phenomenon of the tides. At high-water spring tides, large areas of the shoreline are inundated.

On the sandy beaches of the Manche, such as at Utah, a ridge marks the limit between the land environment and that of the sea.

The evolution of the hard-rock cliffs along the Calvados coast is a result of two influences: that of the sea which batters their base twice a day and that of the damp continental air mass which softens the rock causing fissures to form.

The exposed rock areas along the Calvados coastline, at Omaha for example, consist of the original eroded strata as well as of fallen debris.

The Bobbin tank was equipped with a canvas carpet which could be rolled out onto the sand to provide a solid foundation for vehicles following behind.

■ MARSHLAND AND HEDGEROWS

American parachutist just after landing spilling air from his canopy, prior to folding it and hiding it in the hedgerows.

The *Bocage*, which starts immediately inland from the coast, is characterized by thick hedges bordering sunken roads. The Calvados *Bocage* is made up of parcels of grassland alternating with crop cultivation, while that of Carentan and Sainte-Marie-du-Mont (Plain) was all grassland in 1944. Veys Bay itself is an extension of the Carentan marshes extending to the coast and liable to inundation. These very differing landscapes contributed in many ways to the difficulties faced by the Allies after their landings.

Marsh
Marshes flooded by the Germans

The Douve and the Taute on the one hand, and the Vire and the Aure on the other, are the four rivers which irrigate the Cotentin and Bessin marshlands. The Germans destroyed the sluice gates which hinder flooding at high tide, to render the area impassable.

The Carentan marshes, flat and often poorly drained, rapidly flood during prolonged rain.

During landing, several gliders crashed into stakes planted across the fields, known as "Rommel's asparagus".

BOCAGE

Its dense network forms a labyrinth which in several areas seriously impeded the progress of Allied formations to their objectives.

Vegetation of the *Bocage* grows on top of earth banks, often very high and with steep sides.

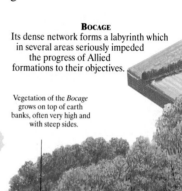

Water circulation in the marshlands is facilitated by ditches known as *limes*, a word derived from the Latin word for limits, which drain into the rivers.

The marsh soil is made up of alluvial deposits, with sea sand in the parts near the coast and peat further inland.

The flooding of this grassy terrain was achieved by the Germans artificially in that they hindered the rivers and streams from emptying towards the sea.

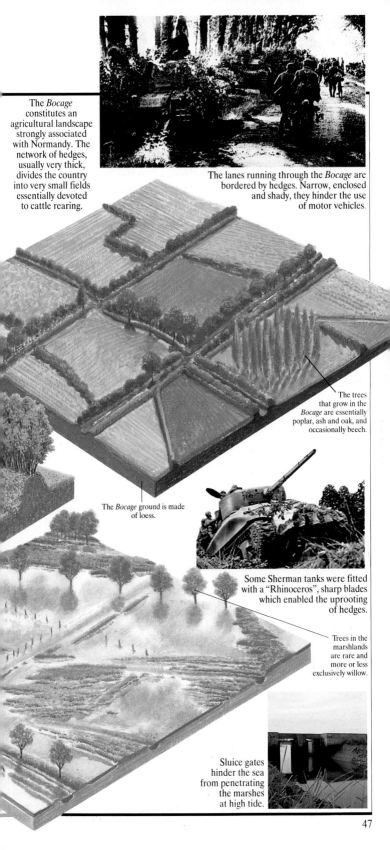

The *Bocage* constitutes an agricultural landscape strongly associated with Normandy. The network of hedges, usually very thick, divides the country into very small fields essentially devoted to cattle rearing.

The lanes running through the *Bocage* are bordered by hedges. Narrow, enclosed and shady, they hinder the use of motor vehicles.

The trees that grow in the *Bocage* are essentially poplar, ash and oak, and occasionally beech.

The *Bocage* ground is made of loess.

Some Sherman tanks were fitted with a "Rhinoceros", sharp blades which enabled the uprooting of hedges.

Trees in the marshlands are rare and more or less exclusively willow.

Sluice gates hinder the sea from penetrating the marshes at high tide.

THE WEATHER FORECAST FOR 6 JUNE 1944

THE STORM ON 19 JUNE
A 70 kph wind devastated the artificial harbour at Saint-Laurent-sur-Mer.

In early June 1944 numerous depressions caused heavy rainfall in Western Europe accompanied by very strong winds. Meteorologists were ordered by the staff officers to predict a "window". Their chief, Group Captain Stagg, forecast a calmer period for 6 June. Thus the landings, originally envisaged for 5 June, were postponed for 24 hours. Paradoxically, the bad weather worked in favour of the Allies as the Germans were convinced that they would wait for a more favourable period, and lowered their guard.

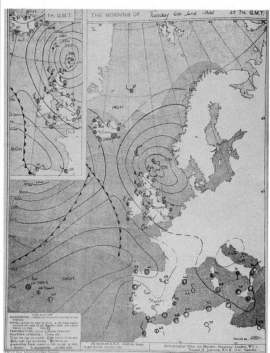

The cold front associated with a depression centred to the north of Scotland crossed France on 5 June. It then moved into Eastern Europe and is practically invisible on the chart.
A second front developed in the Western Approaches but was too far away to influence the weather in Normandy. Broken clouds appeared over Western Europe, notably along the Channel coasts with an east-north-east wind force 4 to 5. Visibility was excellent and the sky was blue, flecked with sufficiently high cumulus clouds. Thus conditions were perfect for the planned air operations.

"Our craft approached the beach. (...) Most of us were floored by sea-sickness. The waves washed vomit over our uniforms, the deck and into the helmets. I felt emptied, annihilated, miserable. Was this the battle we were going into ?"
J. Weiss, *Le Monde*, 24 May 1945.

TIDE TABLES
Because the Germans had obstructed the beaches ● 72, the landings had to be made at low tide. The timing of the tides was one of the fundamental parameters that directed Overlord.

48

MILITARY SCIENCE

ANTHONY KEMP,
JEAN-PIERRE BÉNAMOU

AMERICAN UNIFORMS

From left to right.
12th Army group,
2nd Armored
Division, First Army,
82nd Airborne
Division and
Third Army.

The GI's basic uniform consisted of a beige drill blouse known as the M41, together with mustard-coloured trousers tucked into high laced-up gaiters, which caused them to bag out over the knees. Footwear consisted of fawn lace-up leather boots. Rangers were issued with rubber-soled high laced boots or leather boots and gaiters known as the M44. The sturdy, light, webbing harness was appreciated by the front-line troops. It supported the basic kit made of woven canvas in beige or khaki, and the belt with three rows of copper eyelets onto which the accessories could be hung: pistol holster, water-bottle holder and entrenching tool. In combat the officers' peaked caps and the forage caps of the men were replaced by the heavy US helmet made of special steel. Underneath they wore a helmet liner made of a cardboard and plastic material.

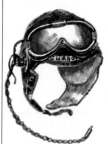

PILOT'S HELMET
Pilots wore a leather helmet and tinted goggles to protect against the very bright light at high altitude.

US ARMY AIR FORCE PILOT
Bomber pilots wore sheepskin-lined two-piece flying suits and boots. This very warm outfit was developed for long-range missions.

AIRBORNE SOLDIER
His equipment included a reserve parachute on the chest, a haversack, M1 hand-grenades, a Thompson cal. 45 sub-machine-gun and a fighting knife.

US ARMY AIR FORCE OFFICER
This fighter pilot is wearing the model A2 leather blouse, a brown peaked cap the same as army issue and mustard-coloured twill trousers.

FLYING GLOVES
A very warm double thickness glove made specially for bomber crews.

The GI's nickname comes from the *government issue* stamp (regulation equipment) that was found on every piece of equipment.

COMBAT DRESS
The airborne jumping smock was reinforced at the elbows. Two slanted pockets on the chest and two strengthened ones on the hip carried grenades. On the left shoulder the divisional insignia were sewn.

OXYGEN MASK
Issued to bomber crews flying at high altitude.

STEEL HELMET
"Don't lose your helmet buddy, you're gonna need it."
The helmet is camouflaged with stripes of coloured tissue. The GIs used them to cook, wash and even develop pictures.

US MEDICAL ORDERLY
He wears over his shoulder a first-aid kit to give primary care on the spot to a casualty prior to evacuation.

US INFANTRYMAN
GI in combat dress with haversack, entrenching tool and helmet covered with camouflage net.

1st Infantry Division "Big Red One".

PARATROOPER KIT, 82ND AIRBORNE
Attached to the belt, the trooper wore a Colt 45, a fighting knife and an aluminium water bottle in a canvas cover.

2nd Infantry Division.

90th Infantry Division.

(Top left) Cartridge belt with pouches containing clips, each with 8 rounds of 30 ammunition.

● BRITISH UNIFORMS

From left to right:
Beach Groups,
1st Canadian Parachute Battalion,
7th Armoured Division,
Combined Operations,
VIII Corps.

Introduced in 1936 by the War Office for the comfort of
the soldier, battledress was the standard uniform: khaki for
the Army, mid-blue for the RAF and dark blue for the Navy.
This battledress was also adopted by the Commonwealth
countries with small differences. The Canadians made their
own khaki woollen cloth and coloured their
webbing green, while the British used a yellow
or deep brown. Helmets were covered with
a net into which strips of hessian or foliage
could be stuck.

**REGULATION AND
NON-REGULATION KIT**
General Montgomery
(below) is wearing
his habitual black
beret with two
badges, a polo-neck
sweater and beige
corduroys. Dempsey
preferred the normal
service dress cap
with the red band
of a general.
The corporal from
a Lowland regiment
is wearing the
traditional Glengarry
cap and trews
in the regimental
tartan.

**YORKSHIRE REGIMENT
CORPORAL**
A Tommy's combat kit
included the flat-
brimmed steel helmet
of 1914-18 and woven
canvas webbing
equipment.

**SCOTTISH REGIMENT
CORPORAL**

**GENERAL
MONTGOMERY**

GENERAL DEMPSEY

FREE-FRENCH SOLDIER

French troops wore the uniform of the army to which they were attached, British or American. They retained, however, their own pattern beret and French Army insignia.

FRENCH OFFICER

A member of the Free-French Air Force (FAFL) wearing the regulation blue uniform of the French Air Force with insignia augmented by the Cross of Lorraine.

CANADIAN SOLDIER

From the Cameron Highlanders of Ottawa Regiment. The Canadians wore khaki battledress with equipment and badges of rank similar to the British.

Standard British parachute.

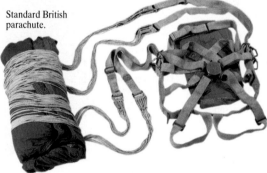

BRITISH SAILOR

Dressed for work on the beach, he wears the traditional beige dufflecoat with a megaphone for calling to incoming landing craft.

RAF PILOT

His regulation uniform consisted of flying boots and a leather flying jacket over the standard blue battledress, together with a yellow "Mae West" life jacket. Most wore their own coloured scarves.

BRITISH GLIDER PILOT

After landing, glider pilots were expected to fight alongside the airborne forces. Therefore they wore the standard airborne helmet and full webbing kit.

● GERMAN UNIFORMS

German uniform patterns were more varied than those of
the Allied nations. Basic colours were grey-green for the Army
and Waffen SS with slight tonal differences, and blue-grey
for the Luftwaffe. The latter was modified for parachutists
who wore special green woollen jumping trousers and soft boots
which laced up at the side. Armoured units wore black which
hid the grease stains, and a double-breasted blouse similar
to the battledress but better fitting. The different camouflage
patterns worn by the Luftwaffe,
parachutists, Army and Waffen
SS in Normandy distinguished
the German combatants.

**WAFFEN SS
CAMOUFLAGE JACKET**
This was a reversible
model to alternate
between spring
and autumn foliage
colours. Worn by
the Waffen SS
when fighting
in the *Bocage*.

DETAIL
Written on the
SS metal belt clasp
were the words *Meine
Ehre heisst Treue*
(my honour
is called loyalty),
which explains
their fanaticism
in combat.

PARACHUTISTS
A number of German
parachute units
fought in Normandy
as infantry. This
one is wearing
the airborne pattern
steel helmet and
a camouflage
jumping smock.

**LUFTWAFFE PILOT
IN FLYING KIT**
The men of
the German Air
Force generally
wore blue-grey with
the eagle badge
of the Luftwaffe
on the cap and
belt clasp.

**WAFFEN SS
OFFICER**
He is wearing
a long black leather
coat as well as
the standard officers'
peaked cap.

GUNNER IN AN ARMOURED UNIT

SIGNALS OFFICER OF A PANZERDIVISION

SOLDIER IN THE 12TH SS PANZERDIVISION
Wearing the black leather combat kit with the soft-cloth peaked cap.

TANK GUNNER
Gunner 2nd Class of the Schwere Abteilung 503 attached to the 21st Panzerdiv., the only battalion in Normandy equipped with Tiger Mk.II tanks.

WAFFEN SS GRENADIER
Grenadiers were motorized infantry. The man below is carrying an MG 42 machine-gun with drum magazine, on a sling.

WAFFEN SS PRIVATE
The uniform shown is practically identical to that of the Army infantry other than the collar insignia. Note the high leather boots.

WAFFEN SS HELMET AND JACKET
Made from Italian cloth, this jacket has a non-standard camouflage pattern used during the Battle of Normandy. The 1940 model helmet was finished either in rough paint or fitted with a reversible cloth cover. 6x30 binoculars have a bakelite case.

The gunner (top left) is wearing a forage cap, a double-breasted camouflage jacket and a leather belt and pistol holster.

55

Allied air superiority had a considerable influence on the success of Operation Overlord. On 6 June the combined Anglo-American air fleets flew 10,742 separate missions, dropped 12,000 tons of bombs and 867 gliders landed in the enemy lines. On the other side the German Third Air Fleet was outnumbered by twenty-eight to one. Being the rulers of the skies over Normandy, the Allies forced the Germans to move only by night or when poor weather conditions grounded the fighters.

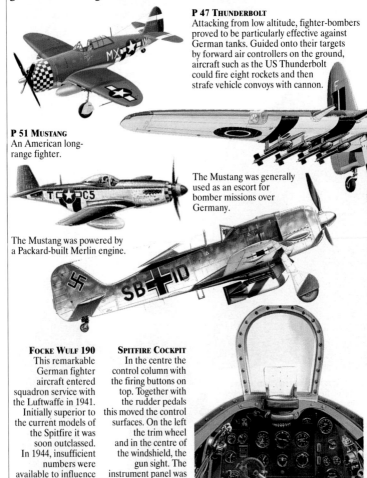

P 47 THUNDERBOLT
Attacking from low altitude, fighter-bombers proved to be particularly effective against German tanks. Guided onto their targets by forward air controllers on the ground, aircraft such as the US Thunderbolt could fire eight rockets and then strafe vehicle convoys with cannon.

P 51 MUSTANG
An American long-range fighter.

The Mustang was generally used as an escort for bomber missions over Germany.

The Mustang was powered by a Packard-built Merlin engine.

FOCKE WULF 190
This remarkable German fighter aircraft entered squadron service with the Luftwaffe in 1941. Initially superior to the current models of the Spitfire it was soon outclassed. In 1944, insufficient numbers were available to influence the battle. Armed with 22-mm cannon housed in the wings it could also carry a 250 kg bomb underneath.

SPITFIRE COCKPIT
In the centre the control column with the firing buttons on top. Together with the rudder pedals this moved the control surfaces. On the left the trim wheel and in the centre of the windshield, the gun sight. The instrument panel was fitted with dials for blind flying as well as engine performance monitoring.

SPITFIRE MARK XIV
The most famous fighter of all times, the Spitfire underwent numerous modifications over the years. The Merlin-engined MK IX was the main British fighter on the Normandy front. The MK XIV, shown in pursuit of a V-I, above, was fitted with the more powerful Griffon engine. Spitfires succeeded in shooting down a number of these pilotless flying bombs designed by the Nazi engineers to attack London.

DE HAVILLAND MOSQUITO
Regarded by many as the most beautiful aircraft of the Second World War, it served as a medium bomber, night fighter and for photo reconnaissance.

HAWKER TYPHOON
By the summer of 1944 this powerful aircraft nicknamed the "Tiffy" was coming to the end of its life, but was still a formidable tank buster. It carried eight rockets mounted on launching rails under the wings and had four 20-mm cannon, also wing-mounted. It was difficult to fly, but once in the air, was fast and manœuvrable.

HORSA GLIDER
Made of plywood and piloted by volunteers, it could transport 18 fully-equipped parachutists or light armaments such as jeeps and anti-tank guns.

Bombers had a vital role to play during the Battle of Normandy. At dawn on D-Day they dropped more than 10,000 tons of bombs on the enemy defences as a preamble to the Allied troop landings. The capture of Caen as well as Cobra, Goodwood and Totalize were all preceded by huge bombardments carried out by British and American squadrons. The inability to bomb accurately, however, caused many deaths among Allied troops on the ground.

MARAUDER
One of a number of types of twin-engined bomber used by the Americans in the Battle of Normandy.

Top centre turret, hydraulically operated and fitted with twin machine-guns.

AVRO LANCASTER
In 1944, this magnificent aircraft, powered by four Rolls-Royce Merlin engines and fitted with radar navigation aids, equipped the bulk of the British squadrons employed on the night bombing of Germany. It could carry six tons of bombs in its racks. For protection against enemy fighters it was armed with machine-guns in rotating turrets.

Radar dome for night navigation

AMERICAN BOMB TYPES
From left to right: Anti-personnel fragmentation bomb, 250-kg high explosive bomb, 2-ton light-case bomb, concrete-piercing bomb.

HANDLEY-PAGE HALIFAX
Numerous versions of this British heavy bomber were built. Fitted with either four Rolls-Royce Merlins or Bristol Hercules it could fly at 460 kph, with a range of between 1,500 and 3,000 kilometres. Flown by a seven-man crew and armed with nine 7.65-mm machine-guns for self defence it could carry almost six tons of bombs in its bomb bay.

FRAGMENTATION BOMBS
Bomb craters seriously hampered the movement of troops on the ground. After Goodwood the Allies went over to using fragmentation bombs which killed the enemy without churning up the soil.

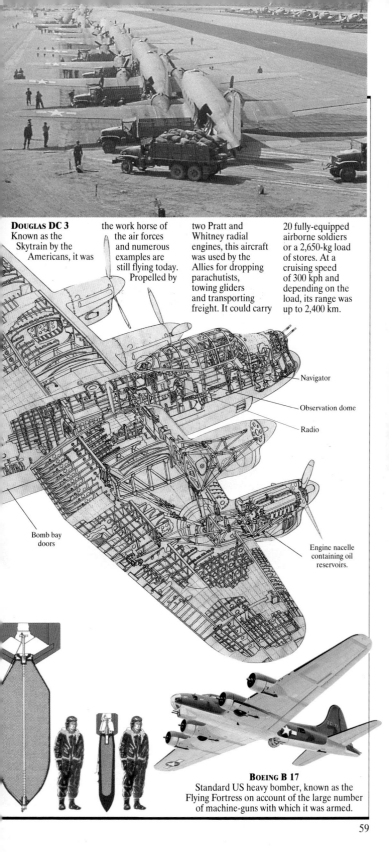

Douglas DC 3
Known as the Skytrain by the Americans, it was the work horse of the air forces and numerous examples are still flying today. Propelled by two Pratt and Whitney radial engines, this aircraft was used by the Allies for dropping parachutists, towing gliders and transporting freight. It could carry 20 fully-equipped airborne soldiers or a 2,650-kg load of stores. At a cruising speed of 300 kph and depending on the load, its range was up to 2,400 km.

Navigator

Observation dome

Radio

Bomb bay doors

Engine nacelle containing oil reservoirs.

Boeing B 17
Standard US heavy bomber, known as the Flying Fortress on account of the large number of machine-guns with which it was armed.

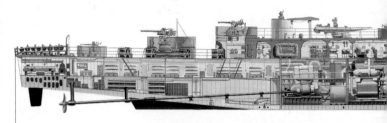

For the naval phase of Operation Overlord, known as
Operation Neptune, Admiral Ramsay had at his disposal
more than 7,000 vessels, ranging from the most powerful
battleships to the smallest assault boats from several nations.
The bombardment fleet remained anchored off
the Normandy coast until the troops who had landed
were out of range of their supporting artillery.

**LANDING-CRAFT
INFANTRY LARGE**
Capable of
transporting
188 fully equipped
men or 75 tons
of stores, it was
armed with several
anti-aircraft guns
for close defence.

LANDING-SHIP TANK
Large vessel able to carry
32 heavy tanks.

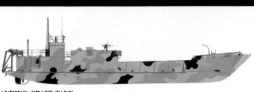

LANDING-SHIP DOCK
This had a floodable
dock at the stern
which could
accommodate
14 assault craft.
After the troops had
embarked, the rear
doors opened and
the assault craft
floated out.

LANDING-CRAFT TANK
Tank-transporting
barge.

LANDING-SHIP INFANTRY
These were converted passenger liners
used to transport troops, and were able
to accommodate a fully-equipped infantry
battalion. The men were embarked in their
assault craft hanging in the davits and
were then lowered into the sea.

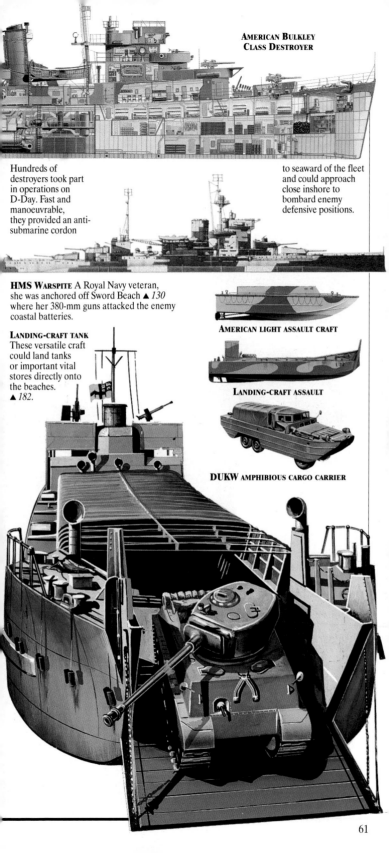

AMERICAN BULKLEY CLASS DESTROYER

Hundreds of destroyers took part in operations on D-Day. Fast and manoeuvrable, they provided an anti-submarine cordon to seaward of the fleet and could approach close inshore to bombard enemy defensive positions.

HMS WARSPITE A Royal Navy veteran, she was anchored off Sword Beach ▲ *130* where her 380-mm guns attacked the enemy coastal batteries.

LANDING-CRAFT TANK These versatile craft could land tanks or important vital stores directly onto the beaches. ▲ *182*.

AMERICAN LIGHT ASSAULT CRAFT

LANDING-CRAFT ASSAULT

DUKW AMPHIBIOUS CARGO CARRIER

Armoured forces are the cavalry of the modern battlefield. By 1944, tanks had reached a high level of sophistication thanks to their firepower and thickness of their armour. On the Normandy battlefield the Allies benefited from greater numbers, but as regards technology, the German ones were superior, being vastly better armed than the lighter Shermans and Cromwells.

M10 TANK DESTROYER

This was a Sherman chassis fitted with an open-topped turret mounting a 3-pdr anti-tank gun. Its purpose was to combat enemy tanks and M10s served in the armoured units of all allied nations.

PANZER MARK IV

Already outdated by the time of the Normandy campaign, the Mk. IV was still the basic equipment for the Panzer divisions ▲ 230. Its all-up combat weight of 25 tons was relatively light but its armour was thicker than that of a Sherman.

TIGER MARK II

Tiger tanks were the kings of the battlefield in 1944, able to take on any of the tanks of the Western Allies. The Mk. II was designed by Ferdinand Porsche, better known post-war for his sports cars. With an all-up weight of 60 tons the front armour was 10-cm thick and at the side 8 cm. and it was fitted with a 700 bhp Maybach engine. The large turret housed a classic 88-mm anti-tank gun.

Spare track links were bolted on the sides of the turret to provide extra protection.

TIGER MARK I

This had a relatively high silhouette and square turret.

SHERMAN M4
The standard American medium tanks
built by the thousand and generally
armed with a 75-mm gun,
although the British used
a version known as the
Firefly with a 17-pdr gun.
Its frontal armour
was 7.6cm thick.

The impressively
long barrel of
the Tiger's 88-mm
gun enabled it
to penetrate Allied
tanks. With a well-
trained crew it could
fire 20 rounds
per minute.

PANZER MARK V Armed with a 75-mm cannon,
low profile and thickly armoured, the Panther
was arguably the best tank of World War II.
Fast and manoeuvrable, it has had a great
influence on the development
of the modern tank.

**SHERMAN DUPLEX
DRIVE (DD)** ▲ *135* This
amphibious tank was fitted
with a flotation screen
and twin propellors at the rear.
On leaving the water
the screen folded, enabling
it to fight on land.

Insignia of the British 79th
Armoured Division
in which all the special
armoured units were grouped.

**MAJOR-GENERAL
PERCY HOBART**
The nickname
"Hobart's menagerie"
referred to the
creator of most of the
special armoured
vehicles.

Lessons learned from the disaster at Dieppe in 1942
led the British staff planners to conclude that it was
impossible to land troops on an enemy-held beach
without strong armoured support. They ordered
the construction of a whole range of vehicles
designed to lay bridges, destroy concrete
bunkers and clear beach obstacles.
Nicknamed the "Funnies", these versatile
devices saved thousands of lives on D-Day
and had the Americans, who viewed
them with suspicion, adopted them,
they would have suffered fewer casualties
at Omaha.

ARC MARK II This consisted
of a turretless tank
chassis which carried
a folding roadway
on top. This could
be deployed to form
a ramp for crossing
concrete sea walls
or the Arc could be
driven into small
streams as well as
anti-tank ditches.

"SPIGOT" MORTAR
This device, nicknamed the "flying
dustbin", was mounted in the turret
of a Churchill tank and fired a 40-lb
charge. This enabled it to knock out
bunkers and concrete buildings.

**CHURCHILL
CROCODILE**
The flame-thrower,
mounted in the
turret, fired a jet
of napalm (made
of liquid petroleum

jelly) within a range
of 150 metres.
The Crocodile
proved itself to be
particularly effective
against concrete
bunkers.

BOBBIN TANK
This tank was fitted with an enormous drum at the front which could unroll a mesh carpet over soft sand, to provide a stable exit road from a beach for other vehicles. The Fascine tank, for its part, carried a large bundle of sticks to fill in ditches.

ARMOURED RECOVERY VEHICLE
At the front it had a derrick capable of lifting a damaged tank turret, and at the rear a jib for towing out bogged tanks.

CHURCHILL BRIDGE-LAYER
This tank could position its bridge, decouple from it, and then fight as a normal tank.

SHERMAN CRAB
The chains on the rotating front drum could flail a passage through a minefield without risking the crew.

OTHER DEVICES
General Hobart's stable also produced the DD ● *63*, ▲ *135* amphibious tank, various vehicles for dealing with beach obstacles and armoured bulldozers.

The Crocodile's armour-plated trailer contained 1,800 litres of fuel for the flame-thrower.

D-Day was without precedent in terms of logistics and the supply services had to move hundreds of thousands of tons of rations and vast quantities of petrol. As an example, an armoured division consumed 600 tons of stores per day and in Normandy the infrastructure was practically non-existent. Therefore it was necessary to create airstrips in open fields, field hospitals, workshops etc. To illustrate this tremendous need, by the end of July a million men were serving in Normandy with the Allies. Opposite them the Germans suffered severe shortages.

CONVOY OF TANKER-TRUCKS
The success of the Allied offensive depended on petrol. Huge tankers were landed to move fuel from the depots on the coast to the troops in the front line.

On average there was one vehicle per ten men landed in Normandy, and the huge industrial capacity of the United States was harnessed to supply them. Below, ambulances parked at Fort Wayne in Indiana at the beginning of 1944, waiting to be shipped.

THE WILLYS JEEP
Robust and cheap, this four-wheel-drive vehicle gave the troops a cross-country capability. It could carry a crew of four men, and their equipment as well as a radio.

THE MULBERRY HARBOURS ● 76
Stores were landed directly onto pierheads which moved up and down with the tides, and from them vehicles were driven ashore along floating pontoon roadways several hundred metres long.

THE "FUNNIES" ● *64* For use on D-Day the Allies adapted certain tanks with devices to enable them to overcome various obstacles placed by the Germans. Here, a Bobbin tank is unrolling a type of canvas mat to enable other vehicles to cross soft ground.

"LIBERTY SHIP" ● *60* Once the bridgehead had been secured, a large proportion of the stores needed was shipped direct from the United States. To do this a new type of cargo vessel was introduced, called the Liberty Ship. 2,700 of these cheap ships were made for transporting stores. They were built in requisitioned shipyards by semi-skilled workers, many of whom came from car factories.

THE DUKW
A true workhorse of the sea, the DUKW was driven through the water by twin propellors and on land by wheels. Nicknamed the *ducks* on account of their beak-shaped fronts, these amphibious cargo carriers were mainly used during the landings for unloading ships anchored off the beaches of Normandy.

PLUTO
The system known as Pipe Line Under The Ocean was conceived in 1942 to provide a proportion of the fuel needs of the forces landed in Normandy. Kilometres of flexible tubes welded together in England were unrolled along the sea bed by vast drums known as conundrums, which were towed across the Channel. A total of 21 lines each 100 km long ran from England to Cherbourg.

67

Both communications and intelligence had a vital role to play. Able to break the German army code, the Allies were well-informed of enemy intentions during the Battle of Normandy. Jamming of German coastal radar ensured the success of deception measures. Communications in the field were by means of transmitter-receivers which were efficient but cumbersome. Use of morse code permitted the exchange of secret information and the maintenance of communication with Eisenhower's HQ in England.

THE BRASSERIE RADAR STATION
The Germans installed numerous radar stations along the coast around Cherbourg. On the left a Giant Würzburg ▲ *148* antenna and on the right, a Wassermann. This was a 40m-high cylinder fitted with reflecting panels designed to detect aircraft at a range of 200 km.

THE ENIGMA MACHINE
Before the war the Germans perfected an encoding device which consisted of a keyboard linked to rotating drums and the British intelligence service managed to obtain one. Decoded messages were known as "Ultra Intelligence", one of the best-kept secrets of the war and which had a vital role to play in the success of Allied operations in Normandy.

THE GIANT WÜRZBURG RADAR
With a 7.5m-diameter rotating parabolic antenna, this radar was mainly used for directing enemy fighters but it could also detect aircraft and ships within a range of 60 km. The cabin contained the screens served by a two-man crew. The Allies could neutralize this radar.

AIR-TO-GROUND COOPERATION
Communication was vital in ensuring
air support for ground troops.
The fighter-bombers flew in groups over
the beaches (the "taxi rank") and were
in radio communication with forward air
controllers right in the front line.
The latter indicated potential targets which
could either be bombed or attacked
with rockets.

RADIO TRANSMISSION
By 1944, battlefield
communications
were relatively
effective although
the sets used were
heavy and
cumbersome.

Their range was
reduced and
messages distorted
by interference,
while their batteries
provided only
a limited
autonomy.

SONIC SOUND DETECTION
A type of sound mirror with amplifier,
this device picked up sound waves reflected
off the surface of the sea. The British
installed these mirrors along the coastline
before the invention of radar for detecting
the approach of enemy aircraft.

**BRITISH FIELD
TELEPHONE**
At the beginning
of the war British
radio was notably
less efficient than
that of the Germans,
but by 1944 the
opposite was

the case.
Large numbers of
British infantry
were equipped with
radios and field
telephones, and
by D-Day wireless
telegraphy could
achieve a range
of up to 150 km.
Radio was used
extensively in
deception which
was effective in
pinning the
German
Fifteenth
Army
in the Calais
area in June
1944.

WINDOWS-CUTTING MACHINE
In 1943 the Allies discovered a means of
jamming enemy radars by dropping
thousands of strips of aluminium foil known
as "windows" from aircraft. (Extreme left)
The effect on an enemy radar screen.

● TROOP RATIONS

MENU No. 2
FOR 5 COMPLETE RATIONS USE CONTENTS OF THIS BOX TOGETHER WITH CANNED GOODS IN BOX MARKED "2ND HALF OF 5 RATIONS"

— BREAKFAST —
CEREAL   BACON
BISCUITS AND JAM
COFFEE AND MILK

— DINNER —
1 K RATION UNIT PER MAN
1 CAN K RATION
CHEESE PRODUCT PER MAN

— SUPPER —
ENGLISH STYLE MEAT AND VEGETABLE STEW
STRING BEANS
BISCUITS AND BUTTER
FRUIT BARS   COFFEE
LOOK FOR A CAN OPENER IN A SMALL ENVELOPE IN THIS BOX

HALAZONE TABLETS ARE INCLUDED TO PURIFY DRINKING WATER

BRITISH FIELD RATIONS
Menus for five daily rations:

Biscuits, jam, bacon, cereals, meat stew, beans, fruit bars, etc., plus halazone water-purification tablets.

Petrol cooker.   Chocolate and sweets.

Sweets, salt and matches.   Two tins of tea.   Emergency ration.   Tin of ointment.   Cigarettes.

Water-sterilisation outfit.   Clasp knife.   Cigarette tin.   Anti-gas protection.   Soldier's pay book.

Metal tins of 50 cigarettes.

Top left, anti-seasickness pills. Left, individual cooker in a packet with flexible tripod and solid fuel block. Right, a box of 250 biscuits with a label inside stating the final date for consumption: 1920!

BISCUITS 7½ lbs C LTD Pac ...

MENU #1 SECOND HALF OF 5 RATIONS
FOR 5 COMPLETE RATIONS USE THIS BOX AND ONE MARKED "FIRST HALF OF 5 RATIONS"

U.S. ARMY FIELD RATION K SUPPER UNIT

AMERICAN FIELD RATIONS
Evening meal field ration.

One-man K-type field ration.

Block of solid fuel for cooker.

Box of five evening meals.

Selection of cigarette packets, matches and a lighter. Some book matches carried advertising for the US war loan, Victory Bonds.

Below left, tin of borax powder for infantry foot care.

Packet of pipe tobacco.   Field ration.

Below right, tin of tooth powder.

Cutlery and tin of Nescafé.

Packet of 5 Chesterfield cigarettes.

Left, water-purification tablets and a cylindrical plastic box of 50 cigarettes.

Tin of sweets.

ARCHITECTURE

ANTHONY KEMP

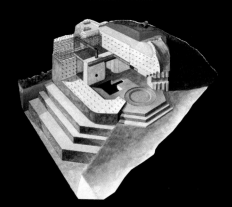

Wooden post supported
by a tripod fitted
with saw teeth to
rip the hulls of
landing-craft
and a mine at
the tip.

Expecting an Allied landing,
the Germans placed obstacles on all the beaches along
the French coast. To rip open landing-craft, there were
mined stakes. To delay progress up the beaches, there were
layers of barbed-wire, minefields, ditches and anti-tank walls
until the troops reached the bunkers of the Atlantic Wall
proper. Those who managed to get through all of this would
be met by infantry armed with mortars,
flame-throwers and
heavy machine-guns.

Floating rafts were
armed either
with mines or shells,
near the surface.

Posts were
armed either
with mines or
shells on top.

If a landing craft
touched one
of these posts it
would swivel
and detonate
a mine or shell in
a concrete housing
at the base.

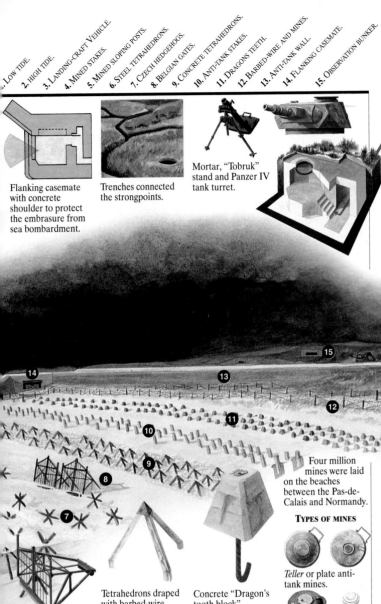

Flanking casemate
with concrete
shoulder to protect
the embrasure from
sea bombardment.

Trenches connected
the strongpoints.

Mortar, "Tobruk"
stand and Panzer IV
tank turret.

Four million
mines were laid
on the beaches
between the Pas-de-
Calais and Normandy.

TYPES OF MINES

Teller or plate anti-
tank mines.

Undetectible mines
in concrete or glass.

Tetrahedrons draped
with barbed-wire.

Concrete "Dragon's
tooth block".

Magnetic anti-tank
mine and anti-
personnel mine.

"Belgian Gates"
anti-tank obstacle.

Coiled barbed-wire or "cheveux
de frise" anchored to stakes.

"Czech hedgehog".

Anti-tank wall made of railway sleepers
backing onto the sand dunes.

Obstacle planted in
the sand with high-
pressure water jet.

Concrete anti-tank wall topped with stakes
and coiled wire.

Jumping mine and a
wooden "shoe" mine.

● THE ATLANTIC WALL

CASEMATES

1. Cutaway plan of artillery type M272 casemate.
2. Shelter for two infantry sections.
3. Artillery casemate at Azeville.
4. Fire-control post type R636.

The concrete works of the Atlantic Wall were based on a number of standard types and Hitler took a personal interest in their design. From the powerful naval shore batteries to simple observation posts, his engineers produced a great variety of structures. The diversity of the armaments, the chronic lack of materials and the low standard of the garrisons in the coast defence units reduced the efficiency of the whole concept.

EFFECTS OF SHELL BURSTS

On a naval-design casemate.

On an army-pattern casemate.

Metal-reinforced ceiling resisted concrete splintering.

Effect of an impact on a non-reinforced ceiling.

ARTILLERY CASEMATE
German naval casemates were built on a stepped foundation sunk well into the ground with an adequate earth covering to absorb shell impacts. This gave them a high degree of stability under repeated bombardment. The gun positions had thick concrete walls reinforced with steel mesh. Their construction required enormous concrete mixers capable of pouring more than 600 cubic metres into wooden shuttering.

JM Guillou '94

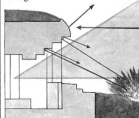

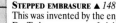

STEPPED EMBRASURE ▲ 148
This was invented by the engineer, Dr. Todt, as a means of giving greater angles of elevation and traverse to long-barrelled guns in casemates, while at the same time having an opening small enough to provide protection for the crews. The lateral grooves, seen in the cut-away drawing above, permitted a traverse of up to 120 deg., and those above the embrasure, an elevation of up to 60 deg.

1

 2

3

 4

THE GUN POSITION
A pit moulded into the floor level housed the actual gun mounting. Behind was a pit for spent cartridges and an ammunition magazine. Pipes evacuated the cordite fumes.

These details show how the steel reinforcing mesh was assembled to strengthen the casemates. To build a bunker 60 kg of steel per square metre was needed. The ends of the mesh were left exposed as hooks for fixing camouflage nets.

Hooks for fixing camouflage nets.

Vegetation planted in recesses.

Traces of wooden shuttering on the concrete.

A faster and more economic method of bunker construction consisted in building two walls of breeze blocks to form a shutter that could be left in place and filling the space between with concrete and mesh lattice.

Method of shuttering for stepped embrasures.

Almost all coast artillery batteries were covered with camouflage netting on top of a thick layer of earth and natural vegetation to protect against impacting shells.

CAMOUFLAGE
The nets came in different versions. Some had cloth strips woven into the mesh in a zig-zag pattern, while some had green and brown hessian strips. Another method was to insert tufts of reeds and other vegetation.

75

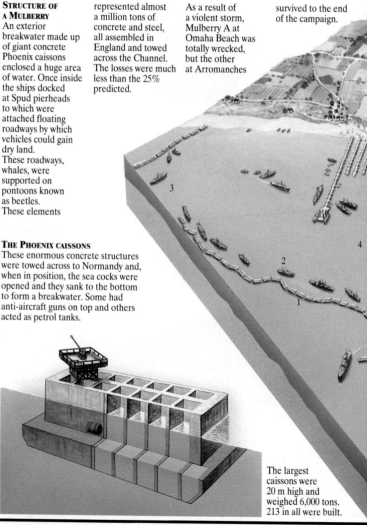

1 2 4 5

The choice of the Normandy coast for the landings imposed the necessity of providing artificial harbours. Each of the two Mulberry harbours had to have the capacity of Dover Harbour to handle the fleet of Liberty ships, remain operational for nine months, and in spite of the strong Normandy tides, be able to cope daily with 12,000 tons of stores and 2,500 vehicles. The latter figures were often surpassed. The secret of the vast building programme was well guarded and most of the 20,000 workers involved remained in ignorance of the true purpose.

STRUCTURE OF A MULBERRY

An exterior breakwater made up of giant concrete Phoenix caissons enclosed a huge area of water. Once inside the ships docked at Spud pierheads to which were attached floating roadways by which vehicles could gain dry land.
These roadways, whales, were supported on pontoons known as beetles.
These elements represented almost a million tons of concrete and steel, all assembled in England and towed across the Channel. The losses were much less than the 25% predicted.

As a result of a violent storm, Mulberry A at Omaha Beach was totally wrecked, but the other at Arromanches survived to the end of the campaign.

THE PHOENIX CAISSONS

These enormous concrete structures were towed across to Normandy and, when in position, the sea cocks were opened and they sank to the bottom to form a breakwater. Some had anti-aircraft guns on top and others acted as petrol tanks.

The largest caissons were 20 m high and weighed 6,000 tons. 213 in all were built.

Cable-laying
barge.

THE LANDING MUSEUM, ARROMANCHES
Working models and an excellent film
explain the building and working of
a Mulberry harbour.

BOMBARDONS
These cruciform
metal caissons,
65m long and 8 m
high were placed
to seaward of the
artificial ports to form
an initial breakwater.

The top arm was
empty, acting as
a float, while the rest
of the bombardon
was filled with 2,000
litres of water to
ensure it remained
in place.

PLAN OF MULBERRY B
Built in front of
Arromanches ▲ *141*,
it was one of
the two artificial
harbours in
Normandy.
Considerable parts
of it can still
be seen.

1. Phoenix caissons.
2. Anchored ships.
3. Entrance.
4. Roadstead.
5. Pierheads, landing
quays (Spuds).
6. Floating roadways
(Whales).
7. Pontoons
(Beetles).

**THE
"SPUDS"**
These pierheads
moved up and down
with the tide
on four steel legs.

A
landing-
ship tank
unloading
vehicles directly
onto the deck of the
Spud from where
they could be driven
ashore along the
floating roadways.

77

The success of Operation Overlord depended on the ability of the engineers to cope with a number of difficult tasks. The landing beaches had first to be cleared of mines and obstacles and, immediately after the assault, beach exits had to be opened up to free the congestion of vehicles and wreckage on the shore. After that, landing strips had to be built and the bridges that had been destroyed to hinder enemy movements had to be repaired. Often working under enemy fire, the engineers suffered proportionally heavy losses.

BRITISH BEACH GROUPS
They coordinated traffic on the beaches and were distinguished by white bands on their helmets.

LOUDHAILER AND LAMP
Naval beach battalions used these to signal landing craft onto the beach.

BRITISH ASSAULT WAVE
A Crocodile with its armoured trailer full of napalm spits a jet of fire at the defenders, while a Crab makes a path through a minefield by beating the soil with its flailing chains. On the extreme left an engineer tank places a hinged bridge over a breach made in the concrete sea wall and a Fascine tank is about to drop its bundle into an anti-tank ditch.

Helmet of the American 6th Naval Battalion sent on Omaha Beach.

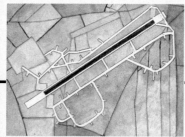

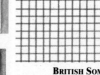

Plan of the advanced landing strip, B2, built near Bazenville.

BRITISH SOMERFELD MESH
Steel-mesh sheet used to strengthen British landing strips. The teams which installed the RAF's advanced airfields fixed the mesh to the ground with special pitons.

AMERICAN PIERCED-STEEL PLANKING
Used for airstrip foundations. Consisted of perforated plates fixed together with tongue and groove, and anchored by pitons.

CATERPILLAR D 7 BULLDOZER
Armour-plated, these were used for levelling beach roadways and the preparation of airstrips.

LANDING ON AN "AMERICAN" BEACH
Landing craft discharge their cargoes directly onto the beach while DUKW's shuttle between the shore and ships anchored out to sea. Stores are piling up, and a roadway inland has been opened past a ruined enemy bunker. Men cluster around the tented headquarters of the Beach Control Unit.

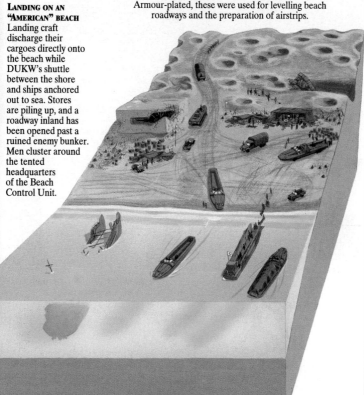

▲ **AMERICAN CEMETERY AT SAINT-LAURENT-SUR-MER** ▲ *166*

▲ **GERMAN CEMETERY AT LA CAMBE** ▲ *174*

▲ **BRITISH HEADSTONE FOR AN UNKNOWN GERMAN SOLDIER**

▲ **AMERICAN CEMETERY AT SAINT JAMES** 4,410 are buried there ▲ *227.*

▼ **GERMAN CROSSES AND TUMULUS AT LA CAMBE**

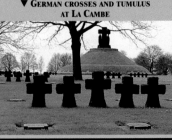

▼ **REVIERS CANADIAN CEMETERY, BÉNY-SUR-MER** ▲ *136*

▲ **BRITISH CEMETERY AND MEMORIAL AT BAYEUX** ▲ *158*

▲ **GERMAN OSSUARY AT MONT-D'HUISNES** ▲ *227*

▼ **FOUR BRITISH HEADSTONES**
Each one has the man's unit badge.

▲ **GERMAN CEMETERY AT SAINT-DÉSIR** (near Lisieux)

▼ **GRAVE MARKER OF ONE OF THE 21,400 GERMAN SOLDIERS BURIED AT LA CAMBE**

▼ **AMERICAN CEMETERY AT SAINT-LAURENT** The headstones indicate the soldier's religion.

● Memorials

Cemeteries and memorials are the visible reminders of the fighting in Normandy. Just visiting one cemetery (21 Allied and 6 German) one realises that one can never do enough honour to the troops who died in the Normandy campaign. Just as the cemeteries differ according to nationality, there are different types of memorial: those of the Comité du Débarquement, massive structures like the prow of a ship, the kilometre stones of the Liberty Way and the isolated monuments to a specific unit.

BIG RED ONE MEMORIAL
This was erected by the Comité du Débarquement on the cliffs above Omaha Beach near Colleville ▲ *169, 171*. It carries the Divisional badge and the inscription: "Allied forces landed on this beach which they called Omaha and liberated Europe."

BIG RED ONE OBELISK ▲ *168*
(Colleville-sur-Mer)

CIVILIAN MEMORIAL AND KILOMETRE STONE ▲ *184*
(Sainte-Mère-Église)

COMITÉ DU DÉBARQUEMENT MEMORIAL
(Carentan ▲ *180*)

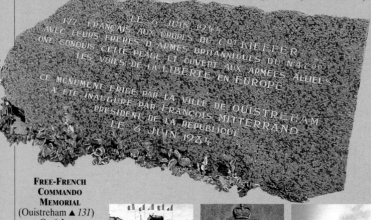

FREE-FRENCH COMMANDO MEMORIAL
(Ouistreham ▲ *131*)
On 6 June, French commandos led by Commandant Kieffer landed there and cleared the casino. In honour of that action the town had a memorial erected, which was unveiled by President Mitterrand on 6 June 1984.

MEMORIAL TO THE 2nd DB
(Écouché ▲ *240*)

REGINA RIFLES REGIMENT PLAQUE
(Courseulles ▲ *135*)

PATTON MONUMENT
(Avranches ▲ *222*)

FILMS AND DOCUMENTARIES

FRANÇOIS JOSEPH

▲ During the crossing a sailor, wearing a lifejacket, cuddles a puppy in his arms: The calm before the storm.

▲ A tank crosses the beach while behind it is the landing craft which brought it in.
▼ Edward G. Robinson, the great American actor, smoking a cigar.

The famous war reporter Jack Lieb was called up into the American Army to cover the war in Europe. Starting in 1943 he filmed the preparations for the landings in England, and at the end of May 1944 he went to the south coast to film the departure of the Allied invasion fleet. He arrived ashore on Utah Beach 4 hours after the first assault wave on 6 June and stayed there for eight days. He made two films, one personal and the other for the army, and received a French decoration for bravery. Below are several scenes.

▲ Ernest Hemingway covered the Battle of Normandy as a war correspondent. He landed with the first assault wave on Omaha Beach.

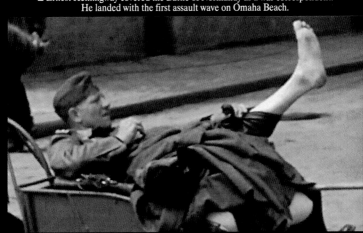

▲ A ludicrous scene of the German defeat: an officer in a wheelbarrow.
▼ An image of the victory: French people offering bunches of flowers.

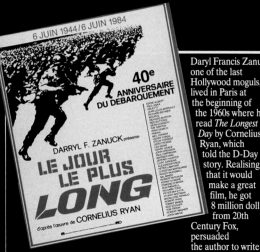

6 JUIN 1944 / 6 JUIN 1984

40e
ANNIVERSAIRE
DU DEBARQUEMENT

EDDIE ALBERT
PAUL ANKA
ARLETTY
JEAN-LOUIS BARRAULT
CURT JÜRGENS
RICHARD BEYMER
BOURVIL
RICHARD BURTON
RED BUTTONS
SEAN CONNERY
RAY DANTON
IRINA DEMICK
FABIAN
MEL FERRER
HENRY FONDA
STEVE FORREST
GERT FRÖBE
LEO GENN
JOHN GREGSON
PAUL HARTMANN
JEFFREY HUNTER
CURT JÜRGENS
ALEXANDER KNOX
PETER LAWFORD
CHRISTIAN MARQUAND
RODDY McDOWALL
SAL MINEO
KENNETH MORE
EDMOND O'BRIEN
RON RANDELL
ROBERT RYAN
TOMMY SANDS
MAURICE SCHELL
ROBERT WAGNER
STUART WHITMAN
RICHARD WYMARK
WOLFGANG PREISS
TOM TRYON
ROBERT WAGNER
JOHN WAYNE

DARRYL F. ZANUCK présente

LE JOUR
LE PLUS
LONG

d'après l'œuvre de CORNELIUS RYAN

Daryl Francis Zanuck, one of the last Hollywood moguls, lived in Paris at the beginning of the 1960s where he read *The Longest Day* by Cornelius Ryan, which told the D-Day story. Realising that it would make a great film, he got 8 million dollars from 20th Century Fox, persuaded the author to write a screenplay and set off for Normandy where he set up his HQ in the Hotel Malherbe in Caen. His intention was to show war on the screen better than ever before. He achieved his aim and *The Longest Day* was the greatest success of his career. The theme music of the film, by Maurice Jarre, was played at his funeral.

Top right. Robert Mitchum playing the American General Norman Cota, encouraging the engineers responsible for opening a breach through the sea-wall which was hindering the GIs, pinned down on the beach by enemy fire, from moving inland. Right. John Wayne, in the role of Colonel Vandervoort, wounded while finding a way through the flooded marshes of the Cotentin with his elite troops.

The Young Lions, E. Dmytryk (1958)

The Big Red

The Second World War has been portrayed frequently on the screen, and the end of the Nazi nightmare and the Allied advance provided material for unforgettable fiction. *The Young Lions*, an American film by Edward Dmytryk (1958) based on the novel by Irwin Shaw, starred Marlon Brando in the main role, Montgomery Clift, Dean Martin and Maximilian Schell. The story was concerned with the long struggle between an SS officer and two GIs.

Le Bataillon du ciel, A. Esway (1946)

Up from the Beach, R. Parrish (1965)

Break Through, A. V. McLaglen (1978)

The Long Day's Dying Collinson (1968)

S. Fuller (1980)

An extract from *Games of Love and War* by the Canadian Arthur Hiller (1964) with James Coburn, concerned with those who hid away. Below, two posters. Left, *Le Bataillon du ciel*, by Alexandre Esway (1946) – screenplay by Joseph Kessel and Pierre Blanchar. Right, *Games of Love and War*. The latest feature film is the Steven Spielberg's *Saving private Ryan*, rewarded with five Oscars in 1999.

THE ART OF THE
BATTLE OF NORMANDY

ODILE GEORGE

● POSTERS

THE POSTER WAR

In 1944 a different
war was raging,
the psychological
one between
Hitler's Germany
and the Allies.
In addition
to the war of
the air waves and
the war on screen,
there was also
the poster war,
an element in
the bitter struggle
to influence minds.
Nazi propaganda
announced at the
end of 1943 that
"Fortress Europe"
defended by the
Atlantic Wall
was invincible.
The various Allied
war ministers
responded with
a series of aggressive
posters hammering
home their message
plainly and effectively,
well designed and
"demanding the
least amount
of reasoning."
The French poster
artist, Carlu, said
when discussing
his work as a poster
propagandist:
"We have to draw
our posters to be
the sort that can
be understood
in the minimum
of time. This
requirement leads
us to provoke the
desired reaction
in the mind of
the viewer using
only visual means
and without
the subterfuge
of words. Because
of that fact, the
graphic symbol
provides a
considerable
intensity of expression
which addresses
the senses without
the need for
reasoning.
In fact the interplay
of lines and colour
together with
sentimental
significance,
immediately induces

the message we wish
to promote.
Thus the poster
has become a sort
of ideogram,
that is to say,
a graphic design
which directly
expresses an idea
without recourse
to words." Here,
the graphic image
takes on different
aspects: the "Gallic"
emphasis of the
cockerel and
the village church
tower, the use
of symbols
(Between
the Hammer and
the Anvil) by Carlu,
and moves onto
the cold, compact
and hostile imagery
of "United we
are strong".

92

ENTRE LE MARTEAU ...

... ET L'ENCLUME !..

UNIS POUR LA LIBERATION

la France éternelle
ses amis, ses alliés

THIS IS THE YEAR !

IT'S UP TO US TO LET 'EM HAVE IT !

4

BUY THAT INVASION BOND!

The exodus of the Normans
fleeing the bombardments.
Edouard Lagnel, July 1944.

WAR FROM THE SHARP END

The drawings of Bromberg (**2, 3, 8** and **9**), an American artist who went to the theatre of war to "obtain a graphic image" are expressions of life. He portrays neither a heroic nor general picture of combat, but rather represents the point of view of the ordinary soldier who suffers: a group kneeling beside a dead comrade, wounded being evacuated in a jeep, loaded with infantry and stretchers. His treatment evokes the exhaustion of the soldier: the imprecise lines do not establish a definitive shape but grow into an impression of suffering and a sense of bewilderment after fear and pain. The compositions appear veiled, the wateriness of dawn and sweat .... The figures are portrayed in a space without perspective, opaque, almost suffocating. A reddish glimmer rises in the background where the assault is being pressed home.

PRAGMATISM

Two Englishmen, one anonymous (**4**) and the other called Alan Ritchie (**6** and **7**), produced a completely different version of D-Day. Without emotion they described three essential phases of the campaign, the Mulberry harbours, the landing of vehicles and an action-packed moment in the battle inland. One does not notice any artistic finesse or emotional outpouring but purely a statement of fact soberly rendered.

1		5	
2		6	7
3	4	8	9

CALVO, THE NORMAN
(1892-1958)
The designer Calvo
had previously been
an innkeeper,
but having had
difficulties he devoted
himself exclusively
to his real passion,
drawing, for which
he had a natural
talent. He had within
himself a certain
delight in his work
which shone through.
It was evident in
his use of space:

Nothing was allowed
to get lost.
He used characters
in profusion, mostly
animals, laughable
when they were
nice and vaguely
disquieting when
they were not,
everywhere in
view and taking part
in the action.
In 1941 he began
to work on *La bête
est morte* (the beast
is dead), a comic
book about the big

bad wolf Hitler
who is held
up to ridicule.
The Americans
are portrayed as
buffaloes and
the British as
bulldogs in a
work which
is both exuberant
and delightful.
When it was
published after
the war the book
incurred the wrath
of Walt Disney,
who thought that

Calvo's wolf
resembled the "Big
Bad Wolf" from
his own cartoons.

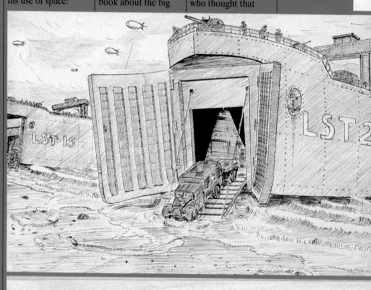

"WE SOON REALISED THAT IN SPITE OF THE SOUNDS,
THE NOISE AND THE TERRIFYING SPECTACLE OF THE BEACHES
WE HAD PROGRESSED SEVERAL MILES."

ALAN RITCHIE, BRITISH WAR ARTIST.

"DO YOU KNOW WHAT I'M THINKING ?
ABOUT MY MOM WHO IS VICTORIOUSLY
BRANDISHING MY LIFE-INSURANCE POLICY."
STATEMENT BY AN AMERICAN LIEUTENANT REPORTED BY ROBERT CAPA

THE MONOCHROME WAR

One does not sense the breath of a saga in this manifestation of war, represented by mechanical force and firepower. The concept of "total war" is portrayed as a climax: the sea, the sky, the earth are all mobilised in the military sense of the word. Individual heroism does not have the meaning that used to be conveyed by a charge of cavalry or infantry fighting hand to hand. In this battle there was no physical contact, no hand to hand. One notices too that the gaudy uniforms of past armies have been succeeded by battledress which tends to hide the soldier from the eyes of the enemy and shelter him from his fire. One wants to undress him, not only to expose him. Modern war is a vast dissimulation exercise, revealed by the almost monochrome palette of the different works presented on these pages. The propitious dawn mist of 6 June 1944 softens the outlines without moderating the impression of a formidable wave of superbly-equipped warriors. The whole natural environment participates in the general conflagration. Even the horizon is at war.

99

Two realistic visions
of the war from
above and below.
On the ground
the infantry patrol
in an apocalyptic
landscape while in
contrast the tanks
appear to be a force
that is on the move.
In the aircraft the
war is far away:
just men doing
their jobs.

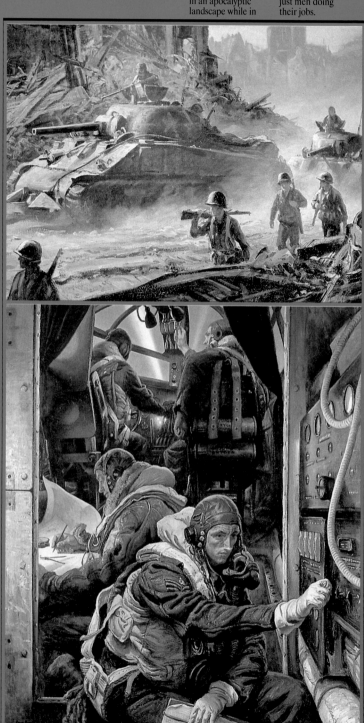

THE BATTLE OF NORMANDY
TEXTS AND TESTIMONIES

A TOUS LES FRANÇAIS

La France a perdu une bataille !
Mais la France n'a pas perdu la guerre !

Des gouvernants de rencontre ont pu capituler, cédant à la panique, oubliant l'honneur, livrant le pays à la servitude. Cependant, rien n'est perdu !

Rien n'est perdu, parce que cette guerre est une guerre mondiale. Dans l'univers libre, des forces immenses n'ont pas encore donné. Un jour, ces forces écraseront l'ennemi. Il faut que la France, ce jour-là, soit présente à la victoire. Alors, elle retrouvera sa liberté et sa grandeur. Tel est mon but, mon seul but !

Voilà pourquoi je convie tous les Français, où qu'ils se trouvent, à s'unir à moi dans l'action, dans le sacrifice et dans l'espérance.

Notre patrie est en péril de mort.
Luttons tous pour la sauver !

VIVE LA FRANCE !

C. de Gaulle

JUIN 1940   **GÉNÉRAL DE GAULLE**

THE PRELIMINARIES TO A MILITARY OPERATION

THE LONELINESS OF COMMAND

Early on the morning of 4 June in the naval headquarters at Southwick House near Portsmouth, the Supreme Commander had to make the most difficult decision in his life – to go or not to go.

❝The final conference for determining the feasibility of attacking on the tentatively selected day, June 5, was scheduled for 4 am. on June 4. However, some of the attacking contingents had already been ordered to sea, because if the entire force was to land on June 5, then some of the important elements stationed in northern parts of the United Kingdom could not wait for final decision on the morning of June 4.

When the commanders assembled on the morning of June 4 the report we received was discouraging. Low clouds, high winds, and formidable wave action were predicted to make landing a most hazardous affair. The meteorologists said that air support would be impossible, naval gunfire would be inefficient, and even the handling of small boats would be rendered difficult. Admiral Ramsay thought that the mechanics of landing could be handled, but agreed with the estimate of the difficulty in adjusting gunfire. His position was mainly neutral. General Montgomery, properly concerned with the great disadvantages of delay, believed that we should go. Tedder disagreed.

Weighing all factors, I decided that the attack would have to be postponed. This decision necessitated the immediate dispatch of orders to the vessels and troops already at sea and created some doubt as to whether they could be ready twenty-four hours later, in case the next day should prove favourable for the assault. Actually the manoeuvre of the ships in the Irish Sea proved most difficult by reason of the storm. That they succeeded in gaining ports, refuelling, and readying themselves to resume the movement a day later represented the utmost in seamanship and in brilliant command and staff work.The conference on the evening of June 4 presented little, if any, added brightness to the picture of the morning, and tension mounted even higher because the inescapable consequences of postponement were almost too bitter to comtemplate.

At 3.30 the next morning our little camp was shaking and shuddering under a wind of almost hurricane proportions and the accompanying rain seemed to be travelling in horizontal streaks. The mile-long trip through muddy roads to the naval headquarters was anything but a cheerful one, since it seemed impossible that in such conditions there was any reason for even discussing the situation.

When the conference started, the first report given us by Group Captain Stagg and the meteorologic staff was that the bad conditions predicted the day before for the coast of France were actually prevailing there and that if we had persisted in the attempt to land on June 5 a major disaster would almost surely have resulted. This they probably told us to inspire more confidence in their next astonishing declaration, which was that by the following morning a period of relatively good weather, heretofore completely unexpected, would ensue, lasting probably thirty-six hours. The long-term prediction was not good but they did give us assurance that this short period of good weather would intervene between the exhaustion of the storm we were then experiencing and the beginning of the next spell of really bad weather. The prospect was not bright because of the possibility that we might land the first several waves successfully and then find later build-up impracticable, and so have to leave the isolated original attacking forces easy prey to German counteraction. However, the consequences of the delay justified great risk and I quickly announced the decision to go ahead with the attack on June 6. The time was then 4.15 a.m., June 5. No one present disagreed and there was a definite brightening of faces as, without a further word, each went off to his respective post of duty to flash out to his command the messages that would set the whole host in motion.❞

DWIGHT D. EISENHOWER,
CRUSADE IN EUROPE.
HEINEMANN, LONDON.

Pre-battle tension

"Waiting"

Charles S. Dedon arrived at Liverpool as a member of the DUKW company in the summer of 1943. They trained in North Devon, Wales and took part in Exercise Tiger on Slapton Sands. As part of 5th Engineer Special Brigade, the DUKWs sailed from Portland on board a LST, bound for Omaha.

❝On the night of June 4th we left the inner harbor and joined a convoy of ships consisting of anything from a battleship down to a LCVp. It turned dark and I went to bed. I awoke about three A.M and looked out the Port Hole to find we were back in the harbor. We later learned that it was too rough and they had decided to wait another day.

The next day June 5th I spent reading "A Tree Grows in Brooklyn". I will always remember that book. Again we pulled out and this time it was the real thing. There was no sleeping. I lay in my bunk for a few hours but could not sleep. The sea was choppy and the moon looked out from behind some scattered clouds. I kept looking out on the deck and going down stairs to see if the men were alright. Most of them slept. There were ships for as far as you could see. They silhouetted against the dark night. We were dressed for the occasion, steel helmets, gas masks, life belts and arm. Our outer clothing was gas proof and smelt like the barn yard of an ancient French farmhouse. We had to be careful of the blackout regulations.

The plan called for us to leave the LST at 02.00 hours about fifteen miles at sea. As the time approached we went below to our DUKWs and waited. We were brought back to the deck a few minutes later by the sound of gunfire in the distance. The attack had started. The naval guns were opening up on the shore installations. The sky was red with flames.

At 04.30 our DUKW, Boston Irish, slid off the ramp of the LST. It was just beginning to get light. The doors of the LST opened up like a giant whale and the quack quacks came off one by one. The lapping of the waves was the only sound. As we hit the water the stern settled low and when it caught hold the rest of the DUKW slid into the choppy ocean. All twelve got off O.K. and we went to a designated meeting place to wait for the Navy escort. Some of the DUKWs with other units which were too heavily loaded went to the bottom as they came into the water.

As dawn approached we could see hundreds of ships all around us. There were some types that we had read about but never seen before. At 05.30 we started for shore. In the distance we could see the outline of land and still hear the Navy fire. Then the planes came over in droves. We ran in a column similar to a mother duck and her ducklings. The faster Navy craft with the infantry aboard who had earlier dates on shore than we did sped by. There was no waving, just a determination to get there.

I kept having trouble with my glasses. The spray from the waves would come over us every time the bow of the DUKW would hit the surf. We rode on top of our cargo which left us out in the open. Two of our DUKWs developed motor trouble. We left them to make out as best they could. It had been agreed beforehand that there would be no turning back...❞

CHARLES S. SEDON.
© MÉMORIAL
DE CAEN.

Letter written on June 1, 1944 by Georges Thierry d'Argenlieu (1889-1864), Commander in Chief of Free-French Navy Forces, to his friend Wietzel, Commander of the *Courbet* battleship ▲ *132.*

INTO BATTLE
BY PARACHUTE

**ASSAULT ON THE GUNS
OF MERVILLE**

*Alan Jefferson was a young
lieutenant commanding a platoon
in the 9th Battalion, the Parachute Regiment,
and took part in the attack on Merville Battery
in the early hours of D-Day. In 1987, he published a thoroughly researched
account of that action.*

"Number 1 was standing in the open doorway, hands gripping it on either side, left foot forward, chin up and looking his own height in the textbook attitude. If he allowed his eyes to look down, he must have had a wonderful view. The dispatcher was staring, mesmerised, at the darkened bulb of the green light. Then it glowed and I could see its reflection on the inside of the fuselage – Green.

The dispatcher danced about gesticulating, emphasising my previous conviction of his simian attributes ; N° 1 had gone, N° 2 followed.

'Go ! Go ! Go !' the dispatcher shouted. And I shouted with him. And then we were all shouting and all moving down the aircraft, faster and faster.

Suddenly there was nobody between me and the door. I caught a glimpse of the dispatcher's grinning face (he'd soon be breakfasting on bacon and eggs) and then the slipstream hit my face. The static line tightened and for a moment the whole weight of my falling body was taken by my left arm. It was flung up across my face, a painful wrench. 'Hell !' I thought, 'I've done it now.' The arm was almost useless though I had to get it up again and secure an even hold on the lift-webs for direction and especially for landing...

The luminous dial of my watch said 00.55 and after the obliterating grind of those aircraft engines it was wonderfully quiet: quieter than I had expected. Twice the moon appeared briefly, and there was a wind. Did I detect some muck and dust blowing about? Not sure. If so it must be coming from the bombing of the Battery.

Two canopies came into view a little below me, so I was not alone. The ground didn't seem far away now. (96-97 ... 100, 101, 102 for luck) 'Watch it! Coming in right. Pull down more on the left lift-web. Can't. Must. Left weak. Try! Here it co-o-omes. Good landing, Hurrah! This is France !'

I smacked the box on my chest to release the straps of the 'chute from my body, bundled up the Nylon and left it there (never done that before) and began pulling up tufts of grass – French grass – Norman grass! 'We're here! We are here! Well, I'm here, but I'm blowed if I know exactly where.'

Major Parry was standing a little away from the main RV position, in fact he was halfway up a tree, shining his lamp and lustily blowing his Ducks, bakelite.

It guided me in towards the RV and as I followed its aggressive call, I met Jimmy Loring, the Signals Officer. He was carrying a large canvas bag which held the Battalion's T-Panel Code – a set of silk panels, red on one side, white on the other. They were intended for use in daylight to give limited messages to our own aircraft above, by arranging them in certain shapes on the ground. To my amazement, Jimmy suddenly flung the bag down a large bomb crater, and walked on.

'Hey, we'll need that tomorrow – I mean today' I said and tumbled down to retrieve the bag. Staggering back to the level, I caught up with Jimmy and gave him back the bag, but again he threw it away. Again I saved it. This was becoming tiresome, and me with my game arm. There was no point in my continuing when he cast it aside for the third time, so I gave up and went my own way, leaving him muttering and cursing to himself. I never discoverd why he had behaved in that way.

When I reached the RV beside a clump of trees, I saw Lieutenant-Colonel Otway standing there, tense and white. I saluted and reported myself to him. He replied in an expressionless tone: 'You're commanding 'C' Company.'

I stood in astonishment. I, the most junior subaltern of the Company in command? Impossible! Where was Ian Dyer, where was 'Robbie' our second-in command? Where indeed were 'Jock' and 'Dizzie', the two other platoon commande? Why, it's ridiculous.

'Well, don't stand there, go and take over your Company.' I went.

And there they were in ditch, all eight of them. CSM 'Barney' Ross had arrived in advance with Major Parry and a couple of men from each company. Private Love was in tears. 'Oh, Sir," he wailed, 'I've lost my rifle and my helmet. What am I going to do?' To lose a rifle, especially at such a critical stage in the proceedings, was a court-martial offence, according to Colonel Otway's stern warning.

'Never mind, Love,' I told him – faintly amused – 'we'll find you another rifle, probably a German one. And keep your head down in the attack !'

ALAN JEFFERSON,
ASSAULT ON THE GUNS OF MERVILLE.
JOHN MURRAY, LONDON.

WITH THE 101ST AIRBORNE DIVISION

"The French battle
has begun."
Charles de Gaulle

Sam M. Gibbons was a 24-year-old captain in the 501st Parachute Infantry Regiment part of 101st Airborne Division who dropped intoFrance with 17 other men from a Dakota. He survived the war and went on to serve as a member of the US Congress.

My parachute snapped open with a loud crack – reflecting the added weight of combat equipment – as I had been taught to do, I looked up to check the parachute canopy – it was functionning perfectly – then looked around to make sure I was clear of other jumpers – couldn't see anyone. Did see and hear rifle and machine gun fire coming up from below me about 75 yards to my right – guess about 15 weapons in action. Could see muzzle blast and occasional tracers – apparently aimed at the waves of planes flying on toward the southeast. Got brief glimpses of small, blacked-out town six or seven hundred yards in front of me. Guessed it to be Sainte-Mère-Église. Guess later proved to be correct. Prepared to land-focused eyes on ground – looking fifty yards ahead of me (looking straight down might cause a broken leg). Knees slightly bent and feet together so that bone and muscle in both legs would absorb the force of landing. Feet hit – knees give – roll forward – end lying flat on my back. Lie quietly, after a noisy landing, my camouflaged parachute settles to ground right above my head. Germans fifty to seventy yards to the southeast would have heard that landing had they not been so noisy shooting at low-flying planes.

Instantly I knew I was in the wrong place – at least six miles from my planned drop zone and far deeper in German territory than planned. The time was 1:26 a.m., June 6, 1944. D-Day was to begin on the beaches at 6:30 a.m. The parachute jump from plane to ground in Normandy, France had taken 35-40 seconds, maybe less. Shortly after 1:26 a.m. while still on my back, I wiggled my feet and legs to make sure they

Les armées

were okay. Then unfastened my reserve'chute and chest straps came off. But I couldn't get the leg straps unbuckled because the harness was tight, so I cut those straps with my switchblade knife. Next off came the life preserver and my personal equipment bag that had been hanging below my reserve chute. I took my folding stock rifle out of the holster – checked the safety and finally rolled over on my stomach. All this probably took less than a minute, but it seemed like an hour. No one had seen me, and I had seen no one else, but there was plenty of shooting by those Germans about seventy yards from me. Their shooting was a blessing because it drowned out any noise I might make and because they were paying more attention to the sky than they were to the ground. **99**

SAM M. GIBBONS. © MÉMORIAL DE CAEN.

THE LANDING

The Rev. Myles Hickey was the Roman Catholic chaplain with the North Shore Regiment, a Canadian unit from New Brunswick. On D-Day he was awarded the Military Cross for his bravery in caring for the wounded.

66 To boats, 'came the command', and in perfect order, groups of thirty stepped into the little gasoline boats on the deck. Slowly they were swung out, then down, down, down, till they struck the water. It was seven o'clock. We pushed away from the 'Brigadier' like life boats leaving a sinking ship. The sea was rough. Soon the area was dotted with our little boats bobbing up and down like sea-gulls on a choppy sea. We lined up in position and started slowly over the ten miles to shore.

The German guns had now opened up, and their shells came screaming back to answer ours. In we moved. The last three miles were to be covered with a burst of speed.

The German small arms fire was now reaching us. Suddenly our boat leaped forward with a burst of speed into the jaws of death! No time was lost; the boats dumped us as they turned ; many were sunk ; the water was covered with wreckage. Joel Murray from Cross Point and I landed together in the water, but we could reach bottom and made shore. A young lad next to me fell, a bullet got him. I dragged him ashore, and there in that awful turmoil I knelt for a second that seemed an eternity and anointed him – the first of the long, long list I anointed in action. There was a long fifty yards of wide, open beach between the water's edge and the cement wall; if you could make the wall, you were safe, for a time at least, from the enemy fire; but ah, so many of our fine young men didn't make it. There on the open beach they lay dead or dying. It was our duty to get to them; so, with our stretcher bearers and first-aid men, Doctor Patterson and I crawled back again across that fifty yards of hell. The beach was sprayed from all angles by the enemy machine-guns, and now their mortars and heavy guns began hitting us. Crawling along in the sand, I just reached a group of three badly wounded men when a shell landed among us, killing the others outright. That is why the report got around that I had been killed in action. Someone saw the shell hit and figured I had

alliées débarquent

gotten it, too. The noise was deafening; you couldn't even hear our huge tanks that had already landed and were crunching their way through the sand ; some men, unable to hear them, were run over and crushed to death. A blast shook the earth like an earthquake; it was the engineers blowing the wall. All the while, enemy shells came screaming in, faster and faster; as we crawled along, we could hear the bullets and shrapnel cutting into the sand around us ; when a shell came screaming over, you dug into the sand and held your breath, waited for the blast and the shower of stones and debris that followed; then, when it cleared a little, right next to you, perhaps someone you had been talking to half an hour before, lay dead. Others, dying, might open their eyes as your reached them.

By the little disc around their necks, I knew their religion. If Catholic, I gave them Extreme Unction with one unction on the forehead; but whether Catholic or Protestant, I would tell the man he was dying and to be sorry for his sins; and often I was rewarded by the dying man opening his eyes and nodding to me knowingly.

It was a hard job to get the wounded on the stretchers and carry them to the shelter of the wall. I will never forget the courage of the stretcher bearers and first-aid men that morning. If some men are living today, next to Almighty God they can thank men like Lieutenant Heaslip of Vancouver and his stretcher bearers; and I will always remember the bravery of these first-aid men from our own regiment, Eymard Hache, Buddy Daley and Bob Adair. They stayed with us on the open beach until we carried all the wounded we could to safety behind the wall and gave them what help we could **99**

> REV R. MYLES HICKEY,
> *THE SCARLET DAWN.*
> INIPRESS. FREDERICKTON, N.B., CANADA.

THE LANDING ON OMAHA BEACH

Joseph P. Doyen was a crew member on board the American LST 506, which arrived at Omaha Beach at 13.00 on D-Day, having sailed from Portsmouth the previous day.

66 Our ship dropped anchor a short, distance out from land because the beach-head area had not yet been cleared of mines, and roads had to be bull-dozed to get the equipment up off the beach.

Our skipper had volunteered to send one of our six landing craft ashore to help in any way we could, so he picked our boat. Our crew of four men and one officer, Ensign Rob't Carter. As we were being lowered from the boat davit, our Captain pointed to the shore and told us to land where all those shells were bursting, find the beach master and report to him for further orders ....

LIBERTÉ

DE NORMA

Organe quotidien du Comité de

Administration et Rédaction : 34, rue Demolo

LIBERTÉ

LES VOILA !
Dimanche 9 juillet. 11 h. 30.
Trois chars allemands s'installent place
des Petites-Boucheries, menaçant de leurs
canons la rue de Bayeux et la rue Guil-

The
beach was loaded with
all sorts of equipment. Lots of oil, wrecked
trucks, tanks, small boats, life jackets and bodies. Some whole,
some not. I noticed a man's head that was no more than two inches thick. Another
with his intestines strung out fifteen feet onto the sand.
Confusion was paramount on the beach, and no one could tell us where to find the
Beachmaster, however a medic asked us if we could take some wounded men out to
one of the ships where there would be doctors and medical supplies. Since we had
made a temporary operating room on our ship and had nine doctors aboard, we
loaded about twenty wounded men and tried to back off the beach.
The extra weight we had taken aboard prevented us from backing off the beach.
There was a landing barge behind us waiting for our spot on the shore-line, so I
grabbed a long line and tried to throw it to them but the strong wind blowing against
us caused the rope to always fall short.
My next idea was to grab the line, jump off the stern of our boat, and wade out far
enough to get the line to them. Well ... since we had tried to get off the sand with the
engine in reverse, we had dug a deep hole in the sand with the huge propeller, about
six feet deep, and I sunk down over my head. Since I had so much clothing which
was now waterproof from the gas repellent, I had sprayed on, I floated to the top.
Earl Barber, our cox'swain, had the good sense to neutral the propeller as he saw
me jump off, otherwise I could have been sucked into it, and chopped to bits.
We finally got off the beach and headed out for our ship in the harbor. One of the
wounded soldiers aboard had his foot and ankle blown off and one of the others had
stepped on a 'Jumping Jack' mine, a type that after you step on it, it jumps up in
the air three to five feet, then explodes. His reproductive organs had been
shattered.
On the way back to the ship, the salt water spray coming over everyone caused by
our flat ramp bow and the rough water was very painful to the soldiers with all their
open wounds. I jumped up onto the bow, extended three feet above the top and
ordered one of the other crew to join me to keep some of the spray off the
wounded. He said he was too cold and didn't want to join me. I mentionned to him
that these men had been through hell today so forget your discomfort and help me
defray the salt spray.
After getting all the wounded out to our ship, we returned to the beach and by this
time it was getting quite dark.
Suddenly, we heard the drone of a low-flying airplane. He was following the
shoreline and he came right over our boat at no more than 100 ft. altitude. I could
have hit him with a rock or better still, if I had known he would come right over us, I
could have shot at him with our thirty-caliber machine gun that we had mounted in
our gun tube.
In the dark we could not find the Beach Master or any wounded men, so we headed
back to our ship. We had no trouble finding it because a few German E boats had
snuck in past the destroyer picket-line and had launched flare-shells in the sky which
came down slowly via parachutes, lighting up the area and making all the ships visible.
I finally saw the Beachmaster, dressed in yellow clothes as I was told he would be. He
was standing there with another man trying to signal an LST that was approaching
the beach for a landing. I started to ask him a question and he interrupted me asking
if I was Navy and could I send a message with semaphore flags. When I said I could,

1ʳᵉ ANNÉE
N° 1

9-13
JUILLET 1944

UN FRANC

DIE
ration
EN

Le premier salut
aux trois couleurs

he told me to signal that ship that he was heading into a mine field, to back off and wait for instructions.

In using flags there are short cuts, so I gave the signalman the letter U. This meant *you* and he acknowledged this word by a wave of his right hand flag over his head. I then gave him a R. This was for *are*, so after I got to the part stating the mine field and to back off, they were in full reverse ... And so was I. Can you imagine that anything that was in the open on that beach got shot at, like the three men trying to get a single truck saved, and here I am with flags in my hand waving wildly to save a big ship and did, yet I did not get killed. All the time I was signaling I had a strong feeling that there was a bullet half way between the cliff and my head.

There is no doubt that the Good Lord had a part in this event.

When I got back to the landing craft waiting on the beach, Barber had loaded up with more wounded to take back out to our ship. As we backed, there was a loud crunch as we hit one of the beach obstacles the Germans had erected, a five-foot steel protrusion set in cement bases. It was underwater and we could not see it.

The wounded men who could walk jumped over to the Rhino, but we had one man on a stretcher who had been shot several times right thru his stomach and couldn't even sit up. He said 'Just leave me here cause I am going to die anyway.' We could not leave him so one of the crew and I grabbed the stretcher and balanced him on the gunnel (ranwale). The water was very rough, and our boat was rising and falling as it banged into the side of the Rhino. I said 'We will have to throw him on the count of three', which we did and he landed on the raft. A heck of a way to treat a wounded man. Our landing craft finally sunk and I had to grab a line that was thrown to me to get up on the Rhino. As I got aboard, I saw one more soldier in the water hanging onto the rope so as I tried to lift him up but could no quite bring him aboard, so I reached under his arm and around his back to get a better grip and my whole fist went into a hole that he received in battle. A wound of this size full of sand and salt water must have been very painful. ❞

JOHN P. DOYEN.
© MÉMORIAL DE CAEN.

A DEFENDER'S PARADISE

Sidney Jary, fresh from training, arrived as a replacement officer in Normandy in July 1944, and was assigned to command a platoon in the Somerset Light Infantry. His baptism of fire came in the assault on Mont Pinçon, and he fought right through to the end of the war with the same platoon.

❝'GENTLEMEN, your life expectancy from the day you join your battalion will be precisely three weeks.' The florid, moustached major who addressed us at the small reinforcement camp, a few miles from Bayeux, obviously had a misplaced sense of humour or he should have been sacked. On second thoughts, he definitely should have been sacked. Not that any of the dozen infantry subalterns took the slightest notice of what, to us, were the ramblings of an old fool. He was probably no more than forty!

It was early July 1944 and I was a reinforcement officer for either 1st Battalion, The Hampshire Regiment, in 50th Northumbrian Division, or the 7th Battalion in 43rd Wessex Division. As events turned out I joined neither battalion.

The 43rd Wessex Division's first major battle had been Hill 112 and owing to their high officer casualties I was sent, with a courteous explanation and a touching apology by the reinforcement-camp commandant, away from my own regiment for the following twelve months. The 4th Battalion, the Somerset Light Infantry, was in 129 Brigade and was a pre-war Territorial Army battalion with close links with Bristol and Bath. In the United Kingdom until late June 1944, it was a close-knit unit

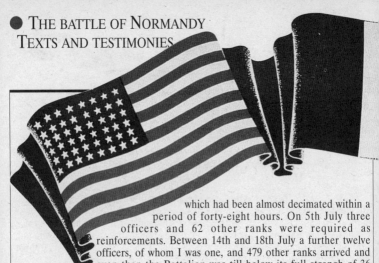

which had been almost decimated within a period of forty-eight hours. On 5th July three officers and 62 other ranks were required as reinforcements. Between 14th and 18th July a further twelve officers, of whom I was one, and 479 other ranks arrived and even then the Battalion was till below its full strengh of 36 officers and nearly 700 NCOs and men. This will give some idea of the appalling level of infantry casualties which had to be accepted in order to enlarge the slender and vulnerable Normandy beach-head.

Normandy was a defender's paradise. It was bad tank country and our poor supporting armour lost many tanks, particularly to Panzerfausts (German bazooka detachments) firing at about thirty yards range or less. We soon learned not to allow our 'tame armour' to wander outside immediate infantry protection. In retrospect, Normandy is now a surrealistic dream, totally lacking the stark clarity of memories of subsequent battles : a pastiche of heat, dust, the stench of bloated cattle, the litter of dead tanks, rusting guns and wildly scattered grenades and small arms ammunition. We fought from one hedgerow to the next, up tortuous, overgrown sunken lanes: ideal country for the German defender but appalling for attacking infantry. However, no arm but infantry could take and hold the Normandy bocage.

It was here that I served my apprenticeship and the Platoon developed its character which, despite constant depletion by casualties over the coming ten months, it would retain until the end of the war. It was also here that, imperceptibly, I became possessive with 18 Platoon. It was mine, to be guarded with an almost maternal jealousy that resented all criticism of my soldiers.

WELCOME TO Y

Most importantly, it was in the *Bocage* that I began to appreciate how vital is grip: grip on oneself, grip on one's soldiers and grip on the situation. Unlike characters in novels and films, most men react nervously to real battle conditions. Discipline and regimental pride are supports but, in decisive moments of great danger, the grip of the leader on the led is paramount. Infantry section and platoon commanders must possess the minds and hearts of their soldiers. Strength of character is not enough. Successful leadership in battle, although complex and intangible, always seemed to me to depend on two factors. Firstly, soldiers must have confidence in their leaders' professional ability and, secondly, they must trust them as men. It helps too, if a leader has the reputation of being lucky. Field Marshal Montgomery placed great importance on the principle of 'making the enemy dance to your tune.' Nowhere is this more important than in the platoon and company battle. It is decisive, because if you do not dominate events your enemy will.

Sound leadership – like true love, to which I suspect it is closely related – is all powerful. It can overcome the seemingly impossible and its effect on both leader and led is profound and lasting.

Even after the passage of forty years, brief mention of the Battalion's finest officers and NCOs brings a smile to the faces of the survivors of my platoon. Their

resentment of those who failed to lead when it mattered most still runs astonishingly deep. 99

18 PLATOON, SIDNEY JARY.
PRIVATELY PUBLISHED.

THE COMMANDOS LAND ON SWORD

Dr. J.H. Patterson was the medical officer of N° 4 Commando which landed at Riva-Bella. The medics were in many ways the unsung heroes in battle as they worked unarmed and under fire, treating both their own wounded and the enemy.

66 We were rolling heavily in a big south-west swell, which broke continually over us, drenching us to the skin. My hands grew numb and dead, and my teeth were chattering with cold and fright. I had a look at my batman, sitting on the thwart. He was looking awful, but gave me a big grin through his green. It was zero hour, and the first infantry were going in. We passed round the rum, and those who were not sea-sick took a good swig. The sea was dotted with 'bags vomit' and I could see the boys on the LCIs rushing to the rail.

I took a look around the boat. Private Hindmarch beside me, polite as ever and looking surprisingly pink. Lieutenant Kennedy – I always remember him as a sergeant in N° 5 – looking grim, but enjoying his rum. Just as well too, as he was never seen again after leaving the boat, Little Sapper Mullen, the artist, as grey as a corpse, who died of wounds later that day. Gordon Webb and Peter Beckett in the bows, peering forward, alert and tense.

U OUR ALLIES

The chaps in the other boats were passing round the rum, and I could hear snatches of song through the hellish din. Hutchie Burt's boat went in singing 'Jerusalem'. We didn't sing in our boat. My mouth was bone-dry and I was shaking all over; I doubt if I could have produced a note.

The shore was obscured by smoke, but I made out the fountains of shell bursts, and the rattle of small arms fire cut through the roar of the heavy shells. Something was hit on our starboard bow, and a huge cloud of black smoke went up, with orange flame licking against the murk of battle. With four hundred yards to go, we were late. Men struggled into their rucksacks – an almost impossible feat. I gave it up until we grounded.

Bullets rattled agaisnt the craft and splinters went whining overhead. 'Ready on the ramp!' We cowered down. The explosions were very near. 'Going in to land',

We touched, bumped and slewed round. This was no true landing. Then the order : 'Ramps down!' The boat began to empty, and, being at the stern, the medics were the last to leave. I seized a stretcher. No one seemed ready to take the other one, so I picked it up too, staggered to the bows and flopped into the water. It was thigh deep, as the craft had grounded on some softish obstacle, probably a body.

The next stretch of time is muddled in my memory. I have no idea how long it took from the boat till I reached the enemy wire. There was thick smoke over the beach,

and tide low but flooding. There were many bodies in the wate; one was hanging round one of the tripod obstacles. The shoals were churned with bursting shells. I saw wounded men among the dead, pinned down by the weight of their equipment. The first I came to was little Sapper Mullen, the artist. He was submerged to his chin and quite helpless. Somehow I got my scissors out and with my numb hands, which felt weak and useless, I began to cut away his rucksack and equipment. Hindmarch appeared beside me and got working on the other side. He was a bit rattled, but steadied when I spoke to him and told him what to do. As I was bending over I felt a smack across my bottom, as if someone had hit me with a big stick. It was a shell splinter, as appeared later, but it hit nothing important and I swore and went on. We dragged Mullen to the water's edge at last. **"**

ATTACK ON A GERMAN STRONGPOINT

Lionel Roebuck volunteered as a schoolboy in 1942, and on D-Day served with the 2nd Battalion of the Yorkshire Regiment, part of 3rd Infantry Division, which landed on Sword Beach. Once inland his company became involved in the attack on the strongpoint near Douvres-la-Délivrande known as "Daimler".

"As the guns laid down their high explosive shells to good effect, our small force of assault troops started to organize ready to be able to attack across the open field. We lightened our loads by stacking big packs and any surplus gear by the track, hopefully for picking up later, and crept forward, nearer to our goal, until we were about fifty yards from the wire fence and then waited for the end of our supporting fire. There was a wide, sloping dug-out pit to the right of the track, (a feature used frequently by the Germans, to protect and house their vehicles) and, for a few of us, including myself, it made the ideal place in which to take temporary cover. Others stood nearby watching from a gateway, curiously tempting providence, as bits of the spent shrapnel, from exploding shells, screaming and singing, winged over towards us. One piece hit an officer hard on his chest giving him quite a shock, slightly winding him. He quickly picked off the hot piece of metal and threw it down with no apparent harm done to him. **"**

Message urgent

du Commandement Suprême des
Forces Expéditionnaires Alliées
AUX HABITANTS DE CETTE VILLE

Afin que l'ennemi commun soit vaincu, les Armées de l'Air Alliées vont attaquer tous les centres de transports ainsi que toutes les voies et moyens de communications vitaux pour l'ennemi.

Des ordres à cet effet ont été donnés.

Vous qui lisez ce tract, vous vous trouvez dans ou près d'un centre essentiel à l'ennemi pour le mouvement de ses troupes et de son matériel. L'objectif vital près duquel vous vous trouvez va être attaqué incessamment.

Il faut sans délai vous éloigner, avec votre famille, pendant quelques jours, de la zone de danger où vous vous trouvez.

N'encombrez pas les routes. Dispersez-vous dans la campagne, autant que possible.

**PARTEZ SUR LE CHAMP !
VOUS N'AVEZ PAS UNE MINUTE A PERDRE !**

THE GERMANS' POINT OF VIEW

THE IMPORTANCE OF PANZERS

After the war, the Canadian journalist Milton Shulman recounted the story of the German defeat, based on interviews with the commanders concerned. In this extract he tells the story of General Bayerlein, the commander of Panzer Lehr Division.

"'At two o'clock in the morning of 5 June, I was alerted,' he said. 'The invasion fleet was coming across the Channel. I was told to begin moving north that afternoon at five o'clock. This was too early. Air attacks had been severe in daylight and everyone knew everything that could fly would support the invasion. My request for a delay until twilight was refused. We moved as ordered, and immediately came under an air attack. I lost twenty or thirty vehicles by night-fall...

'We kept on during the night with but three hours' delay for rest and fuelling. At daylight, General Dollman, commander of Seventh Army, gave me a direct order to proceed and there was nothing else to do. The first air attack came about half-past five that morning, near Falaise. By noon it was terrible; my men were calling the main road from Vire to Beny-Bocage a fighter-bomber racecourse ....

'Every vehicle was covered with tree branches and moved along hedges and the edges of woods. Road junctions were bombed, and a bridge knocked out at Condé. This did not stop my tanks, but it hampered other vehicles. By the end of the day I had lost forty tank trucks carrying fuel, and ninety others. Five of my tanks were knocked out, and eighty-four half-tracks, prime-movers and self-propelled guns. These were serious losses for a division not yet in action. I was just east of Tilly on 6 June and ready to attack.

'My attack took Ellon, and I could have gone straight to the sea down the corridor between the American and British forces, splitting them apart. I was ordered to hold at Ellon because units on my right flank had been delayed. I was a day behind schedule myself, because of air harassment.'

Thus 9 June arrived and still no co-ordinated armored attack had been possible. The Seventh Army telephone journal provides the appreciation of the High Command for that day:

17:30 hours
Conversation of Field Marshal Rommel with the Commander and Chief-of-Staff of Seventh Army at Army Headquarters.
Field Marshal Rommel ... orders that the enemy must be prevented at all costs from:
(a) Getting the fortress of Cherbourg, and harbor, in his hands.
(b) Establishing the connection between both bridge heads; that west of the Orne and that west of the Vire.
The Chief-of-Staff of Seventh Army expresses the opinion that the enemy, because of the increased resistance south of Montebourg, will commit more airborne troops, in order to take possession of Cherbourg rapidly. Field Marshal Rommel does not share this opinion, since the Supreme Command expects a large landing on the Channel coast within the next few days, and therefore the enemy will not have more airborne troops available ....

But it was not until 10 June that bad news in full measure began to flood into the headquarters of Seventh Army. The first part of the day's entries records such pessimistic sentences as these: '3rd Parachute Division must be brought forward piecemeal because of lack of fuel' and 'The advance units of 17th SS Panzer Grenadier Division are stuck in the Saint-Lô area because of lack of fuel.' The first information that the counter-attack of Panzer Group West, of which 'Sepp' Dietrich's 1 SS Panzer Corps was the most important part, had failed, was noted in these words: 'Panzer Group West has sustained enemy attack and is now engaged in local counter-attack. It is evident from reports that Panzer Group West has been prevented from carrying out its basic mission.'

Just how badly that 'basic mission' had fared is vividly described by Fritz Bayerlein of Panzer Lehr Division.

'While I waited for support on my right flank, the British counter-attacked next day (10 June). They massed an unbelievable concentration of heavy artillery and I was glad when we finally were out of it. We pulled out of Tilly on 15 June and the British filled the gap. My chance to drive to the sea was lost. We pulled back south of Aunay, to regroup. We had lost about 100 tanks against the British. Half my striking force was gone ....'

Recognition that the prospects of eliminating the Allied bridgehead were rapidly deteriorating was finally realized at Seventh Army. Instead of the usual orders for

counter-attacks 'to destroy and wipe out the enemy' the evening of 10 June saw this entry made:

'The Chief-of-Staff Army Group 'B' presents the views of the Supreme Commander of the armed forces (Hitler) ... that there should be neither a withdrawal, fighting to the rear, nor a disengagement rearward to a new line of resistance, but that every man will fight and fall, where he stands ....'

With these words vanished the grandiose hopes of a brilliant German offensive and an early victory. The significance of the demand to 'fight and fall' presaged the hard days ahead. It was the first of many similar orders issued in the West. And as defeat followed defeat such orders became more urgent and more demanding and more desperate. They succeeded in so terrifying the German soldier that when at last he had ceased to fight because it was his duty, he continued to fight because he was afraid to do anything else.

Thus less than a week after the invasion had begun the German forces in Normandy were back on the defensive.

Their short-lived opportunity to deny the Allies a foothold on the coast of France was over. The attempts to crush the landings had already cost them over 150 tanks and about 10,000 German prisoners of war. They were dazed, uncertain and weary. They could do nothing but sit back and wait for help to come. When it finally arrived it was far too little and much too late. **"**

MILTON SHULMAN, *DEFEAT IN THE WEST*.
MARTIN, SECKER AND WARBURG, LONDON.

FICTION AND TRUTH

IN THE BACKSTAGE
OF THE EVENT

This poem was written by a woman in her twenties who served as a telegraphist in the Royal Navy. It was she who transmitted Eisenhower's order to launch Operation Overlord, purely because she happened to be on duty that night.

"Behind the ancient chalk-filled hill,
At Southwick House my thoughts return,
Another June, another dawn,
So many since have passed and gone.
Down the years with widows weep,
What tragedy we spread around.
The woods and lanes were bursting then
With no delights of spring but came
To life that long June night and
Rumbled forth towards the shore,
'Embark, embark, and more and more
To leave our precious sacred land
And fight and free and liberate
and stand.'

Two tired Wrens on watch below,
The war room up above says 'Go'
To Overlord, and Omaha and Gold,
Send out Pluto, Mulberry, more ...
The Cypher Queens administered to,
That simple message coming through,
And passed to me with short command,
'On scambler Telex, get it right,
To all Commands, it comes from Ike.'
So I a little Jenny Wren,

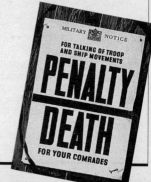

"IT ISN'T THE NATURAL BIRTH OF A NEW DAY.
IT IS AN INTENSE ARTIFICIAL ILLUMINATION."

YVETTE MOREAU-DŒUVRE

Did set the ball in motion then?
And move an army overseas,
To change the face of worlds it seems.
And when the weary watch was done,
Went out into the morning sun,
And walked through country lanes
Upwards up that ancient hill.
And oh the sight and sound of it.
The harbours packed but yesterday were
Empty, peaceful, oh so still. **"**

GERMAN MISCALCULATIONS EXPLAINED

Captain Basil Liddell-Hart was given the opportunity to interview the captured German generals after the war, and from them he gained valuable insights into their thinking about the possible area of the invasion.

"Another hint came from the increased activity of the 'Résistance' in France. We captured several hundred wireless transmitters, and were able to discover the bearing of the code phrases used in communicating with England. The messages were veiled, but the broad significance was evident.

Blumentritt then told me: 'Our Naval Staff always insisted that the Allies would land near a big port. They anticipated an attack on Le Havre – not only because of its value as a port, but because it was the base for our midget submarines. We soldiers did not agree with their view. We doubted whether the Allies would make a direct attack on such a well-fortified place. Moreover, we had information about a big exercise carried out in southern England, where the troops had been disembarked on a flat and open coastline.

'From this we deduced that the Allies would not try to attack a port at the outset. But we had no idea, nor any report, that they were developing artifical harbours – the Mulberries. We thought you were probably intending to lay your ships side by side, to form a bridge over which stores could be unloaded and carried ashore to the beaches.'

Rundstedt said frankly: 'I thought the invasion would come across the narrower part of the Channel, between Le Havre and Calais – rather than between Caen and Cherbourg. I expected the landing to take place on either side of the estuary of the Somme. I thought the first landing might take place on the west side, between Le Tréport and Le Havre, followed by a further landing between the Somme and Calais.' He admitted the point but answered: 'The strength of the defences was absurdly overrated. The 'Atlantic Wall' was an illusion, conjured up by propaganda – to deceive the German people as well as the Allies. It used to make me angry to read the stories about is impregnable defences. It was nonsense to describe it as a 'wall'. Hitler himself never came to visit it, and see what it really was. For that matter the

"ONE COULD NOT SEE ANYTHING BUT THE LOW SKY, EXCEPT
WHEN THE BARGE WOULD DIP FORWARD; THEN ONLY WE COULD
SEE A GREY BLURRY BEACH. FRANCE !"

JEAN AMILA

only time he came to the Channel coast in the whole war was back in 1940, when he paid a visit on one occasion to Cap Gris-Nez.' I remarked: 'And looked across at the English coast, like Napoleon?' Rundstedt nodded, with an ironical smile.

Rundstedt went on to say that another reason for his anticipation that the invasion would come in the Somme-Calais area was that we should be forced to attack the area where V-weapons were located at the earliest possible moment, in order to save London from destruction. He was told that the effect of these weapons would be much greater that it was in reality. Hitler built excessive hopes on them, and that affected strategic calculations.

It was Hitler, however, who guessed that the Allied landings would come in Normandy. Blumentritt revealed this. 'At the end of March O.K.W. issued instructions which showed that Hitler expected an invasion of Normandy. From that time onward we received repeated warnings about it, starting with the words 'The Führer fears...' I don't know what led him to that conclusion. But as a result the 91st Air-landing Division with some tank squadrons was moved down there, and posted in reserve behind the Cherbourg Peninsula – near Carentan.'

Members of Rommel's staff had told me he likewise anticipated that our landings would take place in Normandy, in contrast to Rundstedt's view. I asked Rundstedt and Blumentritt about this, and they said it was correct.

It would seem that Hitler's much derided 'intuition' was nearer the mark than the calculations of the ablest professional soldiers. They were unduly influenced by their tendency to go by what was the proper course in orthodox strategic theory – or by a conviction that the Allied planners were sure to do the conventional thing. The value of doing the 'unexpected' was overlooked.

In this connection Rundstedt made a significant disclosure in answer to one of my questions. 'If the Allies had landed in western France, near the Loire, they could have succeeded very easily – both in establishing a large enough bridgehead, and then driving inland. I could not have moved a single division there to stop them.' Blumentritt added: 'Such a landing would have met practically no opposition. There were only three divisions covering 300 miles of coast south of the Loire, and two of them were training divisions composed of raw recruits. A company commander on that coast had to cycle all day in covering his company sector. We regarded the Loire area as too far from England for air support, and thus assumed it was unlikely the Allied Command would attempt to land there – knowing how much they were inclined to count on ensuring maximum air cover.'

(This revelation was of the more interest to me because in January, 1944, I had written a paper suggesting that the Allied landing should be made on the west coast, near the mouth of the Loire, as 'the surest way of fulfilling the key principle of 'least expectation', and thereby throwing the enemy off his balance'.)

On the same reasoning, the German Command, except Rommel, thought that a landing in Normandy was less likely than where the Channel was narrower, and air support easier. Rundstedt said, too: 'We thought that any landing in Normandy would be limited to an attempt to capture Cherbourg. The American landing near here was thus less unexpected than the British landing round Caen.' 99

LIDDELL-HART, *THE OTHER SIDE OF THE HILL.*
B.H. CASSEL, LONDON.

ITINERARIES
HISTORIC AREA
OF THE BATTLE
OF NORMANDY

▲ Front of a cistern barge, –25 m (Omaha Beach).　　▼ Sherman tank, –15 m (Utah Beach).

▼ The guns of the destroyer USS *Meredith*, –35 m and 12.5 nautical miles (Utah Beach).

▲ LST 523, –35 m (Utah Beach).   ▼ Stern of cistern barge, –25 m (Omaha).

▼ Porthole from troop transport, *Fort Norfolk*, –30 m (Utah Beach).

Sherman tank from wreck of an LST, less than 15 m from Utah Beach.

▲ Pistol found on board an American mine-sweeper YMS 304, –15 m (Omaha Beach).

▲ Helmet discovered on board YMS 304.   ▼ Navigation lamp from YMS 304.

OVERLORD, THE ASSAULT
OVERLORD, L'ASSAUT

THE BRITISH LANDINGS ON SWORD, JUNO AND GOLD.

JEAN-PIERRE BÉNAMOU

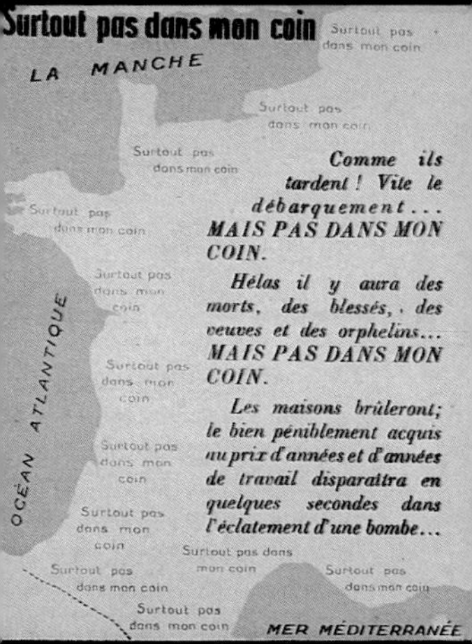

Surtout pas dans mon coin

LA MANCHE

Surtout, pas dans mon coin

Surtout pas dans mon coin

Surtout pas dans mon coin

Surtout pas dans mon coin

OCEAN ATLANTIQUE

Surtout pas dans mon coin

Surtout pas dans mon coin

Surtout pas dans mon coin

Surtout pas dans mon coin

Surtout pas dans mon coin

Comme ils tardent ! Vite le débarquement... MAIS PAS DANS MON COIN.

Hélas il y aura des morts, des blessés, des veuves et des orphelins... MAIS PAS DANS MON COIN.

Les maisons brûleront; le bien péniblement acquis au prix d'années et d'années de travail disparaîtra en quelques secondes dans l'éclatement d'une bombe...

MER MÉDITERRANÉE

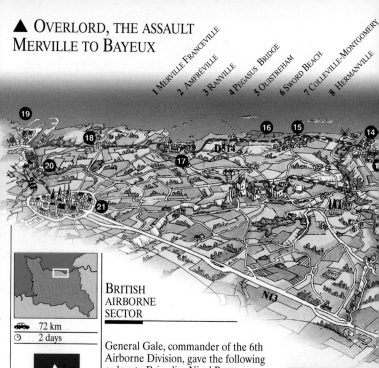

1 MERVILLE FRANCEVILLE
2 AMFRÉVILLE
3 RANVILLE
4 PEGASUS BRIDGE
5 OUISTREHAM
6 SWORD BEACH
7 COLLEVILLE-MONTGOMERY
8 HERMANVILLE

🚗 72 km

🕐 2 days

Logo of
the Battle of
Normandy
Open-Air Museum

**MEMORIAL TO
THE 9TH BATTALION
OF THE PARACHUTE
REGIMENT**
(Merville battery).

MERVILLE BATTERY
● 74
Was defended by
a minefield, a barbed-
wire entanglement,
an anti-tank ditch,
twenty machine-gun
positions, an
automatic 20mm
anti-aircraft gun and
three Schneider
75-mm field guns.
The battery guarded
Sword and the estuary
of the Orne.

BRITISH AIRBORNE SECTOR

General Gale, commander of the 6th
Airborne Division, gave the following
orders to Brigadier Nigel Poett,
commander of the 5th Parachute
Brigade: "Your mission is to seize and
hold the bridges over the Caen Canal
and the Orne, at Bénouville and Ranville.
You will hold and defend the line
Ranville/Bas-de-Ranville/Bénouville
against the inevitable counter-attack by
enemy infantry and armour. The capture
of the bridges intact is important for the
conduct of later operations." Brigadier
James Hill, commander of the 3rd
Parachute Brigade, was given the tasks
of neutralizing the Merville Battery and
of seizing and destroying the bridges over the Dives and its
tributaries from Troarn to Varaville to hinder the arrival
of enemy reinforcements from the east ▲ *232*. (*Coming from
Cabourg take the D223 to Merville.*)

MERVILLE. During the night of 5/6 June, a hundred
Lancasters dropped 400 tons of bombs on the battery without
touching a single bunker. Colonel Otway, commander
of the 9th Canadian Parachute Battalion,
managed to rally 150 men who
lacked the necessary equipment to
attack the battery. The small group
approached the perimeter fence and
found an open passage through the
mines. Hand-to-hand fighting with
the garrison turned in favour of the
Allies. Today there is a museum
there. (*Follow the D514 as far as
Sallanelles then take the D37b.*)

"HAUGER" (LE HOGER). The 9th
Parachute Battalion followed by N° 3
Commando and then N° 4,
which included the Free-French
detachment, fought their way

through the orchards and gardens of the hamlet against opposition from units of the 711th and 346th Infantry Divisions. The Square Colonel-Robert-Dawson is a CAIRN, each stone of which represents a man from N° 4 Commando.

LE PLEIN. Otway, who retired towards Le Plein via Le Hoger, found that the château contained 200 Germans and placed defensive positions around that stronghold. N° 3 Commando cleared the place on the evening of 6 June.

AMFRÉVILLE. N° 6 Commando opened the way from Ouistreham to Bénouville for the 1st Special Service Brigade at midday on 6 June. Lord Lovat led his commandos to Amfréville and they dug in between there and Le Plein.

On 12 June Lovat was seriously wounded, the sole survivor of a group of officers. There is a memorial to N° 6 Commando in the square by the church, and one to the 1st Special Service Brigade at the crossroads on the way to Bréville. At Le Plein there is a square named after COMMANDANT-KIEFFER.

BRÉVILLE. Situated on ground high enough to dominate the whole airborne bridgehead on the Orne, the village was held by grenadiers from the 736th Regiment supported by light tanks

General Rennie commanded the 3rd Infantry Division, which at the time of the landing consisted of the 8th, 185th and 9th Brigades as well as the 101st Beach Group for mine clearance and traffic control.

125

A very British
telephone box
at Ranville.
Below:
the British
Cemetery at
Ranville.

from the 21st Panzerdivision ▲ *230*. With artillery support
from the 1st Corps and some destroyers, 6th Airborne
mounted a combined operation by parachutists, commandos
and some infantry from the 51st Highland Division. On 12
June the 5th Black Watch attacked Bréville but were repulsed.
The same evening, Gale sent in the 12th Parachute and the
12th Devons supported by the Shermans of the 13th/18th
Hussars, to attack the ridge behind a rolling barrage. It was
the latter that wounded Lord Lovat at Le Plein. After hand-
to-hand fighting in the cemetery and the gardens, the 12th
Parachute entered the ruined
village. In front of the church is
the BRÉVILLE MÉMORIAL
dedicated to the men of the
6th Airborne.
LE MESNIL*. *(Follow the
D513 as far as Hérouvillette.)*
The mission of the
1st Canadian Parachute
Battalion was to destroy
the bridge over the Dives
and liberate Varaville. A platoon of Royal Engineers
commanded by Captain Jucke blew up the bridge,
on which there is a commemorative plaque.
There is a MEMORIAL to the Canadian Parachute
Corps at Mesnil, and at Château-Saint-Côme there
is a MONUMENT IN HONOUR of Lieutenant-Colonel
Otway and the 9TH PARACHUTE BATTALION.
HÉROUVILLETTE*. On 7 June the 2nd Ox
and Bucks supported by a company of
the 12th Devons attacked the village below
Bas-Ranville and ran into parts of the 21st
Panzerdivision. A MEMORIAL TO THE 2ND
OX AND BUCKS and the GRAVESTONES OF
TWENTY-SEVEN PARACHUTISTS in the cemetery
testify to the ferocity of the fighting.
Hérouvillette, dominated to the south
by a ridge and the west by the factories
at Colombelles, provided an excellent
observation post for the enemy artillery.
It was not liberated until 18 July during
Operation Goodwood ● *42*, ▲ *210.(Return
to Le Mesnil and continue eastwards.)*

SIR RICHARD GALE
General Gale
commanded
the 6th Airborne
Division which
comprised
the 3rd and 5th
Parachute Brigades
as well as
the 6th Airlanding
Brigade.

Ranville Church.

BAVENT*. The men of the 1st Special-Service Brigade and their commander, Brigadier Mills-Roberts, who succeeded Lord Lovat after he was wounded on 12 June, are

AIRBORNE

remembered in this village. **MANOIR DU BOIS*.** The 8th Parachute Battalion MEMORIAL is on the spot where 60% of the men landed and from where engineer teams from the 3rd and 8th Parachutists left to deal with the bridges at Troarn and Bures. (*Return to Mesnil and take the D37a.*)

TROARN*. The engineers and the 3rd Squadron of 8th Parachute commanded by Major Roseveare reached the bridge at Troarn and blew it up. This deed is commemorated by two memorials, one near the bridge and the other on the wall of the tourist office. (*Follow the D224 from Le Mesnil as far as Bénouville.*)

RANVILLE. The engineers of the 591st Squadron declared Ranville clear at 02.30 hours despite the threat of the 125th Panzergrenadier Regiment which had been forced back by the 13th Parachute Battalion. General Gale installed his advance tactical HQ in BAS-RANVILLE at 04.00 hours. On the Place du 6-Juin one can see A PLAQUE IN MEMORY OF THE 13TH PARACHUTE. and in the Place Général-Gale, a bust of the latter. The British military cemetery contains 2,563 graves of which 323 are German. On the wall of the pigeon loft opposite the cemetery there is a PLAQUE in honour of the Belgians of the Piron Brigade. In the churchyard there is THE GRAVE OF LIEUTENANT BROTHERIDGE, the first man to be killed at Pegasus Bridge ▲ *128* at 0.25 hours, as well as a MEMORIAL to the 8th Parachute Battalion.

BÉNOUVILLE. The 7th Parachute Battalion led by Lieutenant-Colonel Pine Coffin defended the crossroads and the bridge against attacks from 123rd Panzergrenadier Regiment, part of the 21st Panzerdivision. who threw themselves against the light anti-tank guns and Brens of the men holed up in the buildings.

CHÂTEAU DE BÉNOUVILLE
Built by Nicolas Ledoux, it was a maternity hospital run by nuns under the energetic direction of Madame Vion, a member of the local Resistance. She could not prevent the artillery observers of the 21st Panzerdivision from installing themselves there, which drew three shells from Howard's men.

CAFÉ GONDRÉE
The house has preserved its original appearence.

▲ Pegasus Bridge

The bridge at Bénouville, which spanned the canal between Caen and the sea, was the objective for C Company of the Ox and Bucks Light Infantry commanded by Major John Howard. It was assaulted on 6 June at 00.20 by 45 parachutists who scrambled out of three gliders which managed to crash land on the banks of the canal, 200 metres from the target. Shortly afterwards, Lieutenant Sweeney and his section emerged from two gliders on the west bank of the Orne and took the bridge there.

FIRST LIBERATED HOUSE OF FRANCE
High place of the veterans of 1944, the café *Gondrée* transformed itself through the years into a small museum. Today Mme Gondrée (top picture) is the keeper of the café.

PLAQUE HORSA BRIDGE
(Bridge on the Orne).

DETAILS OF THE EXPLOIT
00 . 20: While the five gliders mentioned above landed, the pathfinders and parachute engineers dropped from 27 twin-engined Albemarles.
00 . 50: The 3rd and 5th Parachute Brigades of General Gale's 6th Airborne Division were dropped by 91 four-engined Stirlings, 19 Albemarles, 135 C47 Dakotas ▲ *184* and 17 Horsa gliders.
03 . 20: Horsa and Hamilcar ● *57,* gliders towed by Stirling ● *58,* and Halifax bombers landed the divisional head-quarters, engineer stores and light anti-tank guns.
04 . 30: Three Horsa gliders landed near Merville Battery carrying men from 9th Parachute Battalion.
21 . 00: 250 Horsa and Hamilcar gliders towed by Halifaxs and Stirlings brought in the 6th Parachute. Brigade on both sides of the Orne and the canal.

▲ *184* and 17 Horsa gliders.

LIGHTNING ATTACK
In less than 30 min, with a few grenades and Sten magazines, Major Howard eliminated the garrison defending the bridges.

"HORSA" BRIDGE

SOON AFTER MIDNIGHT ON 5/6 JUNE 1944 A HORSA GLIDER FLOWN BY S/SGTS R A HOWARD AND F W BAACKE GLIDER PILOT REGIMENT LANDED NORTH WEST OF THIS BRIDGE WITH A PLATOON OF OXF. & BUCKS LIGHT INFANTRY LED BY Lt D. FOX AND ROYAL ENGINEERS UNDER Lt J J BENCE? THEY CAPTURED THE BRIDGE. A SECOND PLATOON UNDER Lt H.J. SWEENEY LANDED NEAR BY PILOTED BY S/SGTS S. PEARSON AND L. GUTHRIE, AND REINFORCED THEM

TRES TOT LE MATIN DU JOUR J UN PLANEUR HORSA PILOTE PAR R HOWARD ET F.BAACKE DU REGIMENT DES PILOTES DE PLANEURS ATTERRIT PRES DE CE PONT AVEC DES SOLDATS DU 52e REGIMENT D INFANTERIE SOUS LE COMMANDEMENT DU Lt FOX, ET AVEC DES SAPEURS DU GENIE ROYAL SOUS LES ORDRES DU Lt BENCE?. ILS S'AISIRENT LE PONT UN DEUXIEME PELOTON AVEC LE Lt H.SWEENEY SUIVIT DANS UN PLANEUR PILOTE PAR S PEARSON ET L GUTHRIE ET LES RENFORCA

> **"**The last group of gliders touched down at half past three. Most of the gliders were wrecked but the losses in men were few. The drops were a success: 6,000 men had been landed. They were good blokes ....**"**
> Admiral Lemonnier,
> *Peaceful Normandy*

"HAM AND JAM, HAM AND JAM ...." That was the radio signal that would announce to the high command that Major Howard's mission had succeeded.
The need to control east-west communication across both canal and river necessitated the capture of the bridges intact. The mission of the men was to hold out until commandos at Ouistreham ▲ *130* arrived. They succeeded and around midday they heard the skirl of the pipes of Bill Millin ▲ *157*, personal piper to Lord Lovat ▲ *130*.

THE NEW BRIDGE
Even if since May 1994 the bascule bridge over the Caen canal is not the original of 1944, it resembles it. Carefully dismantled in November 1993, the original bridge dating from 1936 is preserved on a Ouistreham industrial estate three kilometres north of the new crossing.

THE FIRST VICTORY OF THE CAMPAIGN
The capture of the two bridges was a feat of arms which had a high symbolic value in that they were the first objective seized on French territory. A footpath leads to three blocks which mark the spots where the gliders landed. Above there is a British Centaur tank of the 2nd Commando Support Regiment, Royal Marines, mounted on a Royal Engineer bridge span.

LORD LOVAT
Brigadier Lord "Shimi" Lovat, DSO MC, commanded the 1st Special Service Brigade which comprised Nᵒˢ 3, 4 and 6 Commandos and 45 Royal Marine Commando. Nᵒ 4 included the group of Free Frenchmen under the command of Philippe Kieffer. Lord Lovat's charisma was increased by the presence of Bill Millin, his personal piper. (Photo right taken in August 1942.)

There they held out armed only with light weapons, managing with a few PIAT (Projector Infantry Anti-Tank) rounds and phosphorous grenades, to deal with 500 grenadiers from the 192nd Regiment equipped with light tanks and armoured cars. Around midday the green berets of Nᵒ 6 Commando arrived as reinforcements from the direction of Colleville and Saint-Aubin-d'Arquenay, which ended the isolation of the Orne bridgehead. Six weeks later it acted as the springboard for an eventual breakthrough east of Caen ● *42*, ▲ *210*.

SWORD BEACH

(After crossing Pegasus Bridge, take the D514 to Ouistreham.) This long beach is bordered by houses and villas and is dominated by the villages to the east of the mouth of the Orne. Ouistreham is essentially a fishing port, but with its locks forms the entry to the port of Caen, joined to the sea by the canal. The enemy fortifications were designed to hinder an approach to the coast and to protect those locks. The defences continued westwards, consisting of an anti-tank ditch and "dragons' teeth" ● *72* backed up by bunkers armed with cannon, Tobruk stands and mortar pits. Even the famous casino, which recalled the peacetime world, was fortified. The beaches were strewn with obstacles and mines right down to the low-water mark ■ *44* and as far as the rocks at Lion-sur-Mer. Higher up, a bunker every 100 metres armed with 50 or 47mm cannon, flanked a network of trenches and minefields, some of which were fakes, marked with a black death's skull on a yellow background. Three battalions of the 735th Grenadier Regiment, part of the 716th Infantry Division, which had its HQ at Caen, defended the sector. A battery of four 105-mm guns was emplaced south-west of Ouistreham near the water tower. Repeatedly attacked from the air, all that was left was one gun able to fire, a French 75-mm similar to the one at Merville.

THE SWORD LANDING
At 07.30, sixteen Sherman DDs ● *63* from A and B Squadrons of the

ATLANTIC WALL MUSEUM.
Once the port of Ouistreham was cleared all that was left to the troops was to neutralize the 15 metre-high fire-control post, which surrendered on 9 June. This massive bunker (below right) today houses the Atlantic Wall Museum.
Right, a rangefinder in the museum.

Also worth a visit...
OUISTREHAM

13th/18th Hussars rumbled ashore at low tide. The special armoured vehicles of the 79th Armoured Division attacked the defences and cleared minefields and obstacles to open up the beach exits. Two assault companies of the 1st South Lancs., got a foothold on Queen White Sector, east of La Brèche and a further two from the 2nd East Yorks on Queen Red, accompanied by engineer demolition teams. At 08.15, the rest of the 13th/18th Hussars landed dry-shod directly onto Queen White. At 09.30 the 1st Suffolks landed together with the 8th Brigade staff. Hermanville was cleared by 10.30 and the 8th Brigade advanced southwards, while the 1st Special Service brigade moved towards Saint-Aubin-d'Arquenay. N° 4 Commando had to neutralize a fortification that had escaped the air and naval bombardments.

QUEEN RED. At 08.20, 500 green berets of N° 4 Commando led by Colonel Dawson landed. The unit included two troops of 177 Free French participating in the liberation of their country. Numerous bodies were floating in with the tide and the commandos helped the men of the East Yorks who were pinned down in the dunes. Showers of mortar bombs churned

up the sand but grenades got the better of the defenders and a 75-mm cannon in a bunker was silenced.

THE LIBERATION OF OUISTREHAM. On reaching the coast road from Ouistreham to Lion-sur-Mer, Lieutenant Lofi's troop led off eastwards towards the port and its defences. N° 4 Commando advanced under automatic fire from the houses, but a gendarme guided Kieffer to a good position to start his attack. The enemy strongpoint was well armed and consisted of a number of concrete positions joined by tunnels: much too tough an objective for a lightly-armed assault force. Kieffer asked for armoured support and at 15.30 a dozen Churchill AVREs (Armoured Vehicle Royal Engineers) managed to convince the enemy of the futility of further resistance. The Allies blew up the western part of the bridge and took control of the port.

MONUMENTS AT OUISTREHAM/RIVA-BELLA. These two MONUMENTS are facing each other commemorating the memory of the South Lancs and the participation of Kieffer's French commandos. To the south at the roundabout on the D814 is a MEMORIAL LANTERN. A further COLUMN decorated with frescoes was erected for the 50th anniversary on the beach at Colleville. Facing the Casino, which has been rebuilt on the same site as the old one which the Germans replaced with a bunker, the N° 4 COMMANDO MUSEUM commemorates the action of the only French forces that took part on the ground on D-Day. (140 airmen and around 1,600 sailors of de Gaulle's Free French ● 35, ▲ 162 were also involved.) The portion of the beach extending from the canal, which is now the ferry port built in 1988, to Colleville-Montgomery, was not attacked on D-Day. Subject to intermittent shellfire from heavy guns situated at Le Havre or in the Cabourg-Trouville area, it could not be used to bring in supplies for General Crocker's I Corps, which was forced to land stores on Juno Beach. On the wall of a pre-war villa on

Also worth a visit…
THE BEACH OF RIVA-BELLA (above and below).

KIEFFER'S COMMANDOS
The French Marine Commandos led by Commandant Philippe Kieffer formerly belonged to N° 10 Interallied Commando before being attached to N° 4 for Operation Overlord. The monument to N° 4 Commando was unveiled by the President of the French Republic in 1985, on the site of the strongpoint known as the Casino.

Sited on top of a bunker, the names of the 177 marine commandos are engraved in the metal of a symbolic flame. Kieffer himself is portrayed in a relief outline.

German prisoners under escort in Hermanville-sur-Mer.

Boulevard Victor-Hugo, opposite the casino there can be found a plaque commemorating the supreme sacrifice of the first French killed. (*After Riva-Bella take the D60a.*)

COLLEVILLE-MONTGOMERY. Although the abandoned battery at Ouistreham cannot be visited, the strongpoint known as Hillman to the south of Colleville has been well restored and laid out as a memorial to the Suffolk Regiment. (*Return to the D514.*)

LA BRÈCHE-D'HERMANVILLE. At the tourist office can be found an exhibition devoted to the Gooseberry ● 76 breakwater formed by scuttling a dozen old ships, one of which was the French battleship *Courbet* ● 103.

HERMANVILLE-SUR-MER. *(Follow the D60b.)* The beach sectors Queen Green and Queen White were assaulted by the South Lancs and A Squadron of the 13th/18th Hussars whose 6 DD tanks landed with the infantry. Four were blown up on the beach and the 5th Armoured Assault Regiment of the Royal Engineers lost half its effective forces and all its special tanks were pinned down by an 88-mm gun. The only practical route through the flooding ■ 46, induced by the defenders from the 716th Infantry Division, was the one at Hermanville. Resistance on the beach at Hermanville ceased at 10.30 with the exception of the "88" and some mortars. The latter were the responsibility of 8th Brigade which silenced them, opening the way to Périers-sur-le-Dan, where an anti-tank battery of the 21st Panzerdivision was in position. Naval gunfire, assisted by the fighter-bombers of the RAF, participated in the neutralization of the enemy strongpoints. At 20.00 resistance from Hillman grew weaker, thanks to the use of flame-throwers and explosives dropped down the ventilation shafts of the underground bunkers. Resistance from the strongpoint and from the entire 716th Infantry Division ceased the following morning. The 185th Brigade (2nd KSLI

BRITISH MILITARY CEMETERY AT HERMANVILLE Contains 986 graves.

Also worth visiting...
THE CHURCH AT LION-SUR-MER

as well as the Shermans of the Staffs. Yeomanry) suffered losses in brushing aside the anti-tank screen of the 21st Panzer but had to battle with a battery of 122-mm guns which was situated on the reverse slope. That mission accomplished, they beat off a counter-attack mounted by 25 Mark IV tanks ● 62 of the 21st Panzer supported by grenadiers in half-tracks. The Staffords hit 13 enemy tanks on the move, but the remainder managed to reach the coast at 20.30, where the grenadiers of the 736th Regiment fought with the men of N° 41 Commando, Royal Marines. The 3rd British Division memorials at La-Brèche-d'Hermanville are grouped around a Churchill AVRE of the 1st Assault Brigade Royal Engineers. *(Retrace your route to the D514.)*

LION-SUR-MER. It was the sight of thousands of aircraft and gliders almost touching the ground behind Lion-sur-Mer which emphasized the reality of the tactical situation. The remaining enemy Mark IVs turned tail, their retreat harried by the tanks of the 27th Armoured Brigade to Biéville and Mathieu, where they found safety thanks to nightfall. The 27th Brigade tanks should have ensured the liberation of Caen on the evening of 6 June but were delayed by 21st Panzerdivision and 12th SS Panzer which reached the city first. As a result Caen was rendered impassable and useless by air bombardment. The advance to Caen was stopped on the evening of 6 June between Hillman and Périers. Two troops established contact with the South Lancs. from Queen Green and the bulk of N° 41 Commando RM led by Lieutenant Colonel Gray advanced towards Luc-sur-Mer where they joined up with N° 46 Commando RM. The Château at Lion, which was still resisting after the fighting on 6 and 7 June, was taken intact by the 5th Lincolns. The final objective of N° 41 Commando was the capture of the German radar station at Douvres. This action came to a conclusion only after an eleven-day siege. Today one can see the monument to the civilians killed at Lion in the square named in honour of N° 41 R.M. Commando as well as a plaque dedicated to the 77th Armoured Assault Regiment, Royal Engineers,

COMBINED OPERATIONS
On the left the badge of British Combined Operations. (An eagle for air, a sub-machine-gun for land and an anchor for sea.) US beach engineers wore a similar insignia in woven gold on a blue background.

GERMAN RADAR STATION AT DOUVRES-LA-DÉLIVRANDE
Recently restored, the site features a Würzburg antenna and the history of the site is presented in an underground bunker laid out as a museum.

M 8 armoured car

An old picture of Luc-sur-Mer at a time when one could "land" in peace.

133

SAINT-AUBIN-SUR-MER
Near the bunker (above) are two monuments, to the North Shore Regiment and the Fort Garry Horse as well as the British memorial to N° 48 Commando Royal Marines. Below, the plaque of the North Shore.

> SUR CETTE PLAGE DE SAINT-AUBIN, A L'AUBE DU 6 JUIN 1944, A 7"30 FUT ETABLIE UNE TÊTE DE PONT PAR LE RÉGIMENT D'INFANTERIE CANADIENNE DES "NORTH SHORE" OUVRANT LA VOIE AU 48ème COMMANDO DES "ROYAL MARINES"

LANDING AT BERNIÈRES
The monument of the *Comité du Débarquement* can be seen, at La Redoute, those to the Queen's Own Regiment and Regiment *La Chaudière*. In the street named after the latter unit, a plaque marks the headquarters of the 1st Canadian press centre.

mounted on a Churchill tank. *(Continue on the D514 and then turn left onto the D83 after Petit-Enfer.)*

LUC-SUR-MER*. The commune marks the boundary between Sword Beach (British) and Juno Beach (Canadian). N° 46 Commando Royal Marines landed there and advanced to Douvres-la-Délivrande where the second cemetery for those killed on Sword and at Caen was established with 1,123 graves. One can see at Luc the memorial to the first commando RAID ON NORMANDY on 28 September 1941, and at Cresserons, the monument to the 22nd Dragoons who were equipped with flail tanks.

LANGRUNE-SUR-MER. Langrune was attacked by N° 48 Commando Royal Marines who landed at Saint-Aubin-sur-Mer and marched along the coast road. They rapidly cleared the front but fortified houses in the main street held out until 8 June when they were eliminated by supporting tanks. After that the commando joined up with 4th Special Services Brigade in the airborne bridgehead.

JUNO BEACH

(Follow the D514). This beach stretches between Saint-Aubin-sur-Mer and Graye-sur-Mer. This was the Canadian sector which was the goal of General Keller's 3rd Infantry Division, specially trained to crack the German defences. This particular division was composed entirely of volunteers, it numbered 16,000 men, of whom 7,500 were in the front line divided into three brigades.

SAINT-AUBIN-SUR-MER. This was the sector known as Nan Red, where the North Shore Regiment landed. Because the configuration of the beach did not permit an assault along the whole length of 4.5km,

a marine commando was landed to take various German strongpoints from the rear. At Saint-Aubin the preliminary air attacks damaged the German lines of communication but left the defensive system intact. The 50-mm anti-tank gun which can still be seen today was part of a strongpoint which held out for some time against attacks from B Company of the North Shore. The gun destroyed four DD tanks ● 63 which were attempting to get off the beach to the west, but having fired 70 rounds it was eliminated by three Shermans from the Fort Garry Horse which were assisted by an AVRE "flying dustbin" tank ● 64. While B Company took care of the strongpoint, A Company of the North Shore cleared the town, encountering only mines and occasional snipers. C Company moved inland and reached Tailleville at 15.00 where strong resistance around the château occupied the sharpshooters and some Centaur tanks from the Royal Marines. The village was liberated in the evening.

BERNIÈRES-SUR-MER. This was the Nan Green sector that was assaulted by the Queen's Own Rifles of Canada, part of 8th Brigade. B Company landed east of the houses of Bernières in front of La Redoute which was bristling with 50-mm cannon and machine-guns. But as is so often the case, three determined infantrymen were sufficient to silence the defences with bursts from their sub-machine-guns and strings of grenades thrown into the embrasures and rifle-slits of the bunkers. On the other side of the station on the west flank of Bernières, Company A of the Queen's Own suffered from mortar fire when forcing their way inland. The 9th Brigade in reserve landed at 11.00 at Bernières which was finally cleared by the Regiment La Chaudière, while the 8th Brigade advanced towards Anguerny. Only the Nan White sector was used because Nan Red was encumbered by wreckage. The inevitable traffic-jams gave the Germans a respite as they prepared to receive the 9th Brigade and the 27th Armoured Regiment advancing towards their ultimate objective, the airfield at Carpiquet ▲ 205, 206.

COURSEULLES-SUR-MER. East of Courseulles was the Nan Green sector on which the Regina Rifles, part of the 7th Brigade, landed. 19 Sherman DD ● 63, driven at 6 knots by their twin propellors and protected by an inflated canvas skirt supported on a metal frame, approached the eastern arm of the jetty. 15 touched the shore in good condition and engaged the German defences. They were followed by 120 men from the Regina Rifles.

ROYAL WINNIPEG RIFLES MONUMENT (Courseulles). Other monuments there commemorate the landings and the return of General de Gaulle (on the quay). There are PLAQUES to the memory of the Regina Rifles and the Canadian Scottish, as well as a monument to the crew of the FREE-FRENCH DESTROYER, *La Combattante*, which brought de Gaulle to Graye-sur-Mer on 14 June and was torpedoed on 23 February 1945.

Landing on Juno Beach.

SHERMAN "BOLD" (Courseulles) This was recovered in 1970 from 2 km out to sea and is exhibited as a monument to the 1st Canadian Hussars. It serves as a mounting

for several plaques placed by the regimental associations of Canadian units which took part on D-Day.

Bény-Reviers Canadian Cemetery. This contains 2,044 Canadian graves, 335 of these men fell on D-Day. A plaque stands in memory of the Cameron Highlanders of Ottawa.

They attacked the strongpoint. Its two 75mm Pak anti-tank guns each fired 200 rounds before being destroyed by Sherman tanks and AVRE "flying dustbins". On the other side of the River Seulles, an 88mm was neutralized by a direct hit from a destroyer at 07.30. At 17.00, Courseulles was liberated and the Regina Rifles concentrated at Réviers. By 20.00 they had reached Fontaine-Henry and spent the night at Fresne-Camilly.

West Courseulles and Graye. These two communes were fronted by the sectors code-named Mike Red and Mike Green. Immediately to the west of the mouth of the Seulles, Mike Red was a sandy beach bordered by dunes crowned by the usual German defences. Ten Sherman DDs were launched 1,500 m offshore under a hail of mortar bombs which hit two LCTs ● *60*. Only seven reached the beach, six minutes after the assault wave of the Royal Winnipeg Rifles, although others were landed dry-shod shortly afterwards. The tanks avoided the marshy terrain and attacked the bunkers, which, caught between the fire of the tanks and the assault infantry, rapidly gave in. On the border between the communes of Courseulles and Graye, there are several monuments, such as the Cross of Lorraine on the actual spot where General de Gaulle passed en route to make his famous speech at Bayeux. His entourage landed on 14 June ▲ *159*. One can also see a Churchill tank AVRE which was buried on 6 June 1944 and recovered in 1976. This beach exit was also used by Winston Churchill, King George VI and many

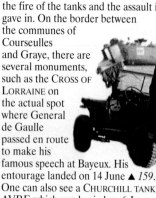

> "THE SECOND BRITISH ARMY, FORMING THE INITIAL ASSAULT WAVE, HAS RECEIVED THE TASK DURING THE DAY OF SEIZING ALL THE TERRITORY SITUATED BETWEEN BAYEUX AND CAEN."

JOHN FRAYN TURNER

other VIPs on their way to visit General Montgomery at his Tactical HQ at the nearby Château de Creullet. Finally, at the same spot is a COMITÉ DU DÉBARQUEMENT monument. **LA VALETTE/GRAYE-SUR-MER.** This was the Mike Green sector, assaulted by C and D companies of the 1st Canadian Scottish supported by the "funnies" of the 26th Armoured Assault Brigade, whose job it was to clear the beach exit and the mines as far as the coast road. All the way from Mike Green to Nan Red, the Crab tanks ● *64* of the 22nd Dragoons flailed the sand looking for anti-tank mines ● *73.* Behind them the leading sections marched towards the N13 road which was the objective of the 3rd Canadian Division led by General Keller. It was almost reached by a troop of tanks from the 1st Hussars under Lieutenant McCormick. The latter came in sight of the hangars of Carpiquet airfield ▲ *205, 206,* and turned around having encountered no opposition. Surprise was the essential element. Had he decided to refuel, pick up some infantry and push towards the objective, the battle for Caen would not have lasted so long, saving the lives of Canadian and British troops as well as a great city.

INLAND FROM JUNO BEACH: FROM REVIERS TO BAZENVILLE*

(From Graye-sur-Mer take the D12 towards Sainte-Croix-sur-Mer or the D79 towards Reviers.) At Sainte-Croix-sur-Mer, various monuments recall 1944. There is a plaque on the wall of the church in honour of the Canadian liberators and a column to commemorate the arrival of the RAF. At Tierceville there is a copy of the Eros statue in memory of the 179 Field Company RE. In Reviers one can see a column dedicated to the Regina Rifles who liberated the village on D-Day. In the village of Bény-sur-Mer (on the D79) there is a plaque to the Chaudière Regiment and not far away, at Basly, there is the Canadian Memorial to the Liberation. The CHÂTEAU DE CREULLET just outside the town of Creully was Montgomery's HQ. The mediaeval castle of Creully itself is destined to house a BBC museum, and finally, one can see a memorial to the 4th and 7th Dragoons who liberated the town on 6 June. From Creully one can continue via the D87 to Bazenville where there is a BRITISH CEMETERY. (*After Bazenville head for Crépon/Ver-sur-Mer on the D112.*)

MEETING POINT OF TWO WARS
In 1944 in Creully, local people accompanied by British and American troops in front of the 1914-18 war memorial.

RYES BRITISH CEMETERY*
(south of Asnelles).

MONTGOMERY
He is seen here, left, arriving on the beach on 8 June accompanied by a beachmaster ● *78.* General Montgomery ● *31, 37,* ▲ *221,* the Commander in Chief of ground forces, arrived on Mike sector as did Churchill, the King and de Gaulle. The village of Colleville did him the honour of adding his name to its own: Colleville-Montgomery ▲ *132.*

CROSS OF LORRAINE
On this memorial at Ver, de Gaulle's speech of 18 June 1940 is reproduced.
"To all the French. France has lost a battle! But France has not lost the war."

BRITISH MEMORIAL
This monument records the establishment of advanced airfield B3 at Sainte-Croix-sur-Mer.

GOLD BEACH

This beach was assaulted and seized by the 50th Northumbrian Division commanded by Major-General D.A.H. Graham. To break through the Atlantic Wall between Ver-sur-Mer (La Rivière) and Asnelles (Le Hamel), the division was doubled in size to a total of 38,000 men of all branches. On D-Day, General Graham issued an order of the day, which read: "To you all, officers and men of the 50th Northumbrian Division, has been given the signal honour of having been chosen to deliver a formidable blow for freedom. I am firmly convinced that with Force G of the Royal Navy, our comrades from the armoured formations, the artillery and the Royal Engineers who are attached to us, and thanks to the support of the RAF and the United States Air Force, we will deliver a decisive blow which the enemy will be incapable of resisting. We will thus proceed towards the glorious final victory, which is what I expect of each and every one of you. Much had been demanded of you in the past and your success has been remarkable, but that which is to come will be the greatest of all your adventures. It will be judged the greatest chapter in the book, already long, which you have written, surely the most glorious.

Also worth seeing…
THE SEA-WALL AT ASNELLES

Good luck to you all." At 07.05 a single squadron of amphibious Sherman DD tanks was launched towards

> "THE TIME HAS COME TO HIT, TO FORCE AND TO SHATTER THE
> WALL TO LIBERATE WESTERN EUROPE."
>
> GENERAL GRAHAM

Gold Beach before Ver-sur-Mer.

94

À SES GLORIEUX
LIBÉRATEURS
La Commune
d'Asnelles le Hamel
RECONNAISSANTE
6 Juin 1944

A commemorative plaque at Asnelles-le-Hamel.

THE ARROMANCHES VIEWING TABLE
This allows an understanding of the lay-out of the Mulberry harbour, "Port Winston". The plans below show the naval convoys and the system of jetties and pontoons. Nearby is ARROMANCHES 360°, in which a circular projection system shows the film. *The Price of Liberty.*

JIG Red, three of which were lost in the heavy swell. The support tanks, 16 Royal Marines Centaurs, were re-routed for technical reasons.

VER-SUR-MER. The 69th brigade landed at La Rivière. The 6th Green Howards on King Green were carried by the current 600 metres west during a 6km journey in their landing craft. The 5th East Yorks landed right on the spot on King Red, but the resistance of the strongpoint at La Rivière caused losses in their ranks. They crossed the beach and charged 1 km inland to the Mont-Fleury coast battery which had been destroyed by 400 tons of bombs during the night, and the garrison raised their hands. The most easterly company of the East Yorks at La Rivière received the brunt of the fire from the intact defence strongpoint, which included an 88mm, mortars and machine-guns. Almost 40 men fell on the beach where two Churchill AVREs caught fire and blew up, causing further casualties: a major, a captain and three lieutenants.

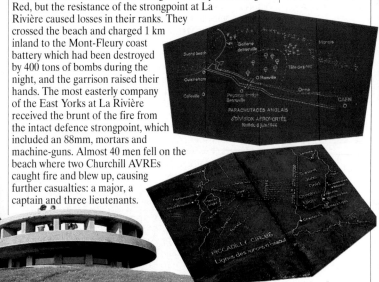

GREEN HOWARDS

The company, joined by another from the reserve unit, the 6th DLI, found themselves pinned down along the sea wall by grenades and mortar bombs, unable to move. Several Shermans joined the infantry on dead ground invisible to the 88 and managed to dislodge the enemy, from the 716th Infantry Division, who were then taken in the rear by the rest of the East Yorks who had landed further west, as well as the company returning from Mont Fleury. Mission accomplished! Well supported by Shermans and specialist tanks, 350 men mounted an assault on La Rivière which surrendered at 09.00. Result: 42 German prisoners and 50 others killed. The 7th Green Howards who had landed at 07.30 crossed through Ver-sur-Mer and forced the garrison of the four armed bunkers at Ver to surrender without putting up a fight.

At 12.30 the 6th Green Howards ▲ *128*, reached Crépon 5 km inland but were stopped by a battery of anti-tank guns in the village.

The sergeant-major of D Company, Stan Hollis, distinguished himself on the beach where he silenced a machine-gun post armed only with grenades and a Sten, and then captured a half section of enemy. At Crépon, armed with a PIAT anti-tank weapon, he was ordered to cover the demolition squad which was threatened by a German anti-tank gun.

As he took aim from a house, the enemy gun, quicker off the mark, opened fire. Bits of the building flew around the ears of the English soldiers and CSM Hollis just got out in time. Under fire and totally without cover, he gave first aid to his comrades wounded by the falling masonry, while giving short bursts of fire from a Bren. Hollis was decorated with the highest British award for gallantry, the Victoria Cross, the only one awarded on D-Day. The GREEN HOWARDS MEMORIAL recalls the courage of the 6th Battalion.

IN 1948, VER-SUR-MER WAS AWARDED THE CROIX DE GUERRE.
At Ver-sur-Mer can be seen the monument to the 2nd Battalion Hertfordshire Regiment and a ship's anchor as a memorial to the liberators. The AMERICA-GOLD BEACH MUSEUM also commemorates the landing of the 69th Brigade. On the sea-wall there is still the bunker which mounted a 75-mm anti-tank gun. At the crossroads of the D514 and the D12 is a house which served as HQ for Admiral Ramsay ● *60*, C-in-C Allied Naval Forces. It is worth seeing THE LIGHTHOUSE for its historical interest as well as its view of Gold Beach.

"DIE WEHRMACHT"
A German magazine dated 10 May 1944.

Street name in Arromanches.

View of Arromanches.

> "VICTORY, NAPOLEON STATED, HINGED ON THE BIG BATTALIONS.
> THE GERMANS ON A FRONT OF 20 KM ONLY TOTALLED A FEW
> THOUSAND MEN. THEY WERE SWAMPED."

ADMIRAL LEMONNIER

Two batteries can be seen in the vicinity: that of MONT-FLEURY (west of the village near the château of the same name) and that of MARE-FONTAINE. (*On the road to Crépon, immediately to your left, take the lane to Sainte-Croix.*)

ASNELLES AND LE HAMEL*.

In the Place Alexander-Stanier, commander of 231st Brigade, is a monument commemorating its actions at Le Hamel. There is also a 75-mm gun BUNKER on which is mounted A MEMORIAL TO THE 147TH REGIMENT ROYAL ARTILLERY.

ARROMANCHES-LES-BAINS

THE 231ST BRIGADE ON JIG.

The unit landed on a 1km stretch of beach well strewn with obstacles, to the west of Hamel. Its task was to capture Ryes, Arromanches and the coast battery at Longues-sur-Mer, while N° 47 Commando RM moved through to Port-en-Bessin. Faced by the attack of the 1st Hampshires at Hamel, the German cannon and mortars put down a curtain of steel and fire on the soaked assailants who managed to take Asnelles after three hours of bitter fighting, well supported by Royal Engineer specialist tanks and watched by some civilians taking part in their liberation. At 17.00 the village was finally cleared and Arromanches was taken at 18.30 by the 1st Hampshires, who lost 120 men including the commander and the second-in-command.The First Dorsets landed to the left of the Hampshires, with the task of taking Ryes. Faced with numerous defences arranged in depth, they reduced it with the help of sixteen Shermans, a dozen self-propelled "Sexton" howitzers from the 90th Field Regiment RA and a few Typhoons ● *56*, ▲ *208*. The enemy had to retire, abandoning their heavy weapons. The 2nd Devons followed the Dorsets, with the task of silencing the 150mm guns at Longues.

PORT WINSTON ● *76*
One can still see several caissons and parts of the jetty of the Mulberry ● *76*. Between 9 and 18 June, 115 caissons were towed from England and formed an 8km breakwater enclosing a roadstead of 1,500 acres. This ensured the back-up for the 21st Army Group: 220,000 men and 40,000 vehicles.

Spitfire ● *56* Squadron above the Anglo-Canadian sector.

47 COMMANDO RM PLAN OF ACTION
This unit had the difficult task of landing hard on the heels of the 231st Brigade at Hamel, marching to Hill 72,3 km south of the village, capturing the cliffs to the east of the harbour by 14.00 and finally clearing the defences with the aid of air support.

SHERMAN TANK ● 63
Weapons and
equipment are
displayed inside the
Arromanches
museum.

**THE LANDING
MUSEUM ♥**
Devoted to D-Day
and the construction
of the Mulberry
harbours, the
Arromanches museum is rich
and varied. The star
exhibits are without
doubt the animated
scale models of
the harbour elements,
which use compressed
air to simulate
the movement of the
waves to demonstrate
how they could move
up and down with

**THE POWER OF
IMAGINATION:
THE ARTIFICIAL
HARBOURS.** They
chose, as a result of
the lesson of Dieppe
● 34, to land well
away from a port, and as
they were deprived of
permanent deep water
facilities, the planning staffs
devised the construction of two
harbours, which they towed over piece by
piece from England. The code-name chosen
was Mulberry ● 76. Huge reinforced
concrete caissons – the famous "Phoenix" -
were designed to form a breakwater around
the system of floating roadways and
pierheads that could move up and down with
the tides. The building work was carried
out in various ports along the south coast,
and in spite of their vigilance, the Germans
did not fathom the purpose. They discounted
Lower Normandy with its lack of ports as a
probable landing area and expected the
invasion in the Pas-de-Calais. The following
comment is from *Defeat in the West* by Milton
Shulman. "Reports of these large contraptions
lying in the Thames were made to Berlin, but
estimates as to their function ranged anywhere
from floating grain-elevators to substitute piers
for use in a captured harbour. Thus the only
correct guess as to Allied intentions was made in direct

contradiction to all military reasoning."
The various elements were assembled
along the south coast of England and
were then towed across the Channel.
By this method, two ports, one for
the Americans (A) at Saint-Laurent-sur-
Mer ▲ 168, and one for the British (B)
at Arromanches were foreseen.
Mulberry A was fully operational on
18 June, but the following day it
happened to be unfortunately wrecked
in a violent storm, which also caused
severe damage to Mulberry B.
The latter, however, was repairable
and was found to play a vital role
in the success of the campaign,
handling 500,000 tons of stores until
Cherbourg ▲ 193, could become
operational. At the port one can find a
MEMORIAL TO THE GROUPE LORRAINE OF

the tides. These are
complemented with
an archive film shown
in a cinema with
a commentary by
a typical voice
of the period.

THE FREE-FRENCH AIR FORCE. Arromanches itself contains
several memorials: a LIBERTY BELL and a COLUMN IN HONOUR
OF THE ROYAL ENGINEERS. The site of the GERMAN RADAR
STATION is also worth a visit. Finally, Arromanches 360° is an
original project which presents a 20-minute film on a circular
screen.

Model figure in the
Arromanches museum.

RYES AND TRACY-SUR-MER*. *(From Arromanches take the D87.)* In the former village there is a British war cemetery containing 979 graves.
(Return to the D514.) In the church at Tracy-sur-Mer there is a stained glass window dedicated to the landings.

THE STRUGGLE FOR THE BATTERY AT LONGUES-SUR-MER ▲ 144. One of the guns was destroyed by the air bombardment and another damaged. The remaining two pieces engaged the cruisers HMS *Ajax* and the *Georges-Leygues* (Free French) on 6 June. The guns also straddled the *Bulolo*, headquarters ship for the 30th Corps, *Ajax*, fired 114 rounds from her 180-mm guns at a range of 15 km silencing the battery at 10.30 hours. The garrison, however, repaired the remaining gun and opened fire again at 15.00. It was the turn of the *Georges-Leygues* to take on the duel, and she managed a direct hit through the embrasure of the casemate at 18.00. More than 170 rounds were fired by the three 155-mm guns at Longues on D-Day before the garrison finally surrendered to the 2nd Devons. Four hundred metres east is the site of the RAF advanced airstrip B11, which was operational from 21 June to 4 September.

LE CHAOS
In the middle of crumbling concrete remains, a footpath just beside the fire control post descends the cliffs to the beach.

125 Wing operated from there and included several foreign pilots, one of whom was the French ace, Pierre Clostermann, with 33 kills to his name. The reserve brigades arrived on Gold Beach at midday. The 151st reached the Caen-Bayeux railway line but retired east of Bayeux for the night, while the 56th Independent Brigade advanced rapidly towards Sully. Patrols of the 2nd Essex entered

Bayeux that evening and tanks ● *63,* were at Saint-Vigord, within sight of the spires of the cathedral. The 69th Brigade reached the Saint-Léger ridge, the highest elevation on the N13 Caen to Bayeux road. At a cost of 413 men killed on D-Day, the 50th Division had achieved practically all its objectives. Bayeux was taken the following morning, Saint-Léger and Ducy in the afternoon. Only the villages of Longues-sur-Mer and Port-en-Bessin still held out.

LONGUES-SUR-MER NAVAL COAST BATTERY.
The battery is unique in that the guns which engaged the Allied naval force are still in place. The fire-control post, situated 500 m in advance of the four casemates is worth visiting. Left, each 155mm gun in its concrete shelter covered a segment of the 120 degree arc of fire of the four-gun German naval battery.

▲ LONGUES-SUR-MER BATTERY

Built in a hurry, the battery was only just operational at dawn on D-Day. During the night of 5/6 June it was attacked by Allied aircraft who dropped 600 tons of bombs, most of which landed on the neighbouring village. At 05.30 its three usable guns opened fire on the Allied fleet, threatening the *Bulolo*, the headquarters ship of Naval Task Force G, but without causing any damage. HMS *Ajax*, a British cruiser, replied and managed to penetrate the embrasures of two of the guns. The battery opened fire again in the afternoon with one remaining gun, before being finally silenced by *Ajax* and the French cruiser *Georges-Leygues*. When British troops arrived in the early evening the battery commander surrendered with 184 gunners.

GERMAN ZEISS BINOCULARS
An observer calculates the distance between the guns and their target, using a rangefinder on a tripod. These were nicknamed "donkey ears".

FORTRESS TELEPHONE TYPE 38
The casemates were linked to the fire-control post by a network of deeply buried telephone cables.

BATTERY CONTROL ROOM
Target information was telegraphed to the guns via dial pointers.

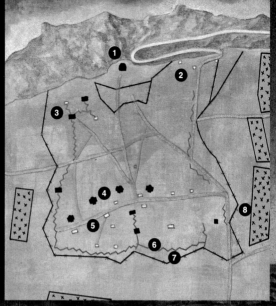

PLAN OF THE LONGUES-SUR-MER BATTERY

This particular coast artillery battery is the only one on the Atlantic Wall with its guns still in place. These installations consisted of four casemates, each housing 150-mm guns with a range of 19 km. It was built at a height of 65 m on top of a cliff between Arromanches and Port-en-Bessin.

1. Fire control post.
2. Tobruk stands.
3. Shelters.
4. Casemates type M272.
5. Magazines
6. Trenches
7. Barbed-wire
8. Mines.

50-MM SHELL
he 150-mm guns
: Longues were
riginally developed
s secondary
rmament for
attleships.
hey were consigned
coast artillery when
e German naval
onstruction
rogramme was
bandoned.

MAGAZINE
Rounds were transported from the magazine
to the guns in wheelbarrows, before being loaded
manually by the gunners.

Hitler intended to construct a "wall of steel from North Cape to the Pyrenees", but his aims were only partially achieved. On D-Day the Atlantic Wall was incomplete and although the Calais area and the Channel Islands were protected by powerful batteries, Normandy was only capable of offering a feeble resistance as a landing in the area was considered unlikely. In spite of many weaknesses, the defensive system was a monument to the ingenuity of the German engineers, both in the design of the fortifications and the methods of camouflage used.

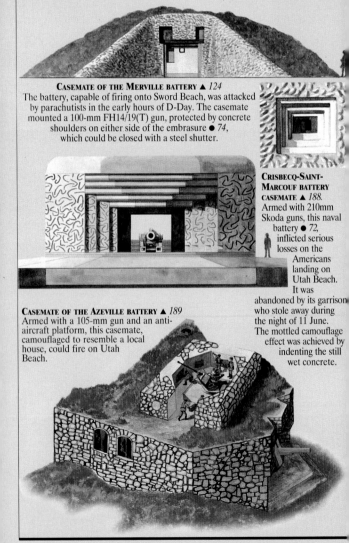

CASEMATE OF THE MERVILLE BATTERY ▲ 124
The battery, capable of firing onto Sword Beach, was attacked by parachutists in the early hours of D-Day. The casemate mounted a 100-mm FH14/19(T) gun, protected by concrete shoulders on either side of the embrasure ● 74, which could be closed with a steel shutter.

CRISBECQ-SAINT-MARCOUF BATTERY CASEMATE ▲ 188. Armed with 210mm Skoda guns, this naval battery ● 72, inflicted serious losses on the Americans landing on Utah Beach. It was abandoned by its garrison who stole away during the night of 11 June. The mottled camouflage effect was achieved by indenting the still wet concrete.

CASEMATE OF THE AZEVILLE BATTERY ▲ 189
Armed with a 105-mm gun and an anti-aircraft platform, this casemate, camouflaged to resemble a local house, could fire on Utah Beach.

VENTILATION

Some works were fitted with manual ventilation systems to expell the gas and fumes caused by firing.

To camouflage bunkers built among the villages facing the beaches, the Germans resorted to disguising the concrete surfaces by painting them to resemble houses and cafés.

From the interior of a casemate, the garrison could defend themselves against an infantry rear attack. Armoured embrasures which could be closed by a sliding shutter were fitted to cover all doorways.

FIRE-CONTROL POST
● *74,* ▲ *172*
Situated at the Pointe du Hoc, this two-storey fire-control post was built into the cliff face. The rangefinder ▲ *144,* was mounted on the upper level, at the summit of the cliff. Below, in the battery-control level, target information was calculated and passed to the guns by dial pointers.

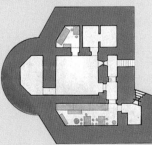

These two leaf stable-type armoured doors, which were fitted to numerous works in the Atlantic Wall, could resist the blast of heavy bombs and were gas-tight.

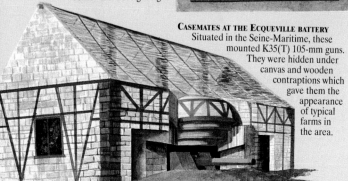

CASEMATES AT THE ECQUEVILLE BATTERY
Situated in the Seine-Maritime, these mounted K35(T) 105-mm guns. They were hidden under canvas and wooden contraptions which gave them the appearance of typical farms in the area.

FLAK 38 ANTI-AIRCRAFT GUN
This gun had four 20-mm barrels loaded
with 20 round clips. With a rate of fire of 700-800
rounds per minute it was a weapon feared by Allied
pilots. Its effective height was 1,900 m.

CASEMATE ● 74
Inside was a ready-use
magazine. Spent cartridges were
ejected into a trap under the floor
directly behind the gun.

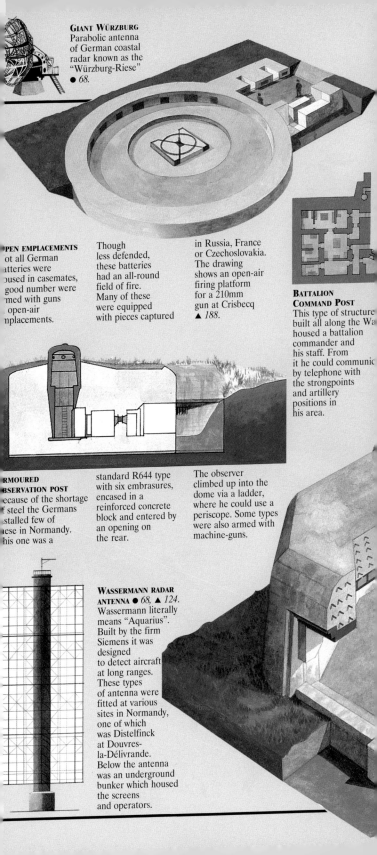

GIANT WÜRZBURG
Parabolic antenna of German coastal radar known as the "Würzburg-Riese" ● 68.

OPEN EMPLACEMENTS
Not all German batteries were housed in casemates, a good number were armed with guns in open-air emplacements.

Though less defended, these batteries had an all-round field of fire. Many of these were equipped with pieces captured in Russia, France or Czechoslovakia. The drawing shows an open-air firing platform for a 210mm gun at Crisbecq ▲ 188.

BATTALION COMMAND POST
This type of structure built all along the Wall housed a battalion commander and his staff. From it he could communicate by telephone with the strongpoints and artillery positions in his area.

ARMOURED OBSERVATION POST
Because of the shortage of steel the Germans installed few of these in Normandy. This one was a standard R644 type with six embrasures, encased in a reinforced concrete block and entered by an opening on the rear.

The observer climbed up into the dome via a ladder, where he could use a periscope. Some types were also armed with machine-guns.

WASSERMANN RADAR ANTENNA ● 68, ▲ 124.
Wassermann literally means "Aquarius". Built by the firm Siemens it was designed to detect aircraft at long ranges. These types of antenna were fitted at various sites in Normandy, one of which was Distelfinck at Douvres-la-Délivrande. Below the antenna was an underground bunker which housed the screens and operators.

RANGEFIELD ROOM
An observer and a gunner
calculate the ship's position
so as to regulate the range
of the guns.

HAND GRENADE
The Allies
nicknamed
these "potato
mashers".

AUTOMATIC PISTOL TYPE P. 38
A standard German army
officer's pistol.

MAUSER KAR 98 RIFLE
A derivative of the famous rifle introduced in 1898.

MACHINE-GUN MAUSER MG 42
7.92-mm calibre, this achieved a rate
of 1,200 rounds per minute.

9-mm
parabellum
machine-pistol
MP40. with
magazine
carriers.

Badge
of the German
coastal
artillery.

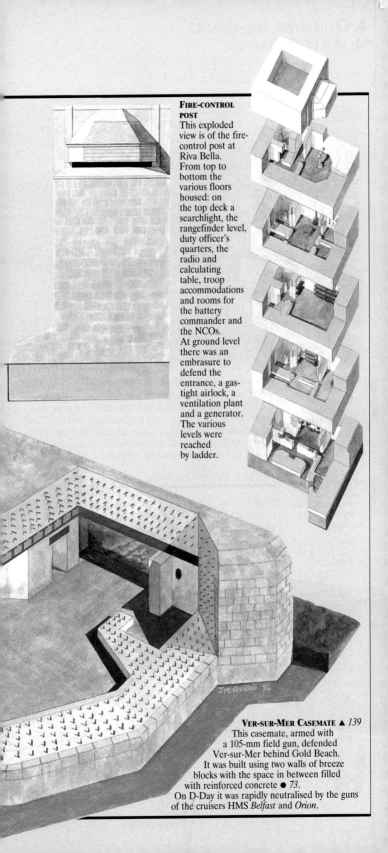

FIRE-CONTROL POST
This exploded view is of the fire-control post at Riva Bella. From top to bottom the various floors housed: on the top deck a searchlight, the rangefinder level, duty officer's quarters, the radio and calculating table, troop accommodations and rooms for the battery commander and the NCOs. At ground level there was an embrasure to defend the entrance, a gas-tight airlock, a ventilation plant and a generator. The various levels were reached by ladder.

JM GUILLOU 94

VER-SUR-MER CASEMATE ▲ 139
This casemate, armed with a 105-mm field gun, defended Ver-sur-Mer behind Gold Beach. It was built using two walls of breeze blocks with the space in between filled with reinforced concrete ● 73.
On D-Day it was rapidly neutralised by the guns of the cruisers HMS *Belfast* and *Orion*.

PAST BATTLES
In the 11th century, Odo, Bishop of Bayeux and half-brother to William, had 40 ships built which accompanied the Conqueror's fleet. ▲ *154, 196, 253*.

PAST WITNESS
The Tour Vauban (above), a defensive structure from the 18th century.

A Bren carrier lands from an LCT ● *60* on 10 June 1944.

MUSÉE DES ÉPAVES (SHIPWRECK MUSEUM). Situated in the village of Commes, this museum is devoted to shipwrecks ▲ *118* which have been explored and recovered since the 1940s (an LCT, howitzers, half tracks, a jeep, DD tanks and gun turrets, etc.), a representative selection of ships which participated on D-Day as well as several wrecks from the last century and the First World War period.

PORT-EN-BESSIN-HUPPAIN

N° 47 Commando R.M. led by Lieutenant-Colonel Phillips, landed at Hamel at 10.00, with the task of reaching the extreme western limit of Gold Beach, the fishing harbour of Port-en-Bessin coveted both by the British and the US 1st Infantry Division. Flanked by high cliffs on each side, the village could only be attacked from

the south which was merely defended by trenches and
a few mines ● 74. The main defences faced seawards.
Three landing-craft hit mines off Hamel causing 70 deaths.
Forty more men were lost in eliminating an enemy company
on their line of advance. By 21.00 the remaining 300 marines
reached and cleared the village of Escures, 2 km south
of Port-en-Bessin. Having lost their radios, the commandos
attacked the eastern cliff, which had not yet been
conquered, at dawn, leaving 15 men behind in Escures as
a rearguard. Street fighting broke out in the town, but by
the evening of 7 June it was in their hands. During the night
the commandos stormed the cliffs and at 04.00 all resistance
ceased. The following morning at 08.00 the 2nd Devons
arrived at Escures. The road from Arromanches to Port-
en-Bessin had been secured at a cost of 200 casualties,
but 47 Commando had seized a harbour 14 km from their
landing place, taken 300 prisoners and killed 60 of the
enemy. Today, Port-en-Bessin remembers its liberators with
a COMITÉ DU DÉBARQUEMENT MEMORIAL on one of the
jetties of the outer port and by a PLAQUE fixed to the wall
of a bunker below the Tour Vauban. This commemorates
the actions of N° 47 Commando R.M. and those of the
marines on board the French ships *Georges-Leygues*
and *Montcalm*. *(From Port-en-Bessin, take the D6.)*

BAYEUX, FIRST FRENCH CITY TO BE LIBERATED

Bayeux was occupied on 18 June 1940, on the day
that de Gaulle issued his famous rallying call to the
French on the BBC. It was there that the maps of
the German defences ● 72, 74, ▲ 144 were drawn
and sent to British intelligence. In fact, in 1944 the city
was the border between two German infantry divisions,
the 716th and 352nd, and very few troops were in position
at strategic points on 6 June; only at the railway station,
the post office and a few intersections ....

ACTIVE FISHING PORT
Two granite jetties
enclose the outer
port, the lock of
which leads to
the inner harbour.

GERMAN DEFENCES
They dominated
the port from
the top of the cliffs.

THE NORMAN PREPARATIONS

Duke William, angered by "treason" on the part of King Harold constructed a fleet to enforce his claim to the throne.

THE ALLIED PREPARATIONS

On the south coast of England a formidable armade was gathered: warships and merchant vessels, tanks, fighter-bombers, commandos, parachutists and assault troops.

HEADING FOR THE COAST OF SUSSEX

William crossed the Channel with a fleet of ships similar to those used earlier by the Vikings.

HEADING FOR NORMANDY

The troop transporters crossing the Channel in heavy seas. The men are alert.

THE BAYEUX TAPESTRY

Exhibited in the William the Conqueror Centre in the city, it tells the story of the rivalry between Harold and William for the throne of England between 1064 and 1066. Falsely attributed in the past to Queen Mathilda, it was made in 1077 to the orders of Odo, half-brother of William, Count of Kent and Bishop of Bayeux. Its 58 panels were embroidered in coloured linen thread on a linen backing. (69,55 m by 55 cm).

The epic in three acts :
1/. Edward the Confessor, King of England, sent Harold to do homage to Duke William of Normandy who had a claim to the throne.
2/. Harold felt he had been tricked and became king on the death of Edward.
3/. William landed in England to assert his claim. During the battle of Hastings, Harold was killed and William became the Conqueror.

TWO ANGLO-NORMAN EPICS
1066 AND 1944

THE OVERLORD EMBROIDERY.
Exhibited at the D-Day Museum in Portsmouth, this recounts the history of the Allied landings in Normandy in June 1944. It was made by the ladies of the Royal School of Needlework between 1968 and 1973 as a patchwork, 82m long and comprising 34 panels. The use of actual cloth from soldiers' uniforms of the period gives it a particular dramatic effect.

Conceived as a replica of the Bayeux Tapestry it also tells its story in three episodes.
1/. The preparations for the invasion of Europe. The necessary resources are assembled.
2/. The crossing of the Channel and the landings.
3/. The Battle of Normandy and the Allied break-out (June-August 1944).

EN ROUTE TO HASTINGS
Dressed in chain-mail shirts and bearing lances and shields, the Norman cavalry advance into battle.

6 JUNE. THE ALLIES LAND
Leaving their landing-craft, rifle in hand, the assault troops storm the beaches under enemy fire.

THE BATTLE OF HASTINGS
On 14 October 1066, William's troops defeated the Saxon forces. King Harold was killed in action.

THE BATTLE OF NORMANDY
August 1944. The German forces hemmed into the Falaise pocket and without tanks or air support, are annihilated.

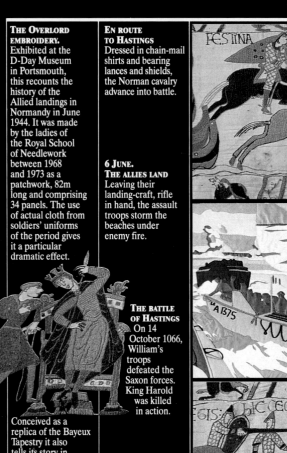

HALLEY'S COMET
The Normans took its
appearance in 1066
to be a sign of Harold's
"treachery". Scene 31
of the Bayeux Tapestry.

INGA: VT CIBVM · RAPERENTVR :

SIMVL · ANGLI   ET   FRANCI :

MEMORIAL MUSEUM
The museum ▲ 160
is situated alongside
the ring-road,
locally known as
the "by-pass", near
the British Cemetery.
As indicated
by the name,
the museum is
devoted to the whole
of the Battle of
Normandy and
features uniforms
and equipment as
well as everything
to do with the period:
newspapers, leaflets,
posters and photos.

There was no fighting or destruction in Bayeux. British troops
patrolled the city on the evening of D-Day and it was officially
liberated at 10.00 the following morning. It rapidly became
a safe haven for civilians forced to flee neighbouring villages,
as well as a British medical centre.
There were five large hospitals, three
casualty clearing-stations and the
city hospital which cared for sick and
wounded civilians. The latter hospital
was named after Captain Robert Lion,
a medical officer with the French
commandos, killed on 6 June at
Ouistreham ▲ 130.

**COMMONWEALTH
CEMETERY**
Contains 4,648 graves.
The monumental
gateway on the other
side of the road
records the names
of 1,837 missing
soldiers. ● 81.

BAYEUX, SEAT OF THE "PROVISIONAL GOVERNMENT"

General de Gaulle was told about the invasion of his country
at a meeting in Churchill's private train which was parked
near Portsmouth on 4 June, after which he was sent back to
Algiers. The Allied commanders were quite
hesitant about
foisting
de Gaulle

> "I MEAN TO STATE WITHOUT FURTHER DELAY,
> THAT ANY POINT FROM WHICH THE ENEMY FLEES,
> IS UNDER THE AUTHORITY OF MY GOVERNMENT."
>
> CHARLES DE GAULLE

BRITISH TROOPS IN BAYEUX ON 27 JUNE
In the cathedral there is a plaque honouring the men of the 56th Independent Infantry Brigade, who entered the city on the evening of D-Day. Another reminder of that period is a stained-glass window unveiled by Queen Elizabeth II in 1989.

Also worth seeing...
BAYEUX HISTORIC CITY ▲ *154, 196, 253*
The beautiful capital of the Bessin region, Bayeux is justly proud of its 12th-century cathedral of Notre-Dame and the tapestry named after Matilda, wife of William the Bastard, Duke of Normandy and King of England. The Baron-Gérard Museum and the Diocesan Museum of Religious Art are also worth visiting.

Also worth seeing...
HALF-TIMBERED HOUSES IN THE OLD PART OF THE CITY

onto the French and were worried about a civil war behind their lines. Finally, to smooth ruffled feathers the general was permitted a short visit to France on 14 June. He arrived at Graye-sur-Mer and was escorted with his entourage to Bayeux where he was able to make a speech in which he thanked "true France, the one of people who fight" and then walked among enthusiastic crowds. Taking on the powers of a head of State he appointed a sub-prefect and installed a number of his supporters in key administrative positions. His activities were tolerated by the Allies, but it was not until October that his provisional government was recognized as a legal entity. Although to many Frenchmen the general was a hero, the British and American governments continued to view him with suspicion.

BAYEUX FREE CITY. The Gaullist administration stamped its personality on the city and issued notes from the Bank of France in an effort to stop the dissemination of "invasion" currency. This currency consisted of dollar bills made in the USA and de Gaulle considered them an insult to the French. The Normans managed to use them, however, to pay their taxes! A fully intact city behind the front and surrounded by airfields, stores depots and thousands of troops, Bayeux became a favourite tourist spot where the famous tapestry, rescued from the clutches of the occupiers, was once again exhibited in the cathedral.

Flags of superior officers' vehicles.

In 1066, William the Conqueror, Duke of Normandy, assembled a fleet of 966 ships which transported 50,000 men to England. Nine centuries later, the 21st Army group of General Montgomery, himself a descendant of Robert de Montgomeri, one of William's companions, launched a million men onto those same beaches in Lower Normandy. Since 1980, the Bayeux Memorial Museum has presented the battle of Normandy both chronologically and thematically: 77 days of combat which ended with the encirclement of the enemy forces and the crossing of the Seine.

A WAR MUSEUM
Several armoured vehicles appear to guard the museum from attack: a Churchill tank, an M10 tank destroyer, a Sherman M4 and a German Hetzer self-propelled gun.

ENGLISH HELMETS
The steel helmets were often marked in regimental colours or with transfers of battalion insignia. The Mark II helmet (left) is covered with sand-effect anti-reflective paint. A circle of stainless steel around the brim neutralised any adverse effect on radio waves or mine detection.

INSTRUCTION POSTER
Thanks to well designed equipment the infantryman of 1944 was independent. This poster shows a typical Tommy armed with a Bren and shows his entrenching tool, water bottle, grenades, spare magazines, etc.

MAP OF UTAH BEACH
(1/25,000 scale showing beach).

British army berets and Scottish headgear.

GENERAL MONTGOMERY'S BERET
This features the woven braid badge of a general and the standard cap badge of the Royal Tank regiment which Monty adopted after the Battle of El Alamein as a personal idiosyncrasy.

FLAG OF THE 7TH ROYAL TANK REGIMENT
During the two months of operations in Normandy, 3,000 tanks for the Anglo-Canadian 21st Army Group were disembarked. After 25 June, columns of tanks no longer got lost in the narrow streets of Bayeux as they could follow the "by-pass", as the local people still call it in honour of the Royal Engineers who originally built it.

HE WAS ONLY 20
Telegram informing the family of the death of a GI (right) of the 5th Infantry Division.

THE OVERLORD HALL
It is divided into two sections, Anglo-Canadian and American. The battle is explained in ten parts, from the beaches to Falaise.

THE EISENHOWER HALL
Field and anti-aircraft artillery are exhibited here. A diorama shows the closing of the Falaise pocket by Americans and Poles meeting at Chambois.

M10 TANK DESTROYER
Used by all the Allied forces in Europe. Its 76.2 shells could destroy a German Panther.

MONTGOMERY AND DE GAULLE
After he landed at Graye-sur-Mer ▲ *135* on 14 June at the same time as a Canadian regiment, de Gaulle had a short meeting with Montgomery whose HQ was on the grounds of the Château de Creullet ▲ *137*.

BAYEUX, 13 JUNE 1944
A civilian watching a convoy from the 30th British Corps.

The British created the by-pass, today's ring-road, to avoid traffic-jams. Camps sprang up all over the place including one for worker-prisoners at Saint-Vigor. In August the railway was reopened to traffic and the pumping stations of PLUTO ● *67* rumbled day and night supplying fuel to the armies. In 1945 a war cemetery containing 4,648 graves was laid out and in 1948 the memorial to the missing, carrying 1,800 names, was inaugurated.

BAYEUX REMEMBERS. The events of 1944 are commemorated in the Musée Charles-de-Gaulle in the former governor's palace. The other monuments include one to war reporters killed in action, the monument to the liberators of the city and the 50th Infantry Division memorial at the Hôtel Doyen. In the Rue Larcher there is the deportees memorial and at the exit of the town towards Caen there is a roundabout named after Eisenhower. In the square named after de Gaulle

BAYEUX, 14 JUNE 1944
The de Gaulle walkabout. After being welcomed by a crowd of 3,000 who listened to him speak in the Place du Château, he travelled to Isigny ▲ *175* and then to Grandcamp. After seven hours spent in Normandy the General re-embarked for England.

there is a monument marking the spot from which he spoke, and a bas-relief on the wall of the sub-prefecture.

CARREFOUR DE VAUCELLES. Driving round the ring-road clockwise you pass the MEMORIAL MUSEUM♥ on the right ▲ *160* and the COMMONWEALTH CEMETERY on the left. At the intersection formed by the Boulevard du 6-Juin, the Boulevard Eindhoven and the Rue Saint-Patrice, there is the MONUMENT COMMEMORATING the landings and the Liberation. Twenty-one blocks of pink granite on an area of 40 square metres evoke the fighting on 6 June and de Gaulle's visit to the city.

D-Day, the Attack
D-Day, le choc
From Omaha Beach
to the liberation of Saint-Lô

Anthony Kemp

▲ D-DAY, THE ATTACK!
BAYEUX TO CARENTAN

1 BAYEUX
2 MANOR OF ARGOUGES
3 PORT-EN-BESSIN-HUPPAIN
4 LE GRAND HAMEAU
5 SURRAIN
6 AMERICAN CEMETERY
7 VIERVILLE-SUR-MER
8 OMAHA BEACH
9 SAINT-PIERRE-DU-M

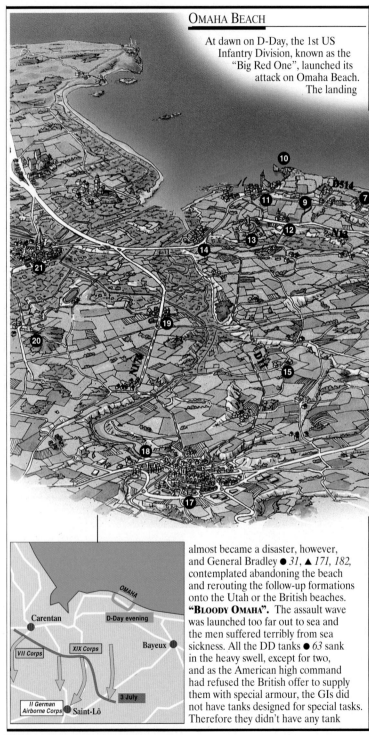

OMAHA BEACH

At dawn on D-Day, the 1st US Infantry Division, known as the "Big Red One", launched its attack on Omaha Beach. The landing

almost became a disaster, however, and General Bradley ● *31*, ▲ *171, 182*, contemplated abandoning the beach and rerouting the follow-up formations onto the Utah or the British beaches. **"BLOODY OMAHA".** The assault wave was launched too far out to sea and the men suffered terribly from sea sickness. All the DD tanks ● *63* sank in the heavy swell, except for two, and as the American high command had refused the British offer to supply them with special armour, the GIs did not have tanks designed for special tasks. Therefore they didn't have any tank

164

designed especially for clearing minefields ● 73, destroying
bunkers and crossing the sea-wall which fronted the beach.
Beyond the wall, high cliffs formed an excellent line of
defence and, shortly before D-Day, the Germans stationed
in the area had been reinforced by elements of the 352nd
Division. The bombers whose task was to destroy
the fortifications dropped most of their loads on open country
too far inland. The result was that when the assault wave

| 🚗 | 130 km |
| ⏱ | 2 days |

Logo of the Battle of
Normandy Open-Air
Museum.

"Bloody Omaha"
The day after
D-Day 3,000 dead
Americans were
counted plus 3,000
wounded or missing
on that infamous
beach.

**P38 over the
Omaha Beach**
This was the first
US aircraft to land
on French soil on 6
June at 09.30: at
Pouppeville (to the
east of Sainte-Marie-
du-Mont ▲ 186).

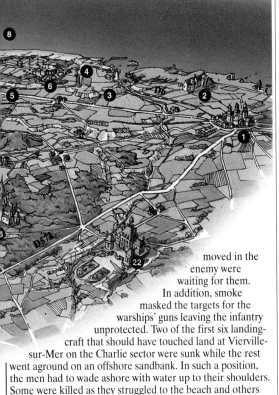

moved in the
enemy were
waiting for them.
In addition, smoke
masked the targets for the
warships' guns leaving the infantry
unprotected. Two of the first six landing-
craft that should have touched land at Vierville-
sur-Mer on the Charlie sector were sunk while the rest
went aground on an offshore sandbank. In such a position,
the men had to wade ashore with water up to their shoulders.
Some were killed as they struggled to the beach and others
drowned. Small groups of men, often without their officers,

HEADING INLAND

By the afternoon of 6 June a few DD tanks had come ashore but, as the beach exits were still mined, it was the infantry who had to take the offensive and attempt to force a way up to the villages on the ridge overlooking the coast.

who had been killed trying to reach the land, sheltered themselves behind the concrete wall. All cohesion was lost and although a few managed to escape the deathtrap on the beach, the following waves simply stumbled into the carnage on the beach. As the tide rose, the narrowing strip of sand became so encumbered with wreckage that those arriving were unable to move. But during the course of the late morning the engineers finally managed to clear narrow passages through the minefields and the Germans were progressively dislodged from their positions. By nightfall a narrow bridgehead had been established extending some 1.5 km inland, which remained extremely vulnerable.

FROM BAYEUX TO COLLEVILLE-SUR-MER. *(After leaving the BATTLE OF NORMANDY MEMORIAL MUSEUM ▲ 158, take the D6 to Port-en-Bessin ▲ 152.)* At Commes can be seen the SHIPWRECK MUSEUM, ● *118,* ▲ *152,* devoted to shipwrecks which have been explored and recovered since the 1940s. After that take the D514 coast road.

AMERICAN CEMETERY OF COLLEVILLE-SUR-MER

SILENCE AND REFLECTION

The name Normandy was given to the cemetery that was inaugurated on 19 July 1956 by President Coty and General Marshall. It covers 170 acres and contains the graves of 9,387 Americans, 307 of whom are unidentified. The layout of the ten square plots made up of thousands of crosses on a lawn overlooking Omaha Beach is impressive.

The Normandy American Cemetery on ground donated in perpetuity by the French government is maintained by the American Battlefield Monuments Commission. According to American tradition, families were offered the right to repatriation of their dead after the war and 14,000 bodies were sent to the United States for burial. Those remaining were collected into a cemetery which contains 9,387 graves carefully aligned. Each one has a headstone of white Italian marble topped either with the Latin cross or the Star of David ● *80.* On the right of the entrance a time capsule has been buried for the instruction of future generations, containing newspaper articles published on D-Day. It was placed there in memory of the war correspondents in June 1969 and is due to be opened on 6 June 2044.

THE MEMORIAL. This consists of a semi-circular colonnade, in the centre of which is a 7 metre high bronze statue by Donald de Lue symbolizing the youth of America. On the base is written: "My eyes have seen the glory of the coming of the Lord." Each colonnade ends in a loggia in which are maps engraved into the stone and highlighted by coloured mosaic. They show three phases of the campaign: the airborne scouts which preceded the main operations, the plan of Operation Neptune and the actual landings themselves on the five beaches. Two large bronze urns, also by the sculptor Donald de Lue, stand at the entrance to each loggia, decorated with allegorical figures. On one of the urns a relief illustrates the phrase from Genesis: "And the Spirit moved upon the face of the waters." From the memorial the visitor looks out over a silent reflective pool to the ranks of white marble headstones, down the central path which ends in a Greek-style temple.

On 6 June
the wounded were
taken off on
the same craft
that had brought
them in.

The Spirit of
American Youth.

THE GARDEN OF THE MISSING. This is located to the east of the main memorial and is in the form of an arc of a circle. On the walls are inscribed the name, rank, unit and the State from which the man originally came, of 1,557 soldiers who have no known grave or could not be identified.

ORIENTATION TABLE. A flight of steps leads from the Memorial down to a viewing platform on top of the cliffs overlooking Omaha Beach. An orientation table is placed there to give visitors a splendid overview of Omaha Beach. To the right in the distance can be seen the remains of the Mulberry harbour at Arromanches ● *76*, ▲ *141*, and closer, the entrance to Port-en-Bessin. To the left the view is terminated by the high cliffs of the Pointe de la Percée. A winding footpath leads down the cliff face to the beach, passing another ORIENTATION TABLE.

MEMORIAL TO THE 5TH ENGINEER SPECIAL BRIGADE
The Croix de Guerre was awarded to this unit by
the French government on 25 May, 1945.

Detail of the 5th
Engineer Special
Brigade Memorial.

SAINT-LAURENT-
SUR-MER CHURCH

In the churchyard
are the graves
of three British
commandos who
were members of
a twelve-strong
raiding party
who landed at Saint-
Honorine in 1942.
Their task was
to sow alarm among
the garrison
and seize a prisoner
or two. Unfortunately
they landed at a
strongly defended
sector and the
three men were
killed in the battle
that ensued.

GERMAN MEMORIAL
(Strongpoint WN62,
Colleville-sur-Mer).
Placed there for their
comrades by
the survivors of
3rd Company, 726th
Regiment, and
716th Infantry
Division, who
defended that sector.

IN HONOUR OF THE "BIG RED ONE". As you leave the
cemetery, a small lane on the left leads down to the site
of one of the ten enemy strongpoints that defended Omaha
Beach. WN62 commanded one of the vital exits and it was
absolutely necessary to eliminate it. Fox Sector was the
responsibility of the 3rd Battalion of the 18th Infantry
regiment. In the middle of a level area of grass there is a
granite obelisk erected in honour of the men of the 1st
Infantry Division who were killed at Omaha. Moving on down
the slope one can see the remains of zig-zag trenches dug by
the Germans. At the edge of the cliff there is a board on
which is inscribed the plan of the strongpoint. Just beside this
is a small wooden cross, the first German war memorial to be
placed on any of the beaches. Finally on the left are the
remains of two large bunkers which could fire along the
beach. On the roof of one of them is a memorial to the 5th
Engineer Special Brigade.

SAINT-LAURENT
SUR-MER

**1942: OPERATION
AQUATINT.**
In the graveyard
of the church there
are three British
war graves dated
13 September, 1942.
These three soldiers
were members of a small
elite group known as the Small-Scale Raiding Force.
The three soldiers were killed while taking part in
Operation Aquatint.

DOG SECTOR. From the village the D517 twists down
to the beach, flanked by steep hills. It is easy to understand
how simple it was for the Germans to defend the exit with
well-sited machine-guns giving them a very large field

of fire. At the bottom is one of the prominent COMITÉ DU DÉBARQUEMENT standard memorials, resembling the prow of a ship. Facing the sea you are on the boundary between Dog and Easy beach sectors. On the left is a small café and beside it there is a narrow road named after the 116TH US INFANTRY REGIMENT. If you walk up it you will see the roof of a German bunker in the garden behind the café, and after about 200 m the memorial in honour of the 6TH ENGINEER SPECIAL BRIGADE: one of the first memorials to be inaugurated, on 26 November 1944. Along the D517, you will find the OMAHA 6 JUIN 1944 MUSEUM, that shows a collection of military vehicles, weapons and uniforms used by the American troops who landed in the area on D-Day.

SECTOR EASY. *(Leave the Comité du Débarquement memorial on your left and drive along the sea-front road to your right.)* Although the present sea-wall is modern, it is easy to understand how difficult it was to cross under fire in 1944. Behind it the soldiers had to find shelter. This was Sector Easy, subdivided into three colours, green, white and red. From there, on the same road, drive as far as you can to the place known as RUQUET. You will see on the right-hand side a flight of steps leading up to the German bunker, which still has its gun in place. This is the memorial to the 2nd US Infantry Division, and there is also a PLAQUE in honour of the dead

Monument to the 1st Infantry Division at Colleville.

FOX, EASY, DOG, CHARLIE
Omaha was divided into four sectors, from east to west, Fox, Easy, Dog and Charlie. These in turn were subdivided by colours: Fox red and green, Easy red and green, Dog red, white and green, etc. Three units from the 1st Infantry Division disembarked on Omaha. The 16th Infantry Regiment on Fox Green and Easy Red (from Colleville-sur-Mer to Saint-Laurent sur Mer), while the 116th Infantry Regiment and the 5th Ranger Battalion attacked Easy Green and Dog, (Saint-Laurent-sur-Mer to Vierville-sur-Mer). Charlie Sector was the target of the 2nd Ranger Battalion.
▲ *172.*

SERVICE AT SAINT-LAURENT-SUR-MER
A chaplain and his organist holding a service shortly after the landings.

← Monument 6ᵉ Brigade de Génie U.S.

Insignia of the 2nd US Infantry Division
This unit ● *50* suffered significant losses during the Normandy campaign and their memorial is sited on Omaha Beach.

of the 6th Engineer Special Brigade. The numerous monuments to engineer units on the beaches are appropriate as they suffered proportionally heavy losses. Landing with the first assault waves, their job was to destroy the obstacles under merciless enemy fire.

To Vierville-sur-Mer. Return to the main monument and continue straight on along the sea front. On the sea-wall on the right is a small plaque commemorating Operation Aquatint, the British commando raid mentioned above. The road runs for about 1.5 km, bordered on the right by the sea-wall. On the left slightly below the level of the road is a plaque indicating where the first bodies were provisionally buried in a field. Driving along the sea-front it is easy to understand the tactical problems faced by the invaders. On the right, the solid concrete wall in full view of the defenders dug in on top of the cliffs on the left, with a perfect field of fire.

From Vierville-sur-Mer to the Pointe du Hoc

The place where the road curves inland was the western extremity of Omaha Beach and the village of Vierville-sur-Mer.

Vierville-sur-Mer. The village formed one of the German strongpoints blocking the exit road from the beach. Facing the sea there is a powerful bunker designed to fire along the beach. Inside it still has its 88-mm gun. To the left is another bunker with embrasures at each end for a 50mm gun which could pour fire all along the American positions. Going further inland onto the cliffs one can see a bunker that served as an observation and fire control post.

To the right beside the café, a footpath leads up to the top of the cliffs from which one can have a good view of the beach. On top of the main bunker, which was a Central Command Post called WN5, a monument has been built to honour the men of the National Guard units which served in the campaign and were killed in the battle. Standing on the monument one can see to the left some remains of the ill-fated Mulberry ● *76*, ▲ *141*, wrecked in the storm, on which a modern jetty has been built. More debris can be

Omaha beach after the landing
"On that beach covered with the wreckage of ships, drowned vehicles and burnt-out tanks, the clusters of soaked shapeless bodies on the pebbles where they fell."
Omar Bradley,
A Soldier's Story

COUNCIL OF WAR
On 14 June there was
a meeting on Omaha
Beach between
the American Rear
Admiral Kirk ● *30*
(wearing the cap)
who commanded
the naval task force
(three battleships,
ten cruisers and
thirty-five destroyers,
General John L.
Hall (carrying
binoculars)
and General
Omar Bradley
(extreme right)
who commanded
the First American
Army ● *31*, ▲ *182*.

From top to bottom:
detail of the Comité
du Débarquement
Memorial at
Colleville-sur-Mer
▲ *169*; view of Omaha
Beach; Memorial
of Vierville-sur-Mer.

seen at extreme low tides. That is all
that's left of this artificial port after
the storm in late June. To your right
is Dog Green Sector where the assault
wave of the 116th Regiment was
decimated by automatic fire from guns
entrenched around the restaurant
of the Casino. As you leave the village,
there stands the monument to the 29th
US Infantry Division, nicknamed the
"Let's Go", which landed as the second
wave later on D-Day. On a wall on
the right beside the road is a PLAQUE
recalling the deeds of the 5th US
Ranger Battalion, which landed on
Omaha on D-Day. Supported by two
companies from the 2nd Rangers they
cleared Vierville-sur-Mer and opened
up the road for the 29th Infantry
Division. If you turn around you can
see a bunker for a heavy machine-gun
cunningly built into the cliffs. The
SENTIER DU LITTORAL (coastal pathway)
runs from Vierville underneath the
cliffs all the way to Grandcamp-Maisy,
passing the celebrated Pointe du Hoc.
CHÂTEAU DE VAUMICEL. (*When you
reach the D514 coast road, turn right
and the château is on the left.*)
A plaque on the wall beside

LUNAR LANDSCAPE AT THE POINTE DU HOC
After two days of fighting, the Stars and Stripes floated over the rocky pinnacle. Above, enemy prisoners being escorted, while for others it was dinner time.

A MILITARY SANCTUARY
The Pointe du Hoc memorial situated on top of the fire-control bunker is a reminder that many bodies from both sides still lie underneath the ruins.

the entrance to the château (below) recalls that it served as headquarters for the US 11th Major Port and the V US Engineer Corps which was responsible for handling all the stores and equipment landed on Omaha Beach throughout the campaign in Normandy. After the destruction of the Mulberry, landing craft beached on the sand and unloaded into waiting rows of trucks.

POINTE DU HOC ♥

(*Continue for six kilometers along the D514.*)
This place is still considered an official war grave as there are bodies, both German and American, which lie undiscovered under the ruins. Having believed that a powerful coast artillery battery, capable of firing both onto Utah and Omaha

beaches, was installed there, allied intelligence decided to neutralize it before H-Hour (06.30 in the morning). Although the site had been regularly bombed since April, it was believed that the guns were still serviceable. The only way to attack the position was to scale the steep cliffs and the mission was entrusted to two Ranger battalions. As the landing-craft containing the men of the 2nd Ranger Battalion moved inshore, the 16" guns of the USS *Texas* anchored out to sea, opened up. The leader of the mission, Colonel Rudder, realized that, in the dark, they were steering towards the wrong area. Unfortunately he was only able to lead seven landing craft in the right direction. When they landed at the base of the cliffs, he had only 225 men left in his command.

THE RANGERS' EXPLOIT. As Rudder approached the Pointe du Hoc, 40 minutes behind the scheduled time, the enemy opened fire on his landing craft, but his men managed to scramble ashore. The Rangers were equipped with grappling hooks fired from mortars, but many of these failed to reach the top as the wet cords were too heavy. They also had two ex-London-Fire-Brigade turntable ladders mounted on DUKWs ● *61*, ▲ *186*, but these

two useful vehicles were unable to get in close enough
to the base of the cliffs. As the Rangers started to climb,
the Germans dropped grenades over the cliff's edge and cut
the few rope ladders. After a vicious battle and with support
from a destroyer which moved in to fire as close as possible
to the cliff, a few intrepid men managed to hoist themselves
over the top where they fought their way from bomb crater
to bomb crater and bunker to bunker against the determined
garrison – only to find that the casemates were empty
of guns. In fact, after the bombardments in April the
Germans had removed the armament and parked the guns
in a field alongside the D514 where they were discovered
some hours later. The Rangers, in spite of the delay due
to the tremendous difficulties they had in expanding the
depth of the Omaha beachhead, fought on alone for two
endless days against an enemy determined to dislodge them
and suffering bombardment by their own artillery. When

ROMMEL'S PROPHECY
"If we cannot succeed
in our task to deny
the sea to the Allies
or to eject them
within the first
48 hours, their
invasion will be
successful .... In the
absence of strategic
reserves and with
the total bankruptcy
of our Navy and Air
Force, we will loose
the war." ● *32, 38.*

Left, a flight of
Typhoons ● *58,*
▲ *209* over the Pointe
du Hoc. Below,
in a photo taken on
12 June, the Rangers
demonstrate
the conditions under
which they had
to achieve their
success.

▲ D-Day, the attack!

"Deutscher-soldatenfriedhof"
Plaque at the entrance to
the cemetery of La Cambe.

finally the time had come to relieve them, Colonel Rudder only had 90 unwounded men left. The whole area has been carefully cleared and sown with grass all around the still impressive ruins of wrecked casemates and massive bomb craters. Near the edge of the cliffs one can also see, on top of the original fire-control post, a monument to the gallant men of the 2nd Ranger Battalion.

Grandcamp-Maisy to Isigny-sur-Mer via La Cambe

The Rangers Museum of Grandcamp-Maisy. (*Continue along the D514 to Grandcamp.*) In this small fishing port a MUSEUM DEVOTED TO THE RANGERS can be found, containing a number of exhibits which tell their story from their foundation to the assault on the Pointe du Hoc. Grandcamp was liberated on 8 June and numerous massive bunkers can still be seen around the harbour. (*From Grandcamp take the D199 and then the D113 to la Cambe. Turning right onto the N13, you will find the cemetery on the left.*)

The German military cemetery at La Cambes. Most German casualties were buried where they fell, in fact, one can still find numerous German graves in British military cemeteries, notably at Ranville ▲ *126* and Bayeux ▲ *158*. The bulk of the corpses were subsequently exhumed and reburied in a number of large cemeteries. One of these cemeteries, the one at La Cambe, is the final resting place of 21,400 men. The laying-out of the cemetery started in 1958 and the names of the soldiers are incised into small stone plaques embedded in the well-kept lawns. In the centre is a 6-metre-high burial mound surmounted by a granite cross flanked by two human silhouettes. The mound is the resting place of 296 members of the Wehrmacht, and the names of those who could be identified are on plaques around the base.

Isigny-sur-Mer. The town was liberated on 10 June by the men of the 29th Division, after having suffered terrible devastation. Caught up in the fighting, the civilian

> "A morning was enough to get an excellent idea of the entire front since the roads, at least in the American sector, were always free. There was one-way traffic from the beaches to the supply depots a few kilometres inland in the fields. Our first fighter base at the side of the road to Isigny remained subject to enemy artillery fire for quite some time. From a distance one could see the heavily laden P47s taking off, flying a few kilometres and launching the bombs carried under their wings, before banking sharply and coming back in to rearm."
> Ralph Ingersoll, American officer/journalist

La Cambe Cemetery

**ON THE ROAD
TO SAINT-LÔ**
This M10 tank
destroyer ● *63,* ▲ *133,
135, 240* is firing at an
enemy strongpoint.
The battle for the
hedgerows involved
thousands of similar
actions.

Also worth seeing...
**THE CHÂTEAU
DE LA COLOMBIÈRE**

population was not always able to appreciate the actions
of the Allies, as Bradley wrote in *A Soldier's Story.* "For
more than four years the people of Isigny waited to be
liberated. And now, from the ruins which cover their dead,
they look at us accusingly." On the war memorial opposite
the town hall is a plaque listing the names of 34 civilians
killed during the liberation. After Isigny, continue along the
N13 towards Carentan. Just before the hamlet of La
Blanche you cross the River Vire which marks the start
of the low-lying area that extends from Isigny
to Carentan, which was flooded by the
Germans. It was vital for the Americans
to gain control of the lowlands in order
to join together their two isolated
beach-heads.

3-19 JULY: THE BATTLE FOR SAINT-LÔ

With the capture of Carentan and the
line of the N13 to Isigny on 12 June, it
was possible to link the two American
bridgeheads and to form a cohesive
front. One of the key objectives for the
Allies in Normandy was the capture of the important town
of Saint-Lô which was the key point in the network of roads
in the *Bocage* country. On 13 June, V Corps had managed to
occupy CAUMONT ▲ *212* and was thus firmly linked to the
British right flank. Attempts to advance further towards
Saint-Lô, however, had been bloodily repulsed. It was not
until Cherbourg had been captured that Montgomery was
able to issue orders for the American breakout which was to
pivot on the axis of Caumont and establish Bradley's
divisions on the line Saint-Lô/Coutances. Starting on 3 July,
the US XIX Corps mounted an attack down the Carentan-
Saint- Lô road starting from the line of the Vire-Taute canal,
and four days later managed to reach Ariel and the northen
parts of Saint-Jean-de-Daye where the bridges over the Vire
were repaired. An attempt was then made to exploit the
bridgehead with the 3rd Armoured Division, which made

**A GI STOOPING
OVER A DEAD GERMAN
SOLDIER**
It was during
the month of July
that the terrible
confrontation
between the
Americans and
the Germans for the
possession of Saint-
Lô took place.
The enemy lost
3,300 men in nine
days. Some of the
American units were
reduced to a third
of their effective
strength.

▲ D-Day, the attack!
Bayeux to Carentan

Also worth seeing…
The Hamlet of La Blanche
Lower Normandy, the home
of camembert

**MONUMENT TO
DE GAULLE AT ISIGNY**
"Here on 14 June,
1944, General de
Gaulle spoke to the
French people
liberated by the
Allied forces.
Homage to the Allied
soldiers, 6 June, 1944
– 6 June, 1969."

Insignia of the US
VII Corps ▲ *189. 225.*

After Bayeux and
Isigny ▲ *162,*
de Gaulle's tour
in Normandy ends
on 14 June 1944
at Grandcamp, where
he's speaking to
the fishermen.

little progress in the *Bocage* country. By 12 July
the Germans managed to gather sufficient strength to
counter-attack the bridgehead, but the 30th Infantry
Division held the line. In nine days they had lost 3,300 men.
VII Corps was then moved into the area and the GIs slowly
fought their way forward through the hedgerows and
the ruined villages. On 15 July some units had reached
the heights overlooking the city, but many of the companies
were reduced to thirty men. On 19 July, the Americans
finally took possession of the cratered landscape
of Saint-Lô, for which they had paid a terrible price.

Saint-Clair-sur-l'Elle. *(Follow the D5 and the D11.)*
Heading south from Isigny along the D5 road, you will
be entering typical *Bocage* countryside where the American
infantry had been struggling forward since late June. Each
hedgerow was stoutly defended by the men of the 17th SS
Panzergrenadier Division. The main axis of the 3 July attack
was along the parallel road from Carentan, however.
Saint-Clair-sur-l'Elle lies one and a half kilometre from
the main road. This village was reached
on 4 July by the men of the 2nd Infantry
Division who fought their way onto
the high ground of Hill 192 to the
south, which was bitterly opposed
by German airborne troops.

Saint-Lô

*(Returning to the main road, drive south until you reach
the outskirts of Saint-Lô, which you enter by following a steep
ravine.)* ▲ *178, 230* On the left is the high ground of
Martinville which was reached on 11 July by elements
of the 29th Infantry Division, which lost 1,000 men in
two days. Once there they could look down on the ruins
of the once beautiful city, the prefecture of the Manche
Department. The old town centre is built on a spur of rock
and surrounded by ramparts. Since the war it has been
totally rebuilt, as hardly a building was left undamaged
when the last defenders left on 19 July. Follow
the signs to the centre ville and park

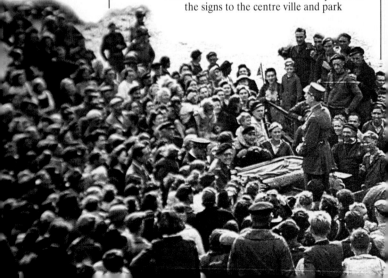

near the Place de l'Hôtel-de-Ville. In the square there is a memorial to forty-two members of the local Resistance who died in their cells when the prison was bombed. It is made from one of the doors of the prison. The other important memorial is in front of Sainte-Croix church and is a bronze bust of Major Thomas Howie.

"THE CAPITAL OF RUINS". The destruction started well before the battle as Saint-Lô was an important crossroads which was the target of a massive bombing raid on D-Day to hinder the flow of German reinforcements. General Marcks, commander of LXXXIV Corps, who was responsible for the defence of Lower Normandy, had his headquarters there. It took the Americans 43 days to capture the town instead of the week forecast. Leave Saint-Lô on the N174 which is the main road to Carentan and Cherbourg. You will be travelling in the opposite direction to the main axis of the US XIX Corps advance. It was up this road that the Germans of General Meindl's Airborne Corps together with some tanks from Panzer Lehr Division attempted their counter-attack on 12 July. In all the small villages along the route, hardly a stone was left standing. (*Follow the N174 as far as Saint-Jean-de-Daye.*)

SAINT-JEAN-DE-DAYE. Continue north to the town of Saint-Jean-de-Daye, which was entered on 7 July after 6,000 men had overwhelmed the Germans defending the canal to the north of the town. The bridges over the Vire River had been destroyed but the American

ISIGNY-SUR-MER
After the bombardment of 8 June, 60% of the town was destroyed.

Isigny today

The Place de l'Hôtel-de-Ville, at Saint-Lô.

Also worth seeing…
THE NATIONAL STUD-FARM AT SAINT-LÔ

PONT-HÉBERT*
The attractive small town of Pont-Hébert, now entirely rebuilt, was the southward extent of the American bridgehead over the Vire River and it was there that the the Germans attacked the GIs of the 30th Infantry Division, who reached the town as early as 8 July.

177

A German soldier surrenders near Saint-Lô.

Also worth seeing…
THE RAMPARTS OF SAINT-LÔ

THE HOWIE MONUMENT
Another important memorial in Saint-Lô, facing the Saint-Front church, is a bronze bust of Major Thomas Howie, commander of the 3rd Battalion of the 116th Infantry Regiment, killed

during the battle. His men placed his body, wrapped in the Stars and Stripes, at the door of the church. Major Howie has become the symbol of the liberation of the city.

engineers rapidly replaced them so that the tanks of the 3rd Armoured Division could cross. In Saint-Jean, turn left in the centre of the town onto the D45 and shortly afterwards take the right fork which is signposted to Graignes. You are now entering territory that was fought over in a completely different phase of the battle: the landings of the 82nd Airborne Division ▲ *185,* in the early hours of D-Day, and the struggle to capture the vital bridges at Carentan.

GRAIGNES*. As you enter the village of Graignes there is a very new church to the right and a small sign to the memorial. Take a right beside the church. A few hundred metres further on there is a small patch of grass with a plaque stating that it is the Rue du 59/507^e Parachute Infantry Regiment, dated 11 June. That regiment was part of the 82nd Airborne Division. Keep to your right past the plaque and at the crossroads turn left up a narrow lane which climbs quite steeply. At the top is the village cemetery and the impressive ruins of the church. The cemetery there has a view over the meadows of the Taute River, which on D-Day were extensively flooded. Graignes was strategically valuable and was therefore destroyed.

Inside the empty shell of the church is a large PLAQUE listing the civilians and the American soldiers who died in the fighting for the village, together with a sign

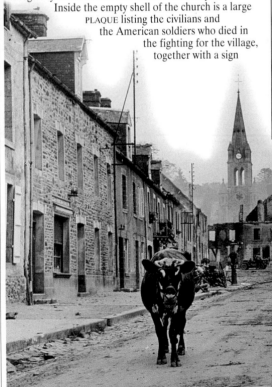

stating that it was inaugurated by David Bruce, the US Ambassador, in 1949.

SAINTENY*. *(From Graignes, follow the D57 to Tribehou where you will be in the centre of the marshes around Carentan which were flooded by the Germans. Then take the D29 and the D971 to Sainteny.)* There is a small memorial plaque on the wall of the town hall dedicated to the men of the 83rd Infantry Division and the 331st Infantry Regimental Combat Team who died fighting in the swamps around Santeny. The line of the road became known as the Isthmus as it was bordered on either side by swamps. In early July the area was defended by the 17th SS Panzer Grenadier Division, elements of the 2nd SS Panzer Das Reich ▲ *230* and the 6th Parachute Regiment, who were holding a line from TRIBEHOU to Raids. The US VII Corps commanded by General "Lightning Joe" Collins ● *31*, ▲ *194*, had been relocated south of Carentan after their victorious advance to Cherbourg, and launched an attack towards Sainteny on 1 July. The town was held by the 6th Parachute Regiment, and on 5 July, the 83rd Infantry advanced 200 metres, captured six prisoners and lost nearly 1,500 men in the process. It took the division until 14 July to finally clear the enemy force from Sainteny, by which time their losses had reached 4,700 men, nearly one third of their effective fighting force. At the crossroads just out of the town on the main road there is another memorial in homage to the 83rd and 4th US divisions,

Saint-Lô at the end of 1944.

MEMORIAL HOSPITAL OF SAINT-LÔ
After the war the American people made a contribution towards the building of a hospital in the Rue Villedieu, on the road to Avranches, in memory of those who lost their lives in the fighting. Above, frescoes by Fernand Léger.

Saint-Lô devastated, August 1944.

An American soldier in the *Bocage*.

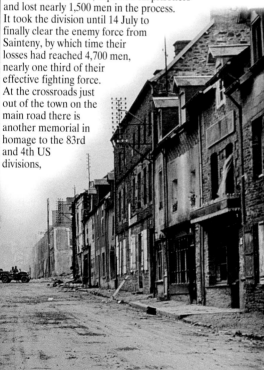

Americans
in Carentan.

Insignia of the V
and XIX US Corps.

Also worth seeing…
CARENTAN
Notre-Dame Church
(right) and the yacht
harbour (below).

flanked by the French and American flags. (*Follow the D971 to Carentan and then turn left onto the D534.*)

MÉAUTIS. The village is on high ground overlooking the Marais de Gorges, which was flooded at the time of the battles there. On a wall near the church is a small plaque which states that this was where Gen. Theodore Roosevelt, who landed on 6 June 1944 at Utah Beach, died. Aged 57, he was the deputy commander of the 4th Infantry Division and a son of the former President Theodore Roosevelt. He persuaded his divisional commander to let him go ashore, seized the initiative and sorted out the tangled traffic on the beach, marching up and down under shellfire supported by a heavy walking stick. He was killed at Mautis on 12 July during the battles for the Isthmus. Leave the village and follow the sign to Carentan. After two hundred metres

there is a memorial on the right to the 50th Fighter Group, who flew from the advanced landing ground in the meadows from 16 August to 15 September 1944.

CARENTAN

In 1944, the main road named in honour of 101st Airborne Division ▲ *185* followed the railway line. Between D-Day and the final liberation, bitter fighting took place in the vicinity and the town suffered heavy damage. The men of the 101st found themselves getting to grips with an elite German parachute unit which had been training in the area which they were unable to dislodge until 12 June. Opposite the station on the right is the town hall, a fine 18th-century building, in front of which is a standard Comité du Débarquement monument ● *82*. At the base of this is a plaque recording the liberation by the "Screaming Eagles" of the 101st Airborne.

OBJECTIVE, A HARBOUR
OBJECTIF UN PORT
FROM UTAH BEACH
TO THE CAPTURE OF CHERBOURG

ANTHONY KEMP

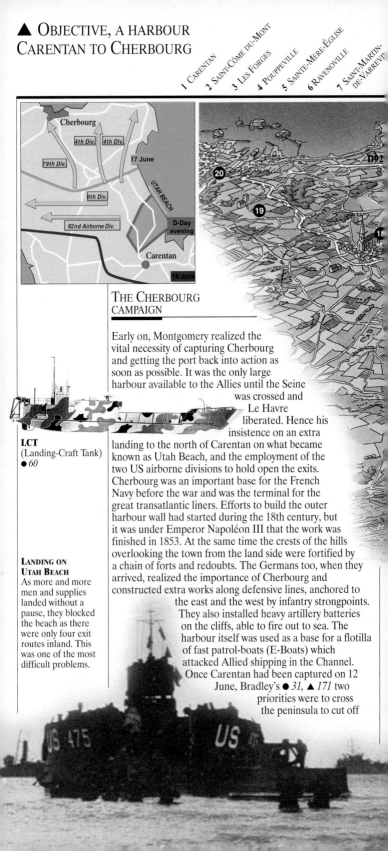

Map labels: Cherbourg · 4th Div. · 4th Div. · 79th Div. · 17 June · 9th Div. · UTAH BEACH · 82nd Airborne Div. · D-Day evening · Carentan · 18 June

D92 · 20 · 19

LCT
(Landing-Craft Tank)
● *60*

**LANDING ON
UTAH BEACH**
As more and more
men and supplies
landed without a
pause, they blocked
the beach as there
were only four exit
routes inland. This
was one of the most
difficult problems.

THE CHERBOURG
CAMPAIGN

Early on, Montgomery realized the
vital necessity of capturing Cherbourg
and getting the port back into action as
soon as possible. It was the only large
harbour available to the Allies until the Seine
was crossed and
Le Havre
liberated. Hence his
insistence on an extra
landing to the north of Carentan on what became
known as Utah Beach, and the employment of the
two US airborne divisions to hold open the exits.
Cherbourg was an important base for the French
Navy before the war and was the terminal for the
great transatlantic liners. Efforts to build the outer
harbour wall had started during the 18th century, but
it was under Emperor Napoléon III that the work was
finished in 1853. At the same time the crests of the hills
overlooking the town from the land side were fortified by
a chain of forts and redoubts. The Germans too, when they
arrived, realized the importance of Cherbourg and
constructed extra works along defensive lines, anchored to
the east and the west by infantry strongpoints.
They also installed heavy artillery batteries
on the cliffs, able to fire out to sea. The
harbour itself was used as a base for a flotilla
of fast patrol-boats (E-Boats) which
attacked Allied shipping in the Channel.
Once Carentan had been captured on 12
June, Bradley's ● *31*, ▲ *171* two
priorities were to cross
the peninsula to cut off

US 475 · US

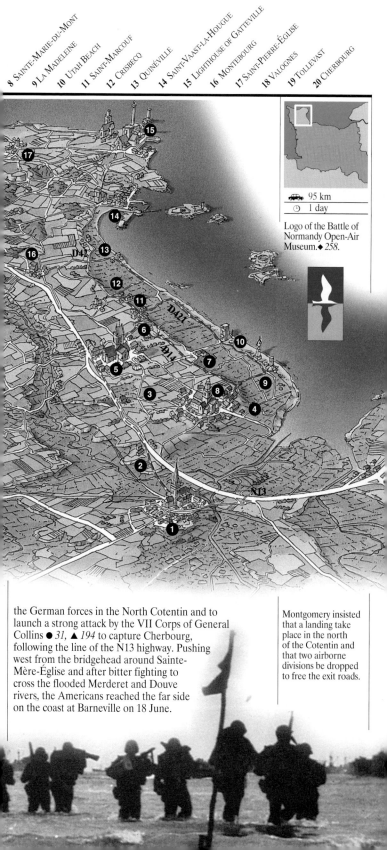

🚗 95 km
🕐 1 day

Logo of the Battle of Normandy Open-Air Museum. ◆ 258.

the German forces in the North Cotentin and to launch a strong attack by the VII Corps of General Collins ● 31, ▲ 194 to capture Cherbourg, following the line of the N13 highway. Pushing west from the bridgehead around Sainte-Mère-Église and after bitter fighting to cross the flooded Merderet and Douve rivers, the Americans reached the far side on the coast at Barneville on 18 June.

Montgomery insisted that a landing take place in the north of the Cotentin and that two airborne divisions be dropped to free the exit roads.

Bollard to mark
kilometre zero on the
Liberty Way at
Sainte-Mère-Église.

THE FIRST FRENCH TOWN LIBERATED

At midnight on 5/6
June a fire broke out
by accident in a house.
The Germans allowed
the inhabitants out to
put out the blaze, just
when parachutists
tumbled out of the
sky: some of them fell
into the fire. The
Germans opened fire
and the civilians took
shelter in the cellars as
a vicious battle raged
around the square. At
04.30, Colonel Krause
hoisted the Stars and
Stripes on the town
hall.

AIRBORNE FORCES MUSEUM

The Dakota C47
aircraft, The Argonia,
and the interior of the
Waco glider.

That had the effect of trapping the remnants of a number of German divisions who were without armoured support and gradually pushed them north into the defended perimeter around Cherbourg. As Collins fought his way northwards against strong opposition, he was able to call on fighter-bombers and support from the guns of the warships offshore. His leading units made contact with the outer perimeter around the port on 21 June and that night the corps commander sent a cheeky message to General von Schlieben, the garrison commander, demanding that he surrender. In fact, several more days of bitter struggle were necessary to overcome resistance in the hills overlooking the town, which had been pounded by bombs and the guns of the US Navy. It was not until 1 July that all resistance in the North Cotentin finally ceased, freeing the American forces to turn through 180 degrees and start their bitter fighting in the hedgerows towards Saint-Lô and Coutances. On 16 July the first Liberty Ships ● 60 entered the harbour but were still unable to come alongside and had to be unloaded by barges and DUKWs ● 61, ▲ 186. It took a further two months of hard work before

SAINTE-MÈRE-ÉGLISE
In the church, a baroque altar
and two stained-glass windows
illustrating the events of 6 June.

Cherbourg could handle the same tonnage per day as was
brought ashore at Utah Beach. On 12 August the first petrol
arrived through the PLUTO ● 67 pipeline and was pumped
inland to Bayeux *(Stay on the N13 beyond Carentan)* ▲ 180.

SAINTE-MÈRE-ÉGLISE ♥

The bridge over the Douve was the scene of persistent
fighting which blocked the American advance and forced
them to use the one over the canal running into the sea, to
attack the Germans from the rear. To the left of the latter
bridge one can still see the original one that crossed the river
at the time. A short distance away near the hamlet of LES
FORGES, the meadows were the landing site of the gliders
which brought in stocks of ammunition, heavy weapons and
jeeps on 7 June. In addition, 3,000 American graves were laid
out there as a provisional cemetery which lasted until 1948.
The area around Sainte-Mère-Église on either side of the
highway between Bayeux and Cherbourg was one of the two
principal objectives of the 82nd Airborne Division. The other
was the crossroads which commanded the flooded terrain
of the Merderet river, to hinder the enemy from attacking
towards Utah Beach.

JOHN STEEL'S STORY. In the square at Sainte-Mère-Église,
named in honour of 6 June, there is a memorial to the mayor
at the time, Alexandre Renaud, who was one of the first
chroniclers of the landings. In the middle of the square is the
church, a mixture of Norman and Gothic architecture, where
in summer you can see a parachute attached to the steeple.
This is in memory of John Steel whose exploit was
immortalised in the film *The Longest Day* ● 86. He found
himself suspended in his harness and used as a target
by the Germans. Seriously wounded, he feigned death
for two hours until his comrades were able to cut
him down.

AIRBORNE-FORCES MUSEUM. To the right
of the church at the corner of the square
▲ 184, there are the two buildings of the
Airborne-Forces Museum, partly built on
the site of the house that caught fire on
6 June. The first, which was opened on
the 20th anniversary in 1964 by
General Gavin, is circular and with a
roof reminiscent of a parachute canopy.
Inside, there is a Waco glider on display
and an important collection of objects
relating to the parachute drops. The
other building was specially constructed to
house a C47 Dakota which was one of those used
for the drops. In the gardens there is a Sherman tank,
a half-track and a 90-mm anti-aircraft gun.

**THE FIRST AMERICAN CEMETERY AND THE LIBERTY WAY
BOLLARD.** ● 80, ▲ 166. In front of the school on what is today
a sports field is the site of the first American cemetery in
which 3,000 men were buried. Exhumed in 1948, those who
were not repatriated to the Unites States now rest in the
cemetery at Saint-Laurent-sur-Mer. At the bottom of the
square turn right past the Auberge *John Steel* to reach the
town hall just where the road climbs a hill. There there is a

Insignia of the 101st
and 82nd Airborne
Divisions.

American parachutist
climbing into a C47
Dakota.

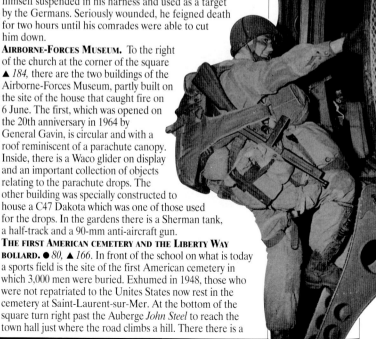

PLAQUE AT SAINTE-MARIE-DU-MONT
"The US parachutist Ambrose had the misfortune to fall onto a house on the corner of this square. Luckily he was not wounded and, unbuckling his harness, pulled himself along the gutter. German soldiers moving from the shelter of the trees pushed him against the wall, ready to shoot him ...."

DUKW ● *61* at La Madeleine memorial to the French 2nd A.D.
▲ *238* Utah Beach Liberty Museum at Quinéville.

memorial to the civilians who were killed during the operations in the area. There is also the bollard "0" of the Liberty Way. "These bollards, which mark the principal route taken by the Allied armies on their victorious march, stretch all the way to the Rhine." Admiral Lemonnier.(*Take the D15 to Ravenoville and then the D14 to Saint-Marie-du-Mont.*)

SAINTE-MARIE-DU-MONT ♥

In the village square and on the walls of the church are a dozen plaques (above left) recounting the events of the first hours of D-Day. Sainte-Marie-du-Mont was situated on one of the main exit roads from Utah, which continued over the area flooded by the Germans. It was absolutely vital for the 82nd Airborne Div. to gain control. The church changed hands several times during the night, and today a stained-glass window recalls some events in the liberation of the village. One of the plaques on a house on the corner of the square records that the building housed the Kommandantur where the villagers were detailed for forced labour on the defences ● *72, 74*. (*Drive along the D913 up to Utah Beach.*)

UTAH BEACH

A RELATIVELY EASY LANDING. Keeping a sense of proportion, one can say that the landings on Utah Beach were relatively easy. After the bombers had, wave after wave, saturated the coast defences which were then mercilessly bombarded by the warships anchored offshore, the first elements of the 4th Infantry Division touched down at low tide at 06.30, well below the beach obstacles placed by the enemy. Two squadrons of DD tanks ● *63*, launched 3 km from the shore, managed to land with the loss of only two, and took the defenders who were dazed from the bombardment, by surprise. Because of a navigational error, one of the assault waves arrived to the south of its objective, and landed between the strongpoints of Varraville and La Madeleine in a less well-defended sector. From there, the first groups of infantry with tank support moved off inland very quickly and at 13.00 joined up with the airborne forces.

B26 of the 9th US Air Force over Utah Beach.

LA MADELEINE. On arrival at the hamlet of LA MADELEINE and just before reaching the sea, a small lane on the left leads via a small road to a chapel, which was severely damaged on 6 June. A modern stained-glass window records the participation of the Free-French forces in the Normandy campaign. All the roads in the Utah Beach area are named after individual American soldiers who were killed there.

Facing you on the sea-front is the German strongpoint W5, where several monuments can be seen, near the beach and all around. The MUSEUM OF THE LANDINGS at Utah Beach is installed inside one of the Atlantic Wall bunkers looking out to sea and tells the story of the landing on Utah Beach with the aid of several models, various archives and objects. The Museum also features a landing craft, a Sherman tank ● 63, ▲ 133, 135, 240 and a 90mm anti-aircraft gun. It was at LA MADELEINE that the principal ceremonies commemorating the fortieth anniversary were held. A plaque beside the path through a gap in the dunes records that President Mitterrand of France welcomed the various heads of State who attended. Two hundred meters to the right of the museum is the monument dedicated to the men of the US Navy who took part in the operation. In front of the museum is a large pink granite obelisk in honour of the men of the 4th US Infantry Division, the D-Day assault force. Various other memorials are on the left, after the LIBERTY WAY BOLLARD "00". There is a pink granite MEMORIAL erected by the United States Government to honour all its sons who died on the beach, and one to the 90th US Infantry, the Texas Oklahoma Division, known as the "Tough Ombres". Beyond that a flight of steps leads to the top of a German bunker on which a 50-mm anti-tank gun is still in place. All around the position are small plaques indicating the position of the various ships which bombarded the coast defences, and the distance to various towns in England. There is also a MONUMENT to the 1st Engineer Special Brigade. Underneath the steps the interior of the bunker has been opened as

KILOMETRE STONE 00
The road to Sainte-Marie-du-Mont is lined by Liberty Way bollards which run from Utah Beach to the German frontier, following the victorious passage of General Patton's ▲ 238 Third US Army ▲ 220.

REPATRIATION OF THE WOUNDED
Jeeps brought the American wounded down to landing-craft, which evacuated them to hospitals in England.

THE DANISH MEMORIAL
At La Madeleine the 800 Danish sailors who took part in Operation Overlord on board Allied ships are remembered.

▲ OBJECTIVE, A HARBOUR CARENTAN TO CHERBOURG

"BEGEL ROAD"
Many street *Plaques* point out places
were such allied soldiers was killed.

B26 MARAUDER ● 56
Used to bomb the battery at Crisbecq on

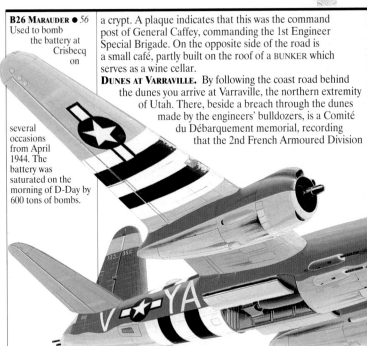

several occasions from April 1944. The battery was saturated on the morning of D-Day by 600 tons of bombs.

a crypt. A plaque indicates that this was the command post of General Caffey, commanding the 1st Engineer Special Brigade. On the opposite side of the road is a small café, partly built on the roof of a BUNKER which serves as a wine cellar.

DUNES AT VARRAVILLE. By following the coast road behind the dunes you arrive at Varraville, the northern extremity of Utah. There, beside a breach through the dunes made by the engineers' bulldozers, is a Comité du Débarquement memorial, recording that the 2nd French Armoured Division

UTAH BEACH
On D-Day 23,750 men, 1,700 vehicles and 1,695 tons of stores were landed, which severely clogged the beach.

landed there at the end of July. Commanded by General Leclerc, the division was in time to take part in the closing of the Falaise-Chambois ▲ *253* Pocket as part of Patton's Third US Army. Beside the monument are two vehicles of the period, an M8 Greyhound six-wheeled armoured car and a half-track.

REMAINS OF A STRONGPOINT. Walk down onto the beach and turn left to visit the remains of two large flanking casemates and several Tobruk ● 73 stands, some of which were fitted with Renault tank turrets captured by the Germans in 1940. Shortly before the landings began at 06.30, 276 bombers ● 56 dropped their 250-lb. bombs on these fortifications. Also on the beach can be found a concrete pontoon. This structure is actually a remnant of the roadway elements from a Mulberry harbour ● 76, ▲ *141*. (*Follow the coast road as far as Grand-Hameau-des-Dunes and take the D269 in the direction of Saint-Marcouf.*)

CASEMATE AT CRISBECQ ▲ 148
The battery was equipped with 210-mm Skoda cannons protected by thick concrete and well sited to defend Utah Beach.

> "THE ASSAULT OF THE 4TH DIVISION (VII CORPS) ON *UTAH*, JUST TO THE WEST OF THE ESTUARY OF THE VIRE, WAS THE ONE AMONG ALL OUR LANDINGS THAT MET WITH THE LEAST RESISTANCE."
>
> GENERAL EISENHOWER

Insignia of VII US Corps. ▲ 217, 225.

SAINT-MARCOUF TO QUINÉVILLE

THE CRISBECQ BATTERY, AT SAINT-MARCOUF. On the plan of the battery you can see the positions of the four casemates linked to a fire-control position. In spite of the Allied bombardments, the battery succeeded in opening fire, and efforts by the infantry to attack it, supported by naval gunfire, were unsuccessful. Commanded by a young lieutenant, Walther Ohmsen, the battery sank an American destroyer on 7 June. Even though he had only one gun left and was badly wounded, Ohmsen held out until 11 June when he gave orders to abandon the site. He was decorated by Hitler with the Knight's Cross.
● *32, 38. (Continue along the D14.)*

AZEVILLE BATTERY. This battery, situated further inland, could not see directly onto Utah Beach which was why its fire control position was linked to that of Crisbecq. Armed with four 105-mm Schneider guns, it fired on Utah besieged by the Americans on D-Day, and was conquered by the 12th Infantry Regiment, part of the 4th Infantry Division, on 9 June.

QUINÉVILLE. *(After Saint-Marcouf take the D69 and then the D421 in a north-westerly direction.)* ▲ 186. One follows the vestiges of the Atlantic Wall as far as the village of Quinéville. At the crossroads, on the right towards the sea, is the MUSÉE DE LA LIBERTÉ which immerses the visitor in the sombre atmosphere of the 1940s and shows the daily life of French people from mobilization to liberation. A large selection of contemporary photographs and newspaper pictures leads the visitor into a reconstruction of a street with its shops and dwelling houses during the Occupation and then to a blockhouse which is part of the museum.

QUINÉVILLE TO VALOGNES

MONTEBOURG. From Quinéville, take the D42 towards Montebourg, which was the approximate start line for the northward advance by General Collins ● *31,* ▲ 194 after him who had mopped up the remaining pockets of resistance inland from Utah Beach. The remnants of the German 709th Division were pursued up the coast by parts of the 4th US Division, whose main thrust was centred on the N13. As you drive into Montebourg, which has been by-passed

Opposite, the fortified island of Tatihou, 1 km off Saint-Vaast-la-Hougue, defended the port.

Also worth seeing…
THE TOUR VAUBAN, ON THE ISLAND OF TATIHOU, AND THE PORT OF SAINT-VAAST-LA-HOUGUE

Also worth seeing…
THE SAINT-MARCOUF ISLANDS
In clear weather you can see the uninhabited Saint-Marcouf Islands, a few kilometres off Ravenoville-Plage. In the early hours of D-Day they were occupied by a small unit, several members of which were killed by stepping on mines ● *72* left by the Germans.

▲ THE CAPTURE
OF THE PORT OF CHERBOURG

The VII US Corps, commanded by General Lawton Collins, landed on Utah Beach on 6 June with the task of capturing the port of Cherbourg, the facilities of which were vital for guaranteeing the necessary reinforcements and supplies for the First US Army in Normandy. When the isolation of the Cotentin was ensured by the arrival of US troops at Barneville, the siege of Cherbourg commenced, with US-Navy ships patrolling in front of the Channel Islands to hinder attempts at resupply by sea. Because of the vital importance of the harbour, Cherbourg was protected by a strong ring of well-buried concrete defences, as well as by German naval batteries.

CHERBOURG

26 JUNE
A main pocket of resistance persisted in the upper parts of the town, delaying the capture of the harbour installations, which were blown up before the Germans surrendered on 28 June.

Tanks and American infantry advanced by leaps, preceded by fighter-bomber attacks and with powerful artillery support.

CHERBOURG, A FREE CITY
In August, Cherbourg became the "Liberty Port", the terminal of the pipe lines which crossed the Channel and followed the armies to supply the precious fuel they needed.

CHERBOURG, 28 JUNE 1944
German prisoners being escorted.
Photo by Robert Capa ● 2.

**CHERBOURG,
30 JUNE 1944**
An American MP
transporting
a jeep-load of
prisoners. Photo
by Robert Capa.

AFTER 28 JUNE
Some of the forts
on the outer
breakwater and
batteries along
the coast continued
to resist, until they
were starved out.

**27 JUNE
1944**
A French
civilian and two
war correspondents,
one British and
the other American,
announce the liberation
of Cherbourg on the radio.
Even though they had taken
3,000 prisoners from the German
navy and army, the Americans
inherited a desert caused by enemy
demolitions. It took an entire month
before the port became progressively
reusable.

FORT DU ROULE

26 June, near Cherbourg
Three US divisions advanced towards Cherbourg. In the evening they entered the city and started to round up the garrison.

Valognes destroyed
The church in 1944.

Also worth seeing…
The Hôtels of Beaumont and Grandval-Caligny, at Valognes

by the main road recently, you will notice that the town has the appearance of being quite new. On 18 June a bitter battle raged for possession of the ruins which had been pounded by bombers, the whole weight of the corps artillery and ships' artillery. In the night, however, the defenders set the ruins on fire and withdrew, leaving the town to the 8th and 12th Infantry Regiments who entered it the following morning. The enemy withdrawal was in compliance with von Schleibens orders to implement Plan Heinrich which called for a fighting withdrawal into the defended perimeter. (*After Montebourg the N13 leads to Valognes.*)

Valognes. "When Hitler realised that Montebourg had been passed, he traced a line on a map which he called the 'Hitler Line', between Vauville and Saint-Vaast, ordering that it be defended to the last drop of blood …. But ignoring La Hague and the Saire Valley, the Americans converged on the port." *Admiral Lemonnier.* While the 4th Divison followed this axis, the 90th Division moved parallel on their left and further left the 9th Division was advancing up the west coast. Valognes has also been by-passed by the modern road, but is well worth a visit as it was once known as the Versailles of Normandy, on account of several fine 18th-century buildings, notably the Hôtel de Beaumont. General von Schlieben had his command post in the town in the period immediately after D-Day, from which he conducted the defence of the area. Valognes was also extensively damaged during the battle, but was occupied on the evening of 19 June after the opposition had departed. Continue north on the N13, a fine dual carriageway which no longer bears any resemblance to the road up which the 4th Infantry struggled in 1944. As you travel, remember that the advance was also being carried out on the network of smaller roads to your left and right as the Germans gradually gave ground. They were not crack units but made excellent use of cover, backed up by their mortars and anti-tank guns.

La Glacerie and Tollevast.
As you enter the outskirts of Cherbourg you are crossing the outer line of the defence which was based around a number of strong bunkers. In La Glacerie just before the second roundabout you can see one of them on the road to your left. This was part of the defensive chain known as Les Chèvres which extended to the left to the village of Tollevast.

The 313rd Infantry Regiment moving up from Saint-Joseph made contact with the Les Chèvres position on 20 June but their advance patrols were repulsed by an artillery barrage. Two days later they by-passed the position to the right of the N13 and entered La Glacerie, which today has altered out of all recognition. The fighting around the fortified area in the village of Tollevast continued for two more days, in spite of a massive bombing raid. Cherbourg was thus surrounded but General Bradley could not afford to tie up a whole army corps in a fruitless siege.

CHERBOURG

Only a deep-water port could enable the unloading of locomotives and other heavy items needed to supply the front, which was rapidly moving forward. In addition, after the wreckage of the Mulberries ● *76,* ▲ *131* in the great storm, Cherbourg was needed to keep up the momentum of supplies, as Bradley was down to only three days' ammunition for his entire army. For General von Schlieben, the situation was clearly hopeless, in spite of orders from Hitler to fight to the last man and the last round of ammunition. Many of his forces, however, were bottled up in the Hague peninsula to the west and of no use to the defence of the port. "Whatever the cost, Rommel signalled, Cherbourg must be held and the cutting-off of the peninsular be avoided." Continue down the road as it winds its way down the hills into Cherbourg itself. By 24 June resistance in the hills had collapsed and the Americans were firmly established on the hilltops.

THE CAPTURE OF FORT DU ROULE.
This is a 19th-century construction which was strongly held by a determined German garrison. About half way up on the left there is a small trackway and if you park there for a moment you can see the blocked up entrances to two tunnels cut into the cliff face. These were built by the Germans as entrances to four firing positions in the cliffs overlooking

A German road sign pointing the way to the great port of the Cotentin.

the town and harbour. There they installed four of their most modern 10.5cm, submarine guns, which had a range of 12,000 metres, complete with a fire control position and a magazine hollowed out from the rock. At the top is the fort itself housing the Liberation Museum, which is well worth visiting. From the terrace on which the American flag was hoisted there is a magnificent view of the town and harbour. Fighting erupted around the fort on 25 June but it was not until the following day that the lower storeys housing the battery

THE GERMAN DEFENCE OF CHERBOURG
General von Schlieben's garrison consisted of remnants of several infantry divisions, the 77th, 91st, 243rd and 709th, plus naval forces, an Organization Todt ● *38, 72, 74* construction battalion and coast artillery units.

June 1944. Americans with prisoners captured in the Cherbourg area.

JULY 1944
Royal Navy frogmen cleared the wrecks that blocked the port while American engineers repaired the quays and cranes.

Also worth seeing…
CHÂTEAU DE TOURLAVILLE

DAMAGED HARBOUR
The Germans had enough time to put into operation a demolition programme. They laid mines everywhere, and sank ships in the various docks. After the liberation of the city it took two months to get the port operating again.

CHERBOURG LIBERATED
Right, the mayor of Cherbourg, Paul Reynaud, and General Manston Eddy, during a ceremony on 27 June in which the city was officially handed over to the French authorities by the Americans.

were captured by enterprising soldiers scaling down the cliffs and throwing explosive charges into the embrasures.

On 25 June, Collins sent a final ultimatum to surrender, and suppression of resistance from Fort du Roule made von Schlieben realise that further fighting was useless.

THE GERMAN SURRENDER. The garrison surendered on 26 June and 10,000 were taken prisoner. The naval commander in the arsenal, however, decided to continue fighting and had to be dislodged the following day. It is impossible to visit the naval port as it is a top-security zone, but it can be seen from the terrace of the fort. Some of the forts on the outer harbour wall continued to hold out for several more days before being shelled and bombed into submission. To the east, the garrison of the strongpoint Osteck continued fighting until the 28th and the Battle Group Kiel in the Hague peninsula to the west until the 30th. In fact it was not until 1 July that all resistance in the North Cotentin ceased. The object of the exercise, the harbour, no longer existed. General Bradley reported: "At Cherbourg the Germans have destroyed all the harbour installations in their zeal to render it unusable. The docks, the cranes, the warehouses, the bridges, the generators and the transformers have been dynamited and burned." Along the cliffs to the east and west of the town, however, there are still extensive traces of the Atlantic Wall coast batteries and strongpoints littered in the fields, which can be visited.

MUSÉE DE LA LIBÉRATION (Fort du Roule).
A remarkable collection of pictures and propaganda posters is displayed in the basement level, start of the visit. The upper levels are devoted to Allied supply problems in Normandy and Cherbourg, the hidden face of the Liberation. Without the prowess of the supply services the landings would have been in vain. British and American engineers succeeded in two months in transforming a port judged beyond repair into a virtual umbilical cord for supplying the front line. From the terrace of the fort there is a magnificent view over the roadstead.

THE CONFRONTATION
L'AFFRONTEMENT
TWO MONTHS OF FIGHTING
IN THE BOCAGE

GILLES HENRY
ANTHONY KEMP

🚗 207 km
🕐 2 days

Logo of the Battle of Normandy. Open-Air Museum.

THE BATTLE OF CAEN

Known as the "Venice of Normandy", the "city of a thousand steeples", and "the Athens of the North", Caen was almost entirely destroyed in 1944. After the war the rebuilding transformed Caen from a mediaeval city into a modern town.

CAEN BOMBARDED. On 6 June 1944, two successive waves of bombers and a deafening artillery bombardment, wrecked the Saint-Jean area and the surroundings of the castle. The hospice was destroyed, residential areas were in ruins, the whole town was covered in rubble and fumes.

A SEA OF FLAMES. On 7 June at 02.40, there was a further raid. SS Standartenführer Kurt Meyer declared that "Caen is a sea of flames where civilians are picking their way through the ruins and streets blocked by rubble. The air is unbreathable. Fine churches have been subjected to irreparable damage and the Allied bombers have

British armoured car in the middle of a field of rubble.

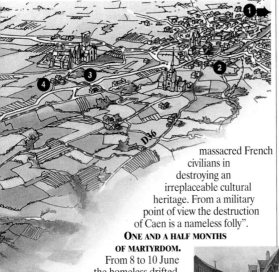

massacred French civilians in destroying an irreplaceable cultural heritage. From a military point of view the destruction of Caen is a nameless folly".

ONE AND A HALF MONTHS OF MARTYRDOM.
From 8 to 10 June the homeless drifted into the refugee centres marked by huge red crosses. On the 11th, fighting started again in the suburbs and the church of Saint-Pierre ▲ *201* lost its tower. The horror continued into July. As a prelude to Operation Charnwood, which cleared the enemy out of the northern half of the city, there was a particularly murderous raid. Caen, which would have been bombed even if the Allies had captured it on D-Day, was already completely destroyed before the raids on 19 July which finally released the German stranglehold around the city: 2,500 aircraft dropped 8,000 bombs. Caen was finally free, but at what a price.

CAEN WIPED OFF THE MAP. Emergency teams made up of a hundred students organised the rescue work. Each member saved on average four persons from the ruins and dragged six bodies from the rubble. In the autumn, 3,000 inhabitants, lacking public buildings and shelter, were without water, gas, electricity, telephones and sewers. What Madame de Sévigné had called "the most beautiful city" was no more.

THE RECONSTRUCTION. The city, "mutilated but as proud as ever" according to General de Gaulle, undertook the reconstruction (8,900 habitations) with the aid of the Allies and thanks to an extraordinary sense of solidarity, although it was to take fifteen years to fashion the Caen of today.

911 Rollo, a Viking leader, was baptised, and exchanged land for peace. In 20 years the future region was established.
1066 William conquered England.
1417 The British occupied the city and founded the university.
1450 Caen became French again.
1480 On 6 June *Horace's Letters* was the first book published in Caen, thus establishing a printing tradition.

Le Lavoir du moulin Saint-Pierre, by Tesnières.

1520 Renaissance architecture with the Lady Chapel of Saint-Pierre and the Hôtel Mondrainville. Caen became "one of the most beautiful, spacious and delectable" cities.
1652 Foundation of the Literary Academy.
1790 Creation of the Calvados Department.
1850 The opening of the canal joining Caen to the sea.

Caen in ruins; Caen reconstructed.

▲ THE CONFRONTATION CAEN TO VIRE

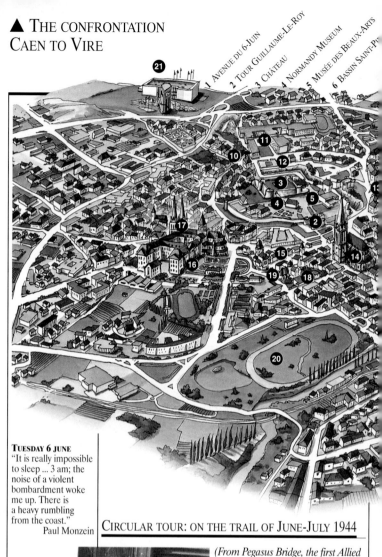

1 AVENUE DU 6-JUIN
2 TOUR GUILLAUME-LE-ROY
3 CHÂTEAU
4 NORMANDY MUSEUM
5 MUSÉE DES BEAUX-ARTS
6 BASSIN SAINT-P...

TUESDAY 6 JUNE
"It is really impossible to sleep ... 3 am; the noise of a violent bombardment woke me up. There is a heavy rumbling from the coast."
Paul Monzein

CIRCULAR TOUR: ON THE TRAIL OF JUNE-JULY 1944

An inhabitant offers a drink to a British soldier lying in ambush during the liberation of the city.

(From Pegasus Bridge, the first Allied bridgehead on 6 June, follow the D515 to Caen via Lébisey.) The British occupied positions to the north of LÉBISEY and were at the gates of the city on the evening of 6 June.

THE AVENUE OF 6 JUNE. After 1944, thousands of cubic metres of rubble were removed in small trucks before the building of a triumphal route between the station and the Castle. What the liberators called "Andy's Alley" became the Avenue du 6-Juin, a symbol born out of the ruins which cut Churchill Bridge. The four-storey stone buildings with slate roofs set in two 45 degree slopes are proof of the harmony sought by the men behind the reconstruction, Mayor Guillou and the architect Brillaud

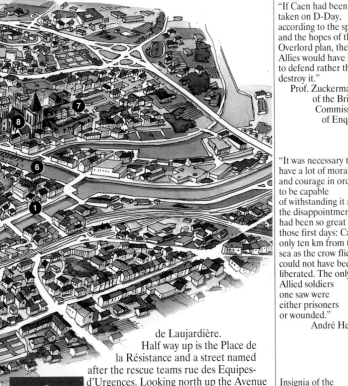

> "If Caen had been taken on D-Day, according to the spirit and the hopes of the Overlord plan, the Allies would have had to defend rather than destroy it."
> Prof. Zuckermann, of the British Commission of Enquiry

> "It was necessary to have a lot of morale and courage in order to be capable of withstanding it all, the disappointment had been so great those first days: Caen, only ten km from the sea as the crow flies could not have been liberated. The only Allied soldiers one saw were either prisoners or wounded."
> André Heintz

Insignia of the VIII British Corps.

The Castle during and after the war.

de Laujardière.

Half way up is the Place de la Résistance and a street named after the rescue teams rue des Equipes-d'Urgences. Looking north up the Avenue one can see KING WILLIAM'S TOWER, THE SYNAGOGUE and WILLIAM THE CONQUEROR'S CASTLE, now freed of surrounding houses after the bombing.

THE CASTLE ♥. Until the end of June 1944 this was used as German barracks, and after 6 June it also served as a transit and sorting centre for prisoners of war captured on the Caen front. Passing through the barbican and crossing the ditch, you can see Saint George's Church with vault bosses and traces of wall paintings, the governor's lodging and the collections of the Normandy Museum. There is also the Hall of the Exchequer which was the seat of the Ducal court of justice. The Fine Arts Museum displays works by Tintoretto, Veronese, Guercino, Rubens and Van der Weyden. There are few traces of the keep, demolished in 1793, where Romme established the Republican calendar. Nearby, the Bassin Saint-Pierre, used by numerous yachts, gives a maritime flavour to the city.

THE ABBAYE AUX DAMES ♥. The Avenue de la Libération leads to the Place Saint-Gilles where you will find the Trinity and the Abbey which is now the seat

199

▲ THE CONFRONTATION
CAEN TO VIRE

The Saint-Jean district and the abbaye aux Dames devastated.

Insignia of the 49th West Riding Division.

THE NEW SAINT-JULIEN CHURCH
Via the Rue des Tilleuls one arrives at the Calvary. Steps lead up to the oval church of Saint-Julien. Facing it is the Botanical Garden, a museum of flowers founded in the 17th century for growing medicinal herbs.

of the Lower Normandy Regional Council. During the war it housed a hospital, the Hospice de la Charité run by nuns. Classified as a protected zone and thus escaping bombardment, it sheltered both civilians and German military personnel. The Abbey church is in Norman style with a majestic nave featuring Byzantine decoration. The crypt, with sixteen pillars which supports low vaults, is the resting place of Queen Matilda, wife of William the Conqueror. The remains of Saint-Gilles church have been preserved, but the bomb damage led to the building of a replacement on the other side of the city, in the Saint-Paul District.

RUE DE LA DÉLIVRANDE. On the right is the ancient CEMETERY OF SAINT-PIERRE. The stones of the entrance wall come from the old prison and one can see prisoners' graffiti dating from the 17th century. On the left is the Rue du Colonel-Usher, director of civil affairs at the time of the liberation. At the corner of the Avenue de Bruxelles is a monument in the form of linked hands, symbolising the rebirth of the city. Further on there is the hospital centre, the new district of Folie-Couvrechef and the Peace Memorial.

7 JULY: THE DESTRUCTION OF SAINT-JULIEN.
On that day, in a raid lasting three quarters of an hour, 450 aircraft dropped 2,276 tons of bombs, engulfing Caen in a sea of flames. The Church of Saint-Julien was destroyed, but it was rebuilt after the war in concrete and glass. The university, the library, the Institute of Chemistry, the rector's palace, the west wing of the town hall and the national emergency stocks were likewise destroyed. A witness noted: "The Allies slept well, confident in the morrow. After such treatment it was impossible to meet a brave German." In fact, Operation Charnwood, for which the raid was a preliminary, only partly achieved the clearing of the northern part of the city on 8 July. Therefore, no progress was made possible south of the Orne. The British regarded it as only a half-victory.

COLONEL USHER
On 9 July, this veteran from the Gordon Highlanders started work as director of civil affairs. Sensitive to the Scottish concern for the destroyed city he founded the Edinburgh – Caen Mutual Aid Committee.

9 JUNE: THE STEEPLE OF SAINT-PIERRE COLLAPSES
The impact of a warship's shell caused the steeple to collapse onto the roof of the 15th-century nave.

The church of Saint-Pierre in June-July 1945.

A MODERN UNIVERSITY. The route takes us around the University which was rebuilt in 1957 according to the plans of architect Bernard. At the time it was the most modern in Europe and was inaugurated by Queen Élisabeth of the Belgians. In the square, the *Phoenix*, by Leygues, symbolizes the rebirth of the ancient institution. Slightly to the south is the Protestant cemetery where Beau Brummel is buried. *(Go down the Gallion, passing in front of the School of Fine Arts as far as the ramparts of the castle, and continue on foot.)*

THE VAUGUEUX DISTRICT.
(Walk up the Rue Montoir-Poissonnerie where one used to land the fish, to reach the Vaugueux district, near the Sepulchre.) On 9 and 10 June the first bombs fell on the district, but the worst was to come. On the evening of 7 July, as part of the preliminary raid for Operation Charnwood, a bomb demolished the SEPULCHRE shelter, killing fifty people. In spite of the damage, this old district

of the city has retained its traditional architecture, being rebuilt in Caen stone with dormer windows and sloping roofs of the 14th and 15th centuries. The cellars have 13th century vaulting.

THE SAINT-PIERRE DISTRICT.
This district was particularly affected by the second raid on the night of 6/7 June. The mediaeval houses around an arm of the River Odon collapsed under the bombs. The CHURCH OF SAINT-PIERRE, which was destroyed, has been restored to its original state in a move to preserve the heritage. On 9 June a warship's shell hit the superb steeple which collapsed onto the 15th-century nave. It was rebuilt thanks to the sale of shipwrecks recovered after the landings. The reflection of the renaissance Lady Chapel, attributed to the architect Sohier, used to be seen in a side stream of the Odon which today has been buried.

HISTORIC WALK

The RUE SAINT-PIERRE is the start of the pedestrian section of the route, which leads us to some ancient buildings, which except for the half-timbered buildings today housing the POSTAL MUSEUM, escaped the bombardments. The RUE FROIDE,

which used to be the printers' street, features numerous carriage entrances leading into courtyards with wooden balconies and secret gardens. Various dates are inscribed on the stones: 1646, 1705, 1750. Saint-Sauveur's Church has lost its rood screen but has

Also worth seeing...
Above right
L'HÔTEL DE THAN
This features pointed pediment windows decorated with pinnacles, set into the roof.

Above left
L'HÔTEL D'ESCOVILLE
Built in 1535, it is decorated with superb statues: Judith holding the head of Holofernes, and David that of Goliath. Inside is the tourist office.

Also worth seeing...
Detail of the Chapel of Saint-Pierre.

Also worth seeing...
LA MAISON DES QUATRANS (above, left in the text). This very ancient half-timbered building faces the Castle. Its two storeys each with six windows and the two dormers are an example of the richness of Caen's architectural heritage before the war.

François de Malherbe (1555-1628).

CAEN BEFORE 1944
Rue Froide with Saint-Sauveur in the background.

The Abbaye aux Hommes and the place Guillouard.

two parallel naves (14th and 15th centuries) and a Norman-style bell tower.

MAISON DE MALHERBE. The house of the Malherbe family is beside another one dated 1593. The poet lived there before becoming an alderman of Caen. The original decorated dormer windows have been faithfully restored. In the Arcisse-de-Caumont and Écuyère streets, the old courtyards, the alleyways and the turrets recall the flavour of pre-war Caen where the stone, slate and water harmonized to form the urban landscape. Continue towards the Palais de Justice and the Place Saint-Sauveur, once the site of the pillory and bounded by fine town houses. From there, rejoin the Rue Caponière and the ancient hospice of Bon-Sauveur, where 2,000 inhabitants found shelter in June 1944. 1,700 wounded were cared for there, after which it became the main hospital for the city owing to the destruction of the Misericord Clinic.

L'HÔTEL DE VILLE (Town Hall). This occupies the monastic buildings of THE ABBAYE AUX HOMMES (right) and its terrace has magnificent gardens. In 1944 the buildings housed the Malherbe High School. A huge red cross was painted on the roof, as on the Bon-Sauveur Hospice and the Girls' High School, in the hope of avoiding

The Boulevard Saint-Pierre.

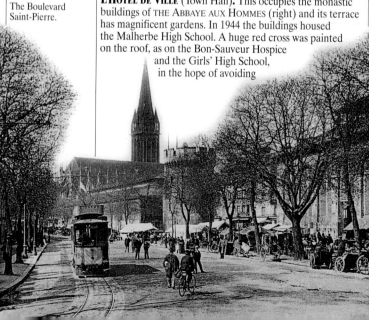

being bombed. Initially intended to shelter 600 refugees, by mid-June it had received 7,000.

ÎLOT SAINT-ÉTIENNE. 1,500 people sought refuge on the Îlot Saint-Étienne (below), stretched out on straw and hoping that the prophecy of the poet Wace would not be fulfilled: "When Saint-Étienne falls the Kingdom of England will perish." An agreement negotiated by the Résistance allowed the refugees to be spared. Even so, shelling caused 50 deaths and more than 100 to be wounded. The first visit that General Montgomery, chief of Allied ground forces, paid to the Norman capital on 13 July, was to the refugees of

The Saint-Sauveur district in June 1944.

Saint-Étienne. Nearby is the municipal library, a rich collection of Norman ephemera. The Avenue Albert-Sorel crosses the Rue Fred Scamaroni (a Resistance hero) and leads to the Lycée Malherbe, decorated with a statue by the sculptor Belmondo.

CHANGE OF NAMES
The Place du Lycée where the first French flag was hoisted, has become the Place Monseigneur-des-Hameaux.

Old houses in the Rue Saint-Pierre.

PLACE DE LA RÉPUBLIQUE. At the centre of the square, flanked by impressive town houses, is the Préfecture of the region in the old Hôtel Gosselin de Manneville built in 1760, and the regional council office. The latter is in the form of a crescent of smooth stonework, and is all that remains of the ancient town hall. Bombed at 03.00 on 7 June the building was cut in two and the shelters in the Place de la République were ploughed up. Those who had confidently taken shelter there (50 civilians and 15 policemen) were buried under the debris. The square in front of THE CHURCH OF NOTRE-DAME-DE-LA-GLORIETTE is closed off by chains taken from the ancient university, which was destroyed in July 1944.

LA PRAIRIE. Situated in the lower part of the city, the park could not be used as suitable defensive ground by the Germans as it was too exposed to Allied aircraft and bombardments. Only a few machine-gun positions joined by trenches were installed. On 9 July, the British, masters of the northern part of the city, bulldozed a road through the park leading to a Bailey bridge over the Orne.

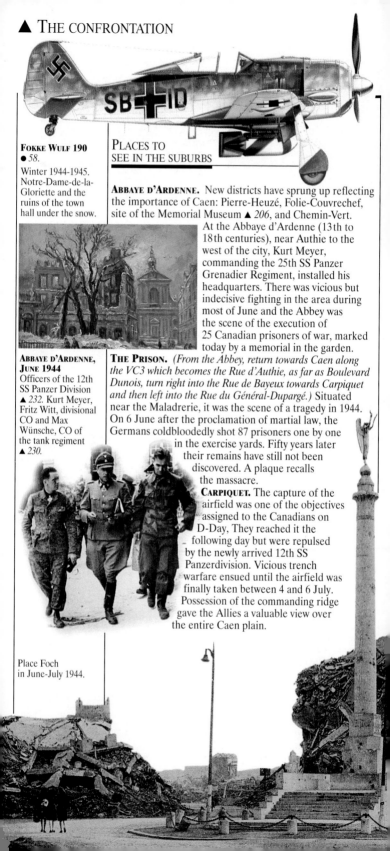

▲ THE CONFRONTATION

FOKKE WULF 190
● *58.*
Winter 1944-1945.
Notre-Dame-de-la-
Gloriette and the
ruins of the town
hall under the snow.

**ABBAYE D'ARDENNE,
JUNE 1944**
Officers of the 12th
SS Panzer Division
▲ *232.* Kurt Meyer,
Fritz Witt, divisional
CO and Max
Wünsche, CO of
the tank regiment
▲ *230.*

Place Foch
in June-July 1944.

PLACES TO SEE IN THE SUBURBS

ABBAYE D'ARDENNE. New districts have sprung up reflecting the importance of Caen: Pierre-Heuzé, Folie-Couvrechef, site of the Memorial Museum ▲ *206*, and Chemin-Vert. At the Abbaye d'Ardenne (13th to 18th centuries), near Authie to the west of the city, Kurt Meyer, commanding the 25th SS Panzer Grenadier Regiment, installed his headquarters. There was vicious but indecisive fighting in the area during most of June and the Abbey was the scene of the execution of 25 Canadian prisoners of war, marked today by a memorial in the garden.

THE PRISON. *(From the Abbey, return towards Caen along the VC3 which becomes the Rue d'Authie, as far as Boulevard Dunois, turn right into the Rue de Bayeux towards Carpiquet and then left into the Rue du Général-Dupargé.)* Situated near the Maladrerie, it was the scene of a tragedy in 1944. On 6 June after the proclamation of martial law, the Germans coldbloodedly shot 87 prisoners one by one in the exercise yards. Fifty years later their remains have still not been discovered. A plaque recalls the massacre.

CARPIQUET. The capture of the airfield was one of the objectives assigned to the Canadians on D-Day, They reached it the following day but were repulsed by the newly arrived 12th SS Panzerdivision. Vicious trench warfare ensued until the airfield was finally taken between 4 and 6 July. Possession of the commanding ridge gave the Allies a valuable view over the entire Caen plain.

> "From the German point of view, an attack towards Caen would not have been taken lightly. A straight distance between Caen and the Seine was less than 90 km."
>
> General O. Bradley

Operations Epsom, Goodwood and Bluecoat

By the evening of D-Day, British and Canadian units moving inland from the beaches had reached the suburbs of Bayeux and were in possession of the N13 road between that city and Caen. However, they failed to take two of their primary objectives: Caen itself and Carpiquet airfield. From then on, British strategy was concerned with outflanking Caen by attacking southwards through the *bocage* country, while at the same time engaging the German armoured units so as to free the Americans to break out to the west. As more and more enemy reinforcements arrived, that task became increasingly difficult to achieve.

The failure of Epsom. While the 3rd Canadian Division remained locked in bitter combat with the newly arrived 12th SS Panzerdivision in front of Carpiquet, British units thrust towards Tilly-sur-Seulles where they came up against the also newly arrived Panzer Lehr Division. At Villers-Bocage on 13 June the British were driven out by a detachment of Tiger tanks. In an attempt to break the deadlock, the British launched Operation Epsom on 25 June, the aim being to cross the Odon and Orne rivers so as to reach the plain south of Caen. Thus defeated by the German tanks and the difficult countryside, the northern part of Caen was not captured until 9 July,

Insignia of the 15th Scottish Division and the 11th Armoured Division.

Goodwood and Bluecoat. Later, Montgomery attempted to go southwards from the airborne bridgehead to the east of the city, codenamed Operation Goodwood. Once again, well entrenched enemy anti-tank weapons managed to defeat the British advance. It was only after the American breakthrough in the west, that a general attack through the *Bocage* (Operation Bluecoat) could be mounted on 30 July, which gained 25 kilometres towards Vire.

Memories in the place Foch
The War Memorial is scarred with bullet and shrapnel damage. Certain buildings have been rebuilt in the original style, including the Hôtel Malherbe which was the Feldkommandantur during the war. The Avenue de Verdun takes you to the church of Saint-Jean, now freed of the surrounding houses.

Two facts lent a strong symbolic value to the original proposal for the Memorial Museum for Peace. It was built in a city that was three-quarters destroyed in the air and naval bombardments in the summer of 1944, and is sited on top of a subterranean command post built by the Germans in an ancient quarry. With its aim of placing the Normandy campaign in the context of two world wars, the Caen Memorial immerses the visitor in the entire history of the twentieth century, using an approach that is at the same time narrative, historical and lyrical. In addition, the aim is to promote the ideal of peace. Created by the City of Caen, it was inaugurated on 6 June 1989 by François Mitterrand and the ambassadors of eleven countries which fought for peace in 1944.

THE PEACE BEACON
Built on the south side and complementing the Memorial is an imposing beacon bordering the cliff on which the museum buildings themselves are found. A Bailey Bridge section joins the two structures. The tower is a symbol which recalls the mission of this living sanctuary: to fight for democracy, human rights and peace.

THE BRITISH NEWS AT 18.30 ON 13 JUNE
"British troops are at Troarn. The Allies have mounted a double thrust which aims to outflank Caen to the south .... Three Panzer divisions are concentrated between Caen and Tilly. Since last Tuesday Allied aircraft have shot down 91 German planes and have themselves lost 65."

10

9

GENERAL RICHTER'S COMMAND POST

The museum is built on top of the command post of the 716th Infantry division (6,000 men) which occupied the coast sector between the Dives and Arromanches. This underground fortress (450 m², 12 m deep) consisted of a telephone exchange, a map room and accommodation. On 6 June the German commanders met there hurriedly to coordinate the armoured counter-attack.

THE ENTRANCE TO THE MEMORIAL

The Esplanade Dwight-Eisenhower in front of the building is bordered on the right by the flags of the combatant nations and closed to the left by a gallery containing a dozen stones from the same countries. On the plain façade of the building are engraved the following words:

"Sadness broke me, fraternity lifted me again, from my wounds has gushed a river of freedom." Thus the martyred City of Caen expressed its gratitude to its liberators. The front is a plain cube of Caen stone in the middle of which is a break dominated by a sombre grey mirror under which is the visitors' entrance.

1. Entrance.
2. Information and tickets.
3. Cloakroom.
4. Toilets.
5. Entry to the museum circuit.
6. Model of a Typhoon.
7. Temporary exhibitions.
8. Children's crèche.
9. Bailey Bridge.

10. Peace Beacon (access to the park and the Nobel-Peace-Prize Gallery).
11. Shop and library.
12. Archive centre.
13. Cinema.
14. Stone from Hiroshima.
15. Glass pyramids (overlooking the basement level).

INTRODUCTION TO THE JOURNEY: THE "GRAND HALL"
Devoid of support the *grand hall* is a meeting space: information centre, bookshop, temporary gallery and cafeteria, leading up to the archive department.

NOBEL-PEACE-PRIZE GALLERY
Access is via the Bailey Bridge. This long vaulted gallery contains a chronological presentation on the walls and the floor (above left) with panels representing each winner since 1902 (left) as well as an audio-visual experience.

THE STAGES TO THE VISIT
In the hall visitors are immediately impressed by the full-size model of the Typhoon which seems to swoop down on them. The visit to the museum starts at the entrance to a huge cylinder and is in two stages: the historical sections (areas 1, 2 and 3) and the audio-visual displays (areas 4, 5 and 6).

THE HISTORICAL PROGRESS
From the cylinder, visitors are guided to the entrance to a sphere which symbolises earth, eternal but powerless in face of the human history, around which they must make their way. The impact of sound enhances the visual exhibits. On the wall, posters, films and newspaper cuttings recount recent world history as it became debased, like a descent into hell. The corridor slopes gently downwards and as the world situation slides into chaos, the lighting is dimmed and the colours become more sombre.

THE BLACK YEARS
After The Frailty of Peace which evokes the Great War, the 1929 crisis and the rise of Nazism, the historical presentation leads into a second area devoted to France under occupation. Visitors proceed at their own pace through a stage-set enhanced by a choice of exhibits, both honest and emotional.

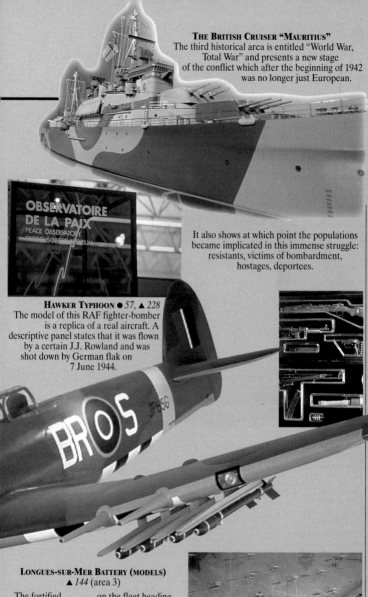

THE BRITISH CRUISER "MAURITIUS"
The third historical area is entitled "World War,
Total War" and presents a new stage
of the conflict which after the beginning of 1942
was no longer just European.

It also shows at which point the populations
became implicated in this immense struggle:
resistants, victims of bombardment,
hostages, deportees.

HAWKER TYPHOON ● *57*, ▲ *228*
The model of this RAF fighter-bomber
is a replica of a real aircraft. A
descriptive panel states that it was flown
by a certain J.J. Rowland and was
shot down by German flak on
7 June 1944.

LONGUES-SUR-MER BATTERY (MODELS)
▲ *144* (area 3)

The fortified
position included
four gun
casemates, numbers
of shelters, anti-
aircraft defence and
a fire-control post.
On 6 June it opened
fire

on the fleet heading
for Gold Beach but
in the afternoon it
was neutralised by
Allied warships.
The following day
the garrison
surrendered.

**ANIMATED MAP: FROM THE LANDING
TO THE LIBERATION**
Emerging back into natural light
the visitor can see three audio-visual
presentations each lasting about 20 minutes.
D-Day on a parabolic screen with split images;
The Battle of Normandy
on four screens flanked by two tanks;
and *Hope* by Jacques Perrin.

▲ THE CONFRONTATION
CAEN TO VIRE

18 JULY: CAEN COMPLETELY LIBERATED
Having poured 24,000 shells onto the enemy entrenched in the south of the city, the Allies succeeded in liberating Caen.

CARPIQUET
A German aircraft destroyed at the airfield.

TOWARDS VIRE

BRETTEVILLE-L'ORGUEILLEUSE. (*Leave Caen via the N13, in the direction of Bayeux.*) Bretteville was reached on 7 June by units of the 3rd Canadian Division, but the following day, elements of the 12th SS Panzerdivision counter-attacked. The village was extensively damaged and fighting continued, finally ending with the capture of CARPIQUET Airfield.

SAINT-MANVIEU-NORREY. (*Take the D83 south.*) Around Saint-Manvieu there was vicious fighting between the Canadians and the Waffen SS. At the start of Operation Epsom on 26 June, 736 guns opened up on the area of Saint-Manvieux, Cheux and Fontenay-le-Pesnil and opened a passage for the 15th Scottish Division. The weather was bad, which precluded support from the fighter-bombers. At Saint-Manvieux there is a British cemetery containing 1,627 graves.

CHEUX. (*Follow the D83.*) At 14.00 on 26 June the arriving tanks of the 11th Armoured Division became involved in fighting with the 12th SS. Repeated German counter-attacks were repulsed and the village was held during the night.

TOURVILLE-SUR-ODON TO THE TOURMAUVILLE BRIDGEHEAD.
(*Follow the D89 along "Scottish Corridor" to Tourmauville.*)
The 11th Armoured Division and the Scots following this route managed to take the bridge at Tourmauville intact on 27 June. A small bridgehead was made on the southern bank of the Odon while 420 British tanks maintained the pressure on 80 German ones in and around Cheux. At TOURMAUVILLE beside the river there is a memorial to the 15th Scottish Division.

HILL 112. (*Follow the D89 to "Bon Repos" and fork left onto the D8.*) The 29th Armoured Brigade occupied this feature in the early morning of 28 June, as a springboard for an advance towards the Orne. All that day and the following one,

At Saint-Manvieu and Tourville-sur-Odon the streets bear the names of Scottish units.

OPERATION GOODWOOD
From 18 to 20 July Montgomery attempted to push three armoured divisions down a narrow corridor to the east of Caen. They were stopped by enemy anti-tank guns.

Villers-Bocage at the end of 1944.

"THE HEAVY 70-TON GERMAN TANKS OUTCLASSED THE LIGHT BRITISH ONES WHICH WERE FORCED TO DIG IN, NOT WITHOUT LOSSES, ALONG THE LINE FROM TILLY TO CAUMONT (...)."

ADMIRAL LEMONNIER

the British tanks clung to the hill under increasing attack from SS units. A strong German offensive towards Cheux was smashed by bombers and artillery. On the evening of the 29th, however, the spearheads of 11th Armoured Division were withdrawn back over the Odon. Memorials stand in the vicinity. At the crossroads is one to the Dorset and Hampshire regiments and on the road to Aunay, one to the 43rd Wessex Division.

VILLERS-BOCAGE. *(Follow the D8 to Évrecy, also severely damaged during the Epsom offensive, and continue to Villers-Bocage via the D174 and then the D675.)* This key town was the scene of the first abortive attempt by the British to move south. On June 13, 13 Tiger tanks ● *62*, ▲ *253* commanded by Major Wittmann ● *253* annihilated the weak British armoured force. The town was once again liberated a month later.

FONTENAY-LE-PESNEL. *(Take the D6 northwards and then the D9 eastwards.)* You cross the plain of Fontenoy where a massive tank-versus-tank combat took place in July. Fontenay itself, or its remains, was not taken until 26 June. A small memorial to the 49th Infantry Division stands on the road to Grainville opposite the British Cemetery.

TILLY-SUR-SEULLES. *(Take the D13 westwards.)* On 8 June, British armour probing south from Bayeux ran into strong resistance from the newly arrived Panzer Lehr Division. The ruins of Tilly were finally conquered on 18 June by the 56th Brigade. A museum at Tilly tells this story and displays objects from the battlefields.

HOTTOT-LES-BAGUES. *(Follow the D6 to the south and then take the D9 which passes the British Cemetery.)* Outside the town hall are memorials in honour of the 231st Brigade and the

Left, a monument in memory of the 49th West Riding Division at Cheux. Above, the insignia of the Divisional Engineers.

On 26 June the Royal Scots Fusiliers engaged in hand-to-hand combat with the 12th SS Hitlerjugend ▲ *248* Division around the church of Saint-Manvieu.

The ruins of the church at Évrecy.

Centre left, the insignia of the 5th Duke of Cornwall's Light Infantry.

▲ THE CONFRONTATION
CAEN TO VIRE

VIRE, LATE 1944
View of the Rue
Saulnerie taken
from the tower.

Dorsetshire Regiment. Continue along the D9 to CAUMONT-L'ÉVENTÉ, captured on 12 June by the American 1st I.D. The town formed the boundary between the two armies.

THE BLUECOAT BREAKOUT. *(After Caumont follow the D53 as far as Saint-Martin-des-Besaces and then the N175 as far as the D56 in the direction of Saint-Charles-de-Percy.)* Caumont was the starting-point for Operation Bluecoat ▲ 224, on 30 July. The aim was to support

the American Cobra breakout, while the main German armour was locked up south of Caen. A vital aim was Hill 309 at Saint-Martin-des-Besaces. Under the weight of air and ground bombing the Germans retreated towards BÉNY-BOCAGE.

MUSÉE DE LA PERCÉE-DU-BOCAGE
Situated at Saint-Martin-des-Besaces, it traces the course of Operation Bluecoat.

The route takes you along the 11th Division axis and you cross the Souleuvre River via TAURUS BRIDGE, captured intact on 31 July. Then the attack began to falter against increasing German opposition. There is a British cemetery at SAINT-CHARLES-DE-PERCY with some 792 graves.

VIRE. *(Take the D577 southwards.)* Vire was reached on 2 August by the 11th British Div. and liberated on 8 August by the 29th U.S. Infantry Division.
From Vire, the route follows the line of the front. On 2 August two SS Panzer Divisions, 9th and 10th, had appeared on the scene. Elements of 11th British Armoured Div., facing Chênedollé, lost numbers of Shermans to the anti-tank guns of the 9th SS. Relieved by the 3rd ID, there was a new attack on 4 August, for which Sergeant Bates of the Norfolk Regiment won a posthumous Victoria Cross.

Insignia of the
7th British Armoured
Division, the "Desert
Rats".

MONT PINÇON. *(Follow the D55 and then the D165 as far as Le Plessis-Grimoult, where you take the D54 northwards.)* In the sector of the 43rd Wessex Division it was the scene of exceptionally heavy fighting until it was captured on 6 August, after the Germans had shortened their line so as to withdraw armoured units to participate in the Mortain counter-attack. ▲ 224.

AUNAY-SUR-ODON. *(Continue on the D54 northwards.)* This village said to have been the most thoroughly destroyed in Normandy was liberated on 5 August. *(Return to Caen via the D8, the D36, the D36B and the D8.)*

Opposite, ruins of
the church at Aunay-sur-Odon
(Summer 1944).

Cobra, the Breakthrough
Cobra, la Percée
The American Thrust down the Cotentin

Anthony Kemp

1 CHERBOURG
2 SAINT-SAUVEUR-LE-VICOMTE
3 LA-HAYE-DU-PUITS
4 MONT CASTRE
5 PÉRIERS
6 MARIGNY
7 COUTANCES
8 AVRANCHES

174 km
2 days

Logo of the Battle of Normandy Open-Air Museum.

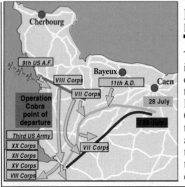

BRADLEY, IN THE COTENTIN *BOCAGE*

The territory covered in this itinerary illustrates several important phases of the Battle of Normandy as far as the American forces were concerned. First, the westward move to cut off the Cotentin peninsula in mid-June, second the southward attacks towards Saint-Lô and Périers through the *Bocage*. Last, the events of Operation Cobra ▲ *216* that finally broke through the crust of the German defence and initiated

"German troops counter-attack south of Avranches." Newspaper headline, 2 August 1944.

the dash to capture Avranches. After Carentan was finally captured, which made it possible to join the two American bridgeheads inland from Omaha and Utah, General Bradley ● *32*, ▲ *171, 225* initiated moves to cross the flooded area of the Merderet River to the west of Sainte-Mère-Église ▲ *184*. The inexperienced 90th Division managed to reach Orglandes by 15 June after bitter fighting in the *Bocage*. To their left, the 82nd Airborne was threatening Saint-Sauveur-le-Vicomte, which they captured the following day after bridging the River Douves. On the right, the 9th Infantry was struggling around Nehou, but by the 18th, managed to reach Barneville on the coast to effectively cut off the North Cotentin. By that stage of the battle, the Germans had been able to bring in sufficient infantry reinforcements by stripping the garrison of Brittany so that they had achieved parity with the Americans, except in terms of air power and mobility. The destruction of Mulberry A ● *76*, ▲ *141* at Saint-Laurent, however, caused a grave shortage of ammunition on the American side. In the enemy's favour was the difficult terrain, perfect for defence and where US armoured superiority could not be exploited. The inexperienced GIs paid a heavy price for their baptism of fire in the Normandy *Bocage*. Having captured Cherbourg, Bradley needed to get through the *Bocage* as quickly as possible to establish his forces on a line of departure to break out to the south and swing into Brittany, while Montgomery ● *31, 52*, ▲ *137, 162* held the German armour around Caen. That at least was the theory. In the general advance that started at the beginning of July, VIII Corps in the west was given the task of fighting their way from Saint-Sauveur to Coutances, parallel to the units aiming for Saint-Lô. At the end of the first week, although La-Haye-du-Puits had been taken, Bradley realized that he would

B17 Bomber ● *58*, ▲ *218*
The nose gunner's position in a Flying Fortress. B17s were used to bomb enemy positions at the start of Operation Cobra.

German prisoners
An American sergeant escorts German prisoners at Saint-Sauveur-le-Vicomte ▲ *217* in July 1944.

SAINT-SAUVEUR,
A GHOST TOWN
16 June:
American parachute
troops entered Saint-
Sauveur-le-Vicomte,
deserted as a result of
the bombardments.

"While Collins cut
the enemy lines with
a column towards the
coast and intended
to encircle the enemy
in the neck of the
Cotentin, Middleton
thrust towards
Coutances, joining
up with Collins at
that point. Then
Middleton headed
for Avranches and
at the corner fanned
out into Brittany."
Omar Bradley,
A Soldier's Story.

Insignia of
the US 2nd ID
● *50*

have to settle for a more modest aim. He therefore selected
the line of the Périers to Saint-Lô road for the start of his
great offensive, in the hope that sufficient forces would have
arrived in Normandy. It was to take eighteen further days
of bitter fighting and 10,000 casualties to reach that objective
only twelve kilometres away.

OPERATION COBRA

On 24 July, Bradley had four army corps in position
and three more in reserve that would form the Third Army
of General Patton ● *31,* ▲ *220,* ready to exploit the
breakthrough. This was to take place along a seven-kilometre
front between Périers and Saint-Lô that was defended by a
weakened Panzer Lehr Division ▲ *230* and a parachute
regiment. A huge carpet of bombs was dropped on the
Germans, but many went wide and hit the Americans. Once
again it was the intrepid General Collins and his men who
punched the initial hole through the German line at Marigny
and on 30 July Coutances was abandoned by the Germans
without a fight.

THE ARRIVAL OF PATTON. That left the way open for
General Patton's army to enter the fray and he sent two
armoured divisions south towards Avranches with orders
not to stop until they got there. Not bothering about their
flanks, they raced into Avranches ▲ *222* and on to
Pontaubault ▲ *227,* which was reached on 1 August
and the bridge captured intact. That opened the way
to turn the corner into Brittany, but did not end
the fighting in Normandy, where other American
units on the left were still struggling through
the *Bocage* towards Vire and Mortain ▲ *227.*
The Germans, although severely mauled by the war
of attrition in the hedgerows, were still a force to be
reckoned with and the British were making only slow
progress against their armoured units around Caen
▲ *196.* From Pontaubault, the 6th US Armoured Division
drove for Rennes, while the XII Corps headed towards
the Loire, The XX Corps for Orléans and the XV Corps
towards the Seine. On 9 August, Le Mans was entered, but
a wide gap had been opened between the Third US Army

and the First US Army on its left, which was ripe for exploitation by a determined enemy.

Along the Liberty Way

(From Cherbourg ▲ 190, 193, take the N13 as far as Valognes. Stay on the by-pass rather than entering the town and turn right onto the D2 road to Saint-Sauveur-le-Vicomte. After two hundred metres on the left, take D24, to Orglandes.)

Liberty Way is clearly marked with kilometre stones of a particular design ● 82, ▲ 184, 187.

Orglandes. At the heart of the *Bocage* country, Orglandes was the target of Americans moving west to cut off the Cotentin. Fighting around the village and to the east erupted on 15 June when the US 90th Division arrived from Pont-l'Abbé and was finally liberated on the 17th. Both the Germans and Americans who were killed fighting in the area were originally buried on the site, but after the war the latter were all moved to the main cemetery at Saint-Laurent ● 80, ▲ 166.

(In the village turn right onto the D126 and then take the D42 to Néhou.)

Néhou. You are now following the main American axis of advance westwards through flooded winding lanes. On the evening of 16 June the 9th Division had cleared Sainte-Colombe but was balked by the village of Néhou which is on high ground overlooking a marshy valley. The Germans, realizing that they were outnumbered, evacuated the severely damaged village during the night. The capture cleared the way for the rapid cross-country advance of the division to Barneville on the far coast which they reached on the evening of the 17th, cutting the route of the enemy units who were trying to escape to the north. *(To reach Saint-Sauveur-le-Vicomte take the D42 and then the D900.)*

NÉHOU

Saint-Sauveur-le-Vicomte*. Liberated on 16 June by the men of the 82nd Airborne Division, Saint-Sauveur was the departure point for the VIII Corps attack south through the *Bocage* to La Haye-du-Puits. Initially, progress was fairly rapid against disorganized opposition, but after crossing the low-lying meadows the Americans were faced with the high ground and *Bocage* as they approached La Haye.

German cemetery at Orglandes ● 80 10,152 German soldiers rest there, their names listed on small stone crosses planted in the lawn.

Also worth seeing…
Saint-Sauveur-le-Vicomte 11th-century castle (above), scene of fighting during the 100 Years War. The Abbey of Saint-Sauveur was secularized at the time of the Revolution, rebuilt during the 19th century, only to be damaged yet again in 1944. The historic centre (below) dominates the town.

▲ COBRA, THE BREAKTHROUGH
CHERBOURG TO AVRANCHES

Insignia of
the 82nd Airborne
Division ▲ 185.

La Haye itself
is dominated by
the hill of
Montgardon to
the west and Mont Castre to the east.

LA HAYE-DU-PUITS. As you enter the town there is
an imposing MONUMENT on your left to the men of
THE 79TH DIVISION, which lists all the subsidiary formations
that made up the complete fighting unit. On the side
is written: "La Haye. Bloody Hill. Hill 84. July 9, 1944."
That refers to the division's battle to take Montgardon
between 3 and 8 July, which cost 1,500 lives. At the same
time the 82nd
Airborne liberated
the town itself.
It was this unit's
last engagement
in Normandy.
After fighting all
the way from
Sainte-Mère-Église
▲ 184, they were
withdrawn back
to England.
Just past the
memorial on
the left are the
ruins of a castle
keep and below
this is the town war memorial which lists the names of a
dozen civilians who were killed, together with a small
plaque recording the gratitude of the people to the men
who liberated them. (*Leave the town on the D903 road
to Carentan and then take the D140.*)

Above, B17s ● 58,
▲ 215 overflying
the Saint-Lô area.
Below, figures in
British uniforms
in the Museum of
the Second World
War at Val-Saint-Père.

MONT CASTRE. After two kilometres you will see the hill
of Mont Castre, a long ridge dominating the plain. The men
of the 90th reached the road on 3 July where they were
regrouped and four days later they began their advance
upwards. It took them two days and they lost 2,000 men in
the process. There is a small road that leads off on the right
towards Mont Castre, on top of which can be found the
traces of a Roman encampment, a castle, as well as a
mediaeval church. These can be reached on foot.
(*To reach Plessis-Lastelle, continue along the D140.*)

> "FURTHER SOUTH THE TERRAIN BECOMES MORE AND MORE PARTITIONED, WOODED AND BROKEN UP, WHICH IS WHY THE REGION TO THE SOUTH OF SAINT-LÔ IS CALLED THE NORMAN SWITZERLAND."
>
> ADMIRAL LEMONNIER

LE PLESSIS-LASTELLE. There is a monument in honour of the men of the 90th Division, from Texas and Oklahoma, who were nick-named the "Tough Ombres".

South of Le Plessis they were held up by the German parachute unit on the high ground around the village of GONFREVILLE, which became known as The Island.

PÉRIERS. (*Take the D24 and then the D900.*) This is still the route taken by the 90th Infantry, who engaged in savage battles with an elite parachute unit in flooded countryside. On the left, one can find a marshy area stretching as far as Sainteny. Although one of the main objectives of the advance, Périers, an important crossroads, was not liberated until 27 July. Severely bombed in June, the town had been totally ruined and burnt before the Americans entered it.

ON THE ROAD TO SAINT-LÔ

The D900 road to Saint-Lô was to form General Bradley's starting-line but was not reached until 18 July. For the first few kilometres the area to the north of the road was still occupied by the 17th SS Panzergrenadier Division ▲ *230* on the 24th, and the actual US attack started to the east of Le Mesnil-Vigot. The road was designated as the objective of a mass bombardment on the afternoon of 24 July. To your left, the 83rd, 9th and 30th Infantry Divisions were dug into the hedgerows about a kilometre back, while on your right were the tanks of the Panzer Lehr ▲ *230, 232* and a parachute regiment. Behind the American front line were two more infantry divisions and two armoured, ready to exploit the breakthrough. The bombardment was a disaster owing to poor visibility. Many of the aircraft turned back and those that did make their run-in dropped short and killed a considerable number of Americans. After a hasty rethink, Bradley decided to postpone the attack for 24 hours, after a further bombardment in the morning. That attack almost totally destroyed the Panzer Lehr, but the cratering slowed American progress southwards.

LA CHAPELLE-EN-JUGER. (*Turn right onto the D89.*) A completely new church bears a memorial plaque recording the events of 25 July. On that day the village became a graveyard for the tanks of the Panzer Lehr in the surrounding fields. From there continue to Saint-Gilles, following the line of the attack by the 4th Infantry Division which encountered only isolated

GERMAN CEMETERY AT MAVIGNY
The entrance is designed in the form of a typical Normandy church. 11,169 German soldiers are buried there who were killed during the fighting in the hedgerows.

LA HAYE-DU-PUITS IN 1944
Below, upper photo, the church square at the end of 1944. The lower photo shows French troops driving through in August. The price of liberation for the village was heavy as three quarters of the houses were destroyed.

▲ GENERAL PATTON

In 1943, George Smith Patton was in command of the Seventh US Army in Sicily, but almost ruined his career by slapping a soldier during a visit to a field hospital, accusing him of being a malingerer. That incident cost him the command of American forces for D-Day, but he was recalled to lead the Third US Army (insignia above) which was being formed in the USA in early 1944. He arrived on the Normandy front on 6 July, subordinate to Bradley, his junior, who entrusted him with the mission of reaching Avranches. His army actually became operational on 1 August.

PATTON IN TUNISIA
Between the two wars he served in the cavalry and was given command of the 2nd Armoured Division in 1940. Two years later as commander of one of the assault forces for Operation Torch, he "conquered" Morocco. Afterwards he led an army corps in Tunisia with Bradley as his deputy.

GENERAL PATTON
George S Patton was born in 1885 at San Gabriel, into a wealthy Californian family.

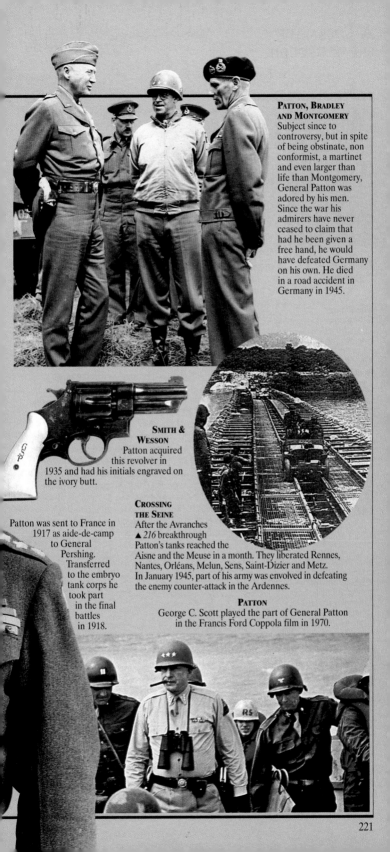

PATTON, BRADLEY AND MONTGOMERY
Subject since to controversy, but in spite of being obstinate, non conformist, a martinet and even larger than life than Montgomery, General Patton was adored by his men. Since the war his admirers have never ceased to claim that had he been given a free hand, he would have defeated Germany on his own. He died in a road accident in Germany in 1945.

SMITH & WESSON
Patton acquired this revolver in 1935 and had his initials engraved on the ivory butt.

CROSSING THE SEINE
After the Avranches ▲ *216* breakthrough Patton's tanks reached the Aisne and the Meuse in a month. They liberated Rennes, Nantes, Orléans, Melun, Sens, Saint-Dizier and Metz. In January 1945, part of his army was envolved in defeating the enemy counter-attack in the Ardennes.

Patton was sent to France in 1917 as aide-de-camp to General Pershing. Transferred to the embryo tank corps he took part in the final battles in 1918.

PATTON
George C. Scott played the part of General Patton in the Francis Ford Coppola film in 1970.

▲ COBRA, THE BREAKTHROUGH

75mm anti-tank gun on a PZ KW II Marder chassis.

pockets of resistance left alive. Saint-Gilles was reached that evening, upon which General Collins felt confident enough to let loose his pursuit units, the 1st Infantry and the 2nd and 3rd Armoured Divisons which headed towards Canisy.

MARIGNY. In the totally rebuilt small town there is a sign for the Marigny German cemetery which is a kilometre to the north. The town was liberated by the 3rd Armoured Division on 26 June.

COUTANCES TO AVRANCHES

Also worth seeing…
**COUTANCES
CATHEDRAL**

**THE PATTON
MONUMENT
AT AVRANCHES**
Commemorating
his famous
Third US Army
● *31*, ▲ *220*.

COUTANCES. Just as you enter the town there is a memorial to the men of the 4th Armoured Division, who were the liberators on the afternoon of 28 July. They had driven south from Périers, while VII Corps were held up on the road from Marigny by a rearguard of SS units.

PATTON REACHES AVRANCHES. It was along this road that the tanks of Patton's Third US Army were launched on 28 July. Three German divisions were retreating in front of the Americans, and in the fields around Roncey on 28 and 29 July, US fighter-bombers spotted a large collection of German vehicles, and swooped down, firing rockets and cannon. The 2nd US Armoured Divison managed to encircle 10,000 men mainly from the two SS divisions, the 2nd's Das Reich ● *41*, and the 17th, Goetz von Berlichingen ▲ *232*. (*Continue south via Lengronne and La Haye-Pesnel.*) At Gavray, a rearguard of 2nd SS Panzer managed to hold up the advance for a few hours and blew the bridge over the Sienne. Driven on by General Patton's invective, the American 4th Armoured Division pushed on round the clock and entered Avranches at dusk on 30 July. The scale of the victory exceeded Bradley's expectations, as Patton's tanks charged on into Brittany. (*The itinerary ends at Val-Saint-Père ▲ 227.*)

An American unit
driving through
Avranches en route
to the front, watched
by the inhabitants.

COUNTER-ATTACK
LA CONTRE-ATTAQUE
THE LAST GERMAN OFFENSIVE AROUND MORTAIN

ANTHONY KEMP

▲ COUNTER-ATTACK
AVRANCHES TO ALENÇON

1 AVRANCHES
2 VAL-SAINT-PÈRE
3 HUISNES-SUR-MER GERMAN OSSUARY
4 MONT-SAINT-MICHEL
5 SAINT-JAMES AMERICAN CEMETERY
6 SAINT-HILAIRE-DU-HARCOUËT

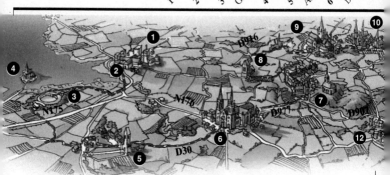

THE LAST GERMAN OFFENSIVE

This particular itinerary covers various elements of
the campaign: the breakthrough into Brittany,
the German counter-attack around Mortain, the start
of the push towards Falaise ▲ *248* and British attacks
as part of Operation Bluecoat ▲ *212* in support
of the Americans.

THE AMERICAN BREAKTHROUGH. At the end of July
the US VIII Corps was heading off into Brittany with
Patton's ● *31*, ▲ *220* Third Army forming up behind it.
To cover the flank of Bradley's ● *31*, ▲ *215* Operation
Cobra ▲ *216*, Dempsey ● *30* launched an attack
southwards code-named Operation Bluecoat, aiming
for Mont Pinçon and Vire ▲ *212*. Not every objective
was achieved but the attack had the effect of diverting
German armoured units that might otherwise have
operated towards the vulnerable bridge at Avranches.
Dempsey, frustrated by the slow progress, sacked the
commanders of XXX Corps and the 7th Armoured
Division on the spot.

🚗 209 km
⏱ 2 days

Logo of the Battle of
Normandy Open-Air
Museum.

**MORTAIN,
AUGUST 1944**
An American soldier,
the sole sign of life,
reading a map on
which the route
of his unit was traced.

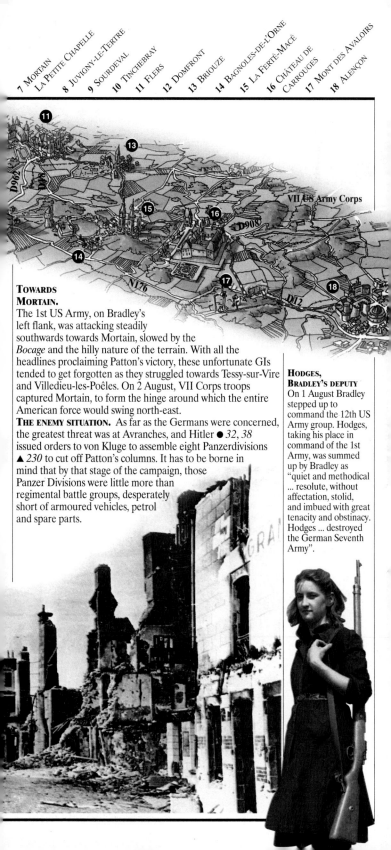

7 Mortain
La Petite Chapelle
8 Juvigny-le-Tertre
9 Sourdeval
10 Tinchebray
11 Flers
12 Domfront
13 Briouze
14 Bagnoles-de-l'Orne
15 La Ferté-Macé
16 Château de Carrouges
17 Mont des Avaloirs
18 Alençon

D962
D909

VII US Army Corps

D908

N176

D12

TOWARDS MORTAIN.

The 1st US Army, on Bradley's left flank, was attacking steadily southwards towards Mortain, slowed by the *Bocage* and the hilly nature of the terrain. With all the headlines proclaiming Patton's victory, these unfortunate GIs tended to get forgotten as they struggled towards Tessy-sur-Vire and Villedieu-les-Poêles. On 2 August, VII Corps troops captured Mortain, to form the hinge around which the entire American force would swing north-east.

THE ENEMY SITUATION.

As far as the Germans were concerned, the greatest threat was at Avranches, and Hitler ● *32, 38* issued orders to von Kluge to assemble eight Panzerdivisions ▲ *230* to cut off Patton's columns. It has to be borne in mind that by that stage of the campaign, those Panzer Divisions were little more than regimental battle groups, desperately short of armoured vehicles, petrol and spare parts.

HODGES, BRADLEY'S DEPUTY

On 1 August Bradley stepped up to command the 12th US Army group. Hodges, taking his place in command of the 1st Army, was summed up by Bradley as "quiet and methodical ... resolute, without affectation, stolid, and imbued with great tenacity and obstinacy. Hodges ... destroyed the German Seventh Army".

▲ COUNTER-ATTACK
AVRANCHES TO ALENÇON

American Soldier
(Juvigny-le-Tertre)

TYPHOON FIGHTER-BOMBER ● *59*, ▲ *256* and **M10** TANK DESTROYER.

PONTAUBAULT
100,000 American vehicles crossed the bridge over the Sélune during the month of August 1944.

AVRANCHES
August 1944.
American tanks on their way to the front passing through the town.

Von Kluge would have preferred an orderly withdrawal to the Seine but, although he knew that he was witnessing the death warrant of his forces, he realized the futility of protesting against the orders of the Führer. In effect, owing to British pressure, he could only assemble four Panzer divisions with a total of 250 tanks between them.

THE DEFEAT OF THE MORTAIN COUNTER-ATTACK.
German preparations could hardly be hidden from air observation, and Bradley took precautions by positioning five infantry divisions with two armoured in reserve, between Vire and Mortain. On 6 August, American and British thrusts were aimed at Vire, and the former captured the town that evening, thus upsetting German preparations for their assault that night. Severely delayed and lacking several units whose moves had been delayed by air attack, the German Panzer group attacked between Sourdeval and Mortain where they managed to advance about seven miles before being halted by the 3rd Armoured Division. They did dislodge the Americans temporarily from Mortain itself, but in the morning Allied aircraft were waiting. It was like a turkey shoot and the roads were littered with the blazing wrecks of the pride of the German army and the SS.

THE GERMAN DEBACLE.
Von Kluge wanted to call off the attack, but Hitler ordered him to pull two more divisions away from the British front. Driven onto the defensive, the Germans were threatened with  encirclement as the Canadians began to drive south from Caen towards Falaise, and Bradley ordered Patton to swing his XV Corps northwards towards Alençon to close the noose around the neck of the Seventh German Army. At Mortain Hitler threw away the chance to withdraw the bulk of his forces in Normandy with some resemblance of order.

AVRANCHES TO SAINT JAMES

AVRANCHES ♥. The PATTON MONUMENT, erected on the spot where he set up his headquarters, is flanked by a Sherman tank. (*Turn right at the monument and descend the hill.*) There is a remarkable view over the estuary of the Sélune and in the distance, Mont-Saint-Michel. At VAL-SAINT-PÈRE visit the MUSEUM OF THE LIBERATION ◆ 260 which features uniforms, equipment and weapons used by the troops of the period.

AMERICAN CEMETERY (Saint James)

GERMAN OSSUARY ● 81 (Huisnes-sur-Mer)

PONTAUBAULT. (*Follow the D43 as far as the bridge.*) It was this road that unit after unit of Patton's army swept along at the end of July. Senior officers acting as traffic policemen pushed units over the bridge at Avranches in any order and down the bottleneck to Pontaubault, where other officers allotted them roads for their further advance. Seven divisions were rammed through in seventy-two hours, a remarkable achievement, in spite of German efforts to bomb the bridges. In Pontaubault at the far end of the bridge is a plaque recording this achievement.

THE GERMAN OSSUARY AT HUISNES-SUR-MER ◆ 260. (*Go on west along the D43 and take the D75 towards Le Mont-Saint-Michel ♥.*) This is in the form of a circular two-storey building. In each level there are thirty-four chambers containing a total of nearly 12,000 human remains which were collected there in 1961 from as far afield as the Channel Islands.

THE AMERICAN CEMETERY AT SAINT-JAMES ◆ 260. (*Continue towards Ardevon on the D280, at Brée take the D80 and then the D30 to the east.*) Here are buried 4,410 soldiers killed in the fighting in Brittany and towards the Loire. (*From Saint-James, take the D30 to SAINT-HILAIRE-DU-HARCOUËT. From there, take the D977 towards Mortain via the CARREFOUR DES CLOSEAUX.*) It was along this road that the 2nd SS Panzer intended to travel on their way to capturing the Pontaubault Bridge, but when the column reached the hamlet of La Salais they met a strong defence mounted by the 80th US Infantry.

MORTAIN. Situated on a high knoll overlooking the plain and an important road crossing, Mortain itself was only weakly held by troops of the 30th Infantry, who were dislodged during a night attack by the 17th SS Panzer Grenadiers. An American battalion was surrounded on the ridge overlooking the town (Hill 314) and strongly attacked from all sides. Supplied by air, the small group held out for five days until finally relieved. In the town, which was virtually wrecked by the fighting, there is the abbey and the 13th-century church of Saint-Évroult. Continue on the D977 through LE NEUFBOURG where the ancient iron mine sheltered 800 civilians dislodged by the fighting.

MEMORIAL ON HILL 314 Erected near the small chapel in memory of the men of the 30th Infantry Division who liberated Mortain.

On 6 August on Hitler's orders, two relatively weakened armoured corps launched an attack westwards. Their aim was to advance to Avranches and cut the communications of the Third Army which was already fanned out in Brittany, having managed to liberate Rennes on 4 August.

After having travelled 70 km during the night, 200 heavy tanks and 9,000 motorized infantry fell on the advance positions of the 30th Infantry Division at Mesnil-Adelée which were under the cover of a smokescreen at dawn on 7 August. The sunken roads bordered by high banks were filled with Panther tanks and armoured half-tracks which reached Mortain at midday, pushing back with this effort the advance posts of the 9th Infantry Division.

At 12.35 Typhoons from 174 Group RAF destroyed 60 tanks and 200 soft-skinned enemy vehicles on the road between Saint-Barthélemy and Chérencé-le-Roussel ▲ 234.

Two squadrons swooped on the head of the column and two others attacked the tail, paralysing the German advance.

CHÉRENCE-LE-ROUSSEL

The battalion of the 30th Infantry Division surrounded by the SS Panzergrenadiers on the ridge south-east of Mortain exchanged blow for blow. Parachuted ammunition and hollow shells filled with medical supplies kept them going. The GIs were, however, on the point of being overrun when, on 10 August, Allied air power compelled the Germans to retreat.

At 12.45 24 P47 Thunderbolt fighter Bombers ● 56 located and bombed another important enemy column at Sourdeval, while 16 other aircraft loaded with rockets attacked the SS Division Das Reich west of Mortain.

At 13.00 the mist lifted. A Mustang, flying a reconnaissance mission, discovered the densely packed columns.

GERMAN FRONT COLLAPSING

A squadron of rocket-firing Typhoons operated from its advanced landing strip north-west of Caen. Fifty aircraft got the better of a Panzer army and the GIs applauded the exploits of the RAF pilots.

"GERMAN FRONT COLLAPSING"
At Mortain Hitler played his last card – in vain. For the first time in military history air power alone had halted an adverse land offensive.

MORTAIN

By the end of the day, 137 tanks had been destroyed.

Influenced by General Heinz Guderian, the Germans developed their theory of armoured warfare before the war began. The successful conquest of Poland and the "Blitzkrieg" in the West proved the efficiency of the concept and ensured the supremacy of the German armoured divisions. The latter, however, lost many of their effectives in the East, at the battle of Kursk, and during the Normandy campaign, Allied air supremacy was an effective counter to their fire power.

THE TIGER ● 62
These heavy tanks, present in small numbers during the Normandy campaign, were integrated into the armoured divisions. They were well armed with a Krupp 88-mm cannon and the thickness of their armour was capable of resisting most Allied armour-piercing shells. In spite of this quasi-invulnerability, their heavy weight and its corollary in terms of excessive fuel consumption limited their radius of action and independence.

PANZER LEHR DIVISION
Units of this division engaged in Normandy comprised a whole hierarchy of different divisions. One could count in it the divisional staff, the headquarters company, two tank battalions (Mk.IVs and Panthers), two grenadier regiments, one self-propelled anti-tank battalion, one artillery regiment, and an anti-aircraft battalion. In addition to all this, the division also included an engineer battalion, a reconnaissance battalion, plus workshop for the maintenance of the material and technical support, medical, administrative, police and supply companies.

A well-camouflaged German observing enemy movements with the aid of a periscope on the Normandy front in July 1944.

TANK IN COMBAT (JUNE 1944)
The German tanks were superior to those of the Allies both in terms of protection and armament. In Normandy they were equipped with the latest models: the Mark V Panther and the Tiger.

A soldier cleaning his machine-pistol.

In June 1944, a division in theory was made up of 14,500 officers, NCOs and men. In terms of vehicles the complement was 188 tanks and 674 half-tracks for carrying the infantry.

The divisional artillery park comprised at that time: 18 88mm anti-aircraft guns, 30 150-mm guns, 48 81-mm mortars 24 105-mm howitzers, 48 75-mm PAK anti-tank guns.

THE 21st PANZERDIVISON
Field Marshal Rommel inspecting the 21st Armoured Division with which he already had fought in North Africa
● *18.*

PANZERGRENADIER
In keeping with the strategy of Guderian, once the enemy lines had been penetrated by the tank spearheads and a breach had been opened, the infantry (grenadiers) poured through. Any remaining pockets of enemy resistance were left to be mopped up by infantry following on foot. This young Panzergrenadier is carrying an MG42 machine gun and has grenades hanging from his belt.

On 6 June, Panzergruppe West consisted of two armoured corps held in reserve, unable to move without direct orders from the high command. The units of 1st SS Panzerkorps were the 1st SS Panzer Division at Antwerp, the Panzer Lehr Division in the Le Mans/Chartres area and the 12th SS Panzer around Évreux. XLVII Panzerkorps comprised the 116th Panzerdivision west of Paris, 21st Panzer near Caen and the 2nd Panzer at Abbeville. The tangled command structure and the difficulty in transmitting orders ensured that the only armoured division capable of mounting an attack on D-Day, the 21st, remained ineffective. Time was wasted until Hitler released the nearest reserves.

GERMAN CONVOY
● *62*
On the one hand Allied air supremacy and on the other a chronic lack of fuel considerably slowed down the deployment of German armour. The 2nd SS Panzerdivision took two weeks to get from Toulouse to Normandy instead of three days.

ARRIVAL OF THE II SS PANZERKORPS
This unit en route from the Russian front by rail was forced to stop on 26 June in eastern France and continue by road because Allied bombing had destroyed the railway network.

A COLUMN OF GERMAN PRISONERS
By the summer of 1944, heavy losses on the Russian front had caused a grave shortage of experienced officers and NCOs in the armoured divisions. The ranks were often filled with Luftwaffe ground crews and other ill-trained replacements.

AN SS OFFICER BEING SEARCHED BY AN MP
On 10 June the 17th SS Panzergrenadier Division Götz von Berlichingen arrived in the Saint-Lô area. On 12 June the II SS Panzerkorps was ordered to leave Russia and its divisions, 9th SS Hohenstauffen and 10th SS Frundsberg, arrived in time to block the Epsom offensive on 25 June. At the same time the 2nd SS Panzer arrived at Saint-Lô and the 1st SS Panzer Leibstandarte Adolf Hitler arrived south of Caen, where it was immobilised for lack of petrol. On 8 August, the 9th SS Panzer moved from Le Mans to Mortain.

Also worth seeing...
AT MORTAIN ♥
From left to right.
The Grand Waterfall,
the Abbaye Blanche
(12th cent.) used as
a German hospital
in June 1944, and
the abbey cloisters.

**THE RUINS
OF MORTAIN**
A general view
of the town at the end
of the war. The battle
for Mortain cost
VIII US Corps the
lives of 4,300 men.

Insignia of the
12th US Army
Group.

FLERS
The Normandy
Bocage Museum
devotes certain rooms
to the war.

Also to see...
**THE CHÂTEAU
AT CARROUGES** ♥
Built below the town
it dates from the 14th
century, but was
progressively rebuilt
up to the 17th cent.
It is square in form,
surrounded by a moat
and consists of
towers alternating
with red brick
pavilions.

SAINT-BARTHÉLEMY AND JUVIGNY-LE-TERTRE. *(Take the D33 from Neufbourg towards the north.)* In this area, determined resistance by the 30th Infantry delayed the 17th SS, totally destroying their timetable of advance. Follow the D5 to JUVIGNY, which was defended by American infantry who barred the route of a battle group from the 1st SS Panzer, the Leibstandarte.

CHÉRENCÉ-LE-ROUSSEL. *(Take the D55 northwards, passing through LE-MESNIL-TÔVES.)* The 2nd Panzer achieved a breakthrough along the winding small roads leading to the west, hitting the divide between the 30th and the 4th Infantry. They were attacked, however, in the flank by the US 3rd Armoured Division.

SOURDEVAL. *(Follow the D911 eastwards.)* The route follows the beautiful winding valley of the Sée towards Sourdeval, from where a battle group of the 116th Panzerdivision started, aiming to reach Avranches. It managed only about five kilometres before being halted by the 4th Infantry. The Germans dug in and the Americans had to fight against strong rearguards pushing eastwards. They liberated Sourdeval only on 15 August, while elements of the 30th Infantry were racing towards Domfront. The Germans retreated eastwards, escaping the trap that was about to be sprung.

TINCHEBRAY AND FLERS. *(Keep on the D911 up to Tinchebray, take the D924 to La Fontaine, then the D229 to Saint-Georges-des-Groseillers and the D962 to Flers.)* The road towards Tinchebray follows the 29th US I.D. which pushed back the remnants of Eberbach's Fifth Panzer Army, also threatened by the British advance southwards towards Flers. At SAINT-GEORGES-DES-GROSEILLERS there is a memorial to the 11th British AD commanded by General "Pip" Roberts. *(From Flers, take the D924 as far as Briouze and then the D20 towards LA FERTÉ-MACÉ.)* The route crosses the line of the great German retreat and heads towards where US troops were squeezing up from the south to close the grip of the vice. The route ends at ALENÇON.
▲ 236.

THE ENCIRCLEMENT
L'ENCERCLEMENT
THE SOUTHERN ARM
OF THE PINCER

ANTHONY KEMP

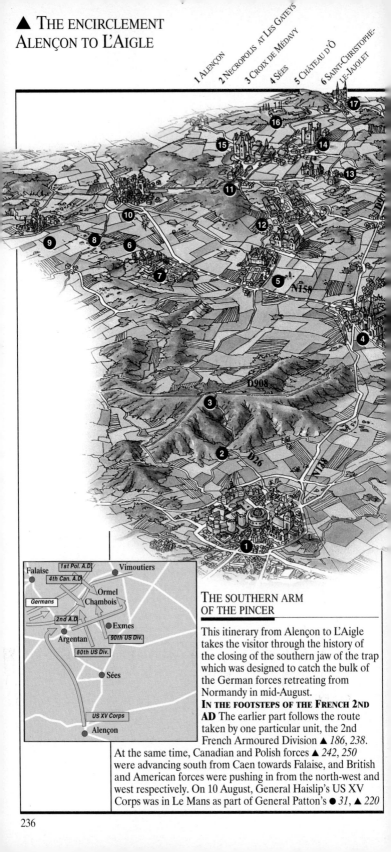

1 ALENÇON 2 NECROPOLIS AT LES GATEYS 3 CROIX DE MEDAVY 4 SÉES 5 CHÂTEAU D'Ô 6 SAINT-CHRISTOPHE-LE-JAJOLET

THE SOUTHERN ARM OF THE PINCER

This itinerary from Alençon to L'Aigle takes the visitor through the history of the closing of the southern jaw of the trap which was designed to catch the bulk of the German forces retreating from Normandy in mid-August.

IN THE FOOTSTEPS OF THE FRENCH 2ND AD The earlier part follows the route taken by one particular unit, the 2nd French Armoured Division ▲ 186, 238. At the same time, Canadian and Polish forces ▲ 242, 250 were advancing south from Caen towards Falaise, and British and American forces were pushing in from the north-west and west respectively. On 10 August, General Haislip's US XV Corps was in Le Mans as part of General Patton's ● 31, ▲ 220

🚗 162 km
🕐 2 days

Logo of the Battle of Normandy Open-Air Museum.

Third Army when it received orders to change its axis of march and turn north towards Alençon. The corps consisted of the following units: the 90th and 79th Infantry, and two armoured divisions, the 5th US and 2nd French.

NORTHWARDS TO CLOSE THE TRAP.
The army corps moved towards the Orne against sporadic resistance and entered Alençon on 12 August, capturing two bridges over the Sarthe intact. The 2nd French Armoured Division headed for the Forêt d'Ecouves while the 5th Armoured Division drove towards Sées, which it entered that evening. The further those units advanced northwards, the more desperate the German resistance became, as the enemy frantically tried to keep open the two jaws of the trap steadily closing in on them.

ALLIED HESITATION ENABLED 100,000 GERMANS TO ESCAPE.
On 13 August Haislip was ordered to stop his advance as both Bradley and Montgomery ● 31, ▲ 137 were worried that the Canadians and the Americans might bump into each other, and Argentan was the original Canadian objective after Falaise. This was with hindsight a grave error of judgement on the part of the Allied high command, as 100,000 Germans escaped through the corridor while XV Corps remained static until 17 August. The 90th Division and 2nd A.D. were detached to the US V Corps with orders to seize Chambois and plug the narrowing gap through which another 100,000 Germans were still trying to escape.

Insignia of French 2nd Armoured Div.

OTTO ELFELDT
A major-general, he was the fourth to surrender in the Argentan area, in command of the LXXXIV German Corps.

THE JOY OF THE LIBERATED INHABITANTS
Alençon, 14 August 1944. Young women throwing apples to French troops passing through.

▲ THE ALLIED ARMOURED FORCES

The Allies learned rapidly from the Germans in 1940 and from then on, armoured divisions were featured in both the British and American order of battle. The Americans subdivided their divisions into three Combat Commands, independent tank/infantry battle groups made up from a battalion of each arm. The British used two brigades, one each of tanks and infantry, each of three battalions, plus artillery, reconnaissance and support units. Each division was fully motorized and required 600 tons of supplies per day to keep fighting.

ALLIED TANKS
The Americans supplied various models of Sherman tanks to all the Allied formations, providing a high degree of standardization. The British also retained their own designs, such as the Cromwell, Churchill and Centaur which were used in the Normandy campaign.

FIELD COMMAND POST
A divisional commander had his own headquarters company and a small team of staff officers. By 1944, radio communications had developed a reasonable degree of efficiency, enabling the commander to remain in touch with his units when on the move.

ARRIVAL IN NORMANDY
Divisions landed directly on the beaches, and this was a major operation. An American division consisted of 12,000 men and over 3,000 vehicles: jeeps, tanks, trucks, half-tracks and self-propelled artillery.

GENERAL LECLERC
One of the most successful armoured commanders at divisional level was the French General Leclerc who escaped to England in 1940 and later fought in North Africa with Montgomery.

ARMOUR ON THE MOVE
A division advancing required several kilometres of road, and the distance travelled was limited by wear of the tracks and ensuring regular fuel supplies.

THE LECLERC MONUMENT AT ALENÇON

After landing at Utah Beach ▲ *182, 238* on 30 July, the division was integrated into Patton's Third Army to receive its baptism of fire under the orders of its brilliant commander, General Leclerc, during the liberation of the Orne Department.

Also worth seeing…
ALENÇON
The Alençon Lace Museum. The Fine Arts and Lace Museums. The birthplace of sainte Thérèse.

Also worth seeing…
THE CHÂTEAU D'Ô ♥
This superb château near Mortrée, built in the middle of a lake formed by the River Thouanne, was started in the reign of Louis XII and finished in the classical period.

SHERMAN TANK "VALOIS" ● *63* (at the Croix-de-Médavy crossroads).

ALENÇON TO SÉES

ALENÇON ♥. This was the first town in France to be liberated by French troops. The Museum dedicated to General Leclerc and the Liberation ◆ *260* was built to honour the men of the 2nd French Armoured Division. The events of the liberation of the town as well as the exploits of French troops in the area are emphasised in the displays. For the French, the fact that they had their own division in combat has strong emotional connotations to do with national pride and has helped to soften the shame of the defeat in 1940 and the collaborationist Vichy regime.

NATIONAL NECROPOLIS AT LES GATEYS. *(On the D26.)* Over a bridge you will see the cemetery surrounded by a low wall and set in a peaceful park landscape with a forest in the background. In it are a dozen graves with headstones in the form of crosses, Islamic pattern and one Jewish. There is also a plaque recording the men of the division killed in the department. Back on the road heading north, after a hundred metres there is a stone memorial on the right. This is in memory of Roger Rémy who served in the 1st Régiment de Marche des Spahis marocains and who died on 12 August aged eighteen years. He was in fact the son of the colonel commanding that regiment.

THE CROIX-DE-MÉDAVY CROSSROADS. *(Continue through the forest on the D26.)* There is a Sherman tank of the divison preserved as a memorial. In the gentle greenery of the forest it is difficult to imagine the thundering of tank guns as the 2nd AD, in their first serious battle, destroyed the remnants of the 9th S.S. Panzerdivision ▲ *230*.

SÉES* ♥. *(Continue on the D26 and then take the D908.)* While the French armour swung left towards Carrouges, you take the right-hand fork towards Sées where you join the march route of the 5th US Armoured. Sées is a historical town well worth a visit with the magnificent 13th/14th-century cathedral of Notre-Dame which was relatively undamaged by the fighting.

SÉES TO VIMOUTIERS

The countryside in this area is perfect for tank warfare, over flat and rolling plains without hedges.

SAINT-CHRISTOPHE-LE-JAJOLET*. *(Take the N158 and then the D219.)* After a few kilometres you can see a Sherman Tank, named Keren, on the Butte de Montmerrei, the access to which is difficult. It belonged to the Warabiot column commanded by Roger Denormandie and has been left where it was disabled on 12 August.

FLEURÉ*. *(Continue along the D219.)* To the north of the village on the left is a monument unveiled on 28 November 1947, recording that on that spot, General Leclerc set up his headquarters for twelve days while his men cleared the Germans from the surrounding countryside.

ÉCOUCHÉ. *(Rejoin the D219.)* Bombed on 6 June, the town of Écouché was liberated on 13 August by a unit from the 2nd French Armoured Division and the 9th Compagnie de Marche du Tchad which comprised Spanish Republicans. The capture of the bridge hindered the enemy from escaping westwards and the French troops caught and annihilated 300 members of an SS unit.

THE "MASSAOUA", AT ÉCOUCHÉ
The tank is a symbol of the severe fighting which shook the small town liberated on 13 August.

Also worth seeing...
THE CHÂTEAU OF SASSY
Dating from the 18th century, it is built of stone and brick. The French-style garden is surrounded by a moat.

THE DECISION TO LIBERATE PARIS. The Allies were unwilling to take on the responsibility for the liberation of the city and afterwards feeding its population, which they regarded as a political rather than a military objective. De Gaulle exerted enormous pressure on General Eisenhower to undertake the liberation of Paris and to allow French troops to do the job. In the background were Allied suspicions of de Gaulle's motives and personal political ambitions. In the end the local Resistance, mainly Communist, took matters into their own hands by starting an insurrection and Eisenhower was forced to intervene. Leclerc's division was moved sideways across the American front and permitted to race for the capital, which it entered to tumultous scenes of welcome.

On 19 August the Falaise pocket seemed closed after the junction between the 1st Polish Armoured Division and the 90th US Infantr Division at Chambois. In fact the battle of the pocket was just starting as the Germans desperately tried to keep a passage open for units still attempting to escape. Dominating the valley of the Dives was the 262-metre-high ridge of Mount Ormel, renamed Maczuga (iron club or mace) by the Poles, on which the Poles, anxious to avenge their defeat in 1940, joined battle with the Germans who were desperate to dislodge them from the high ground which stood betwen them and safety. On 21 August at midnight, after two days of fighting on their own, the Poles and the Canadians succeeded in ending the enemy escape.

In the Dives valley around Chambois, the retreating German forces were subjected to continuous artillery and air bombardment by the Allies. The area was nicknamed the Death Corridor. In four days 10,000 Germans were killed and 40,000 taken prisoner.

CHAMBOIS

OMMÉEL

August 1944. Polish officers studying a map.

On the south west side of Mount Ormel, retreating enemy units attacked the Poles as they attempted here and there to evade the blockade. Bitter fighintg, often hand to hand, ensued.

August 1944. Sergeant McVay from Whitby (2nd left) chatting with Polish comrades.

Coming from Vimoutiers to the east, SS armoured units attempted to take the Poles from the rear in the hope of driving them off Mount Ormel.

On the evening of 20 August on Mount Ormel, only four Polish officers out of 60 and 110 men out of 1,500 were still fit to fight.

COUDEHARD

MONT ORMEL

Memorial tank on Mount Ormel.

RESISTANCE MONUMENT (Argentan) Eisenhower regarded the efforts of the Resistance as equivalent to that of 15 divisions. The first Resistance groups appeared in Normandy in July 1940. Apart from certain well-known actions ● *40*, it is well to remember that it was the Normandy Resistance which supplied the Allies with the plans of the Atlantic Wall ● *72, 74* ▲ *144* from Cherbourg to Honfleur, hid Allied aircrews who had parachuted into the area after being shot down, and saved numerous parachutists who had fallen into the marshes around Carentan ▲ *180* and Sainte-Mère-Église ▲ *184* on 6 June.

Also worth seeing…
LE HARAS DU PIN ♥

THE KEEP OF THE CASTLE AT CHAMBOIS ♥

THE TANK "MACZUGA" (on Mont Ormel).

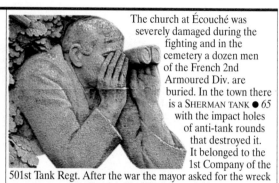

The church at Écouché was severely damaged during the fighting and in the cemetery a dozen men of the French 2nd Armoured Div. are buried. In the town there is a SHERMAN TANK ● *65* with the impact holes of anti-tank rounds that destroyed it. It belonged to the 1st Company of the 501st Tank Regt. After the war the mayor asked for the wreck as a permanent memorial. The War Memorial honours the memory of forty-four civilians killed in the bombing on 6 June and a further dozen killed in another raid on 20 August.

ARGENTAN. *(Take the D29 to Montgaroult and after the village turn onto the D15 to Argentan.)* On your right, the village cemetery contain the graves of the pilot and navigator of an RAF aircraft shot down on 5 July 1944. Argentan was held by the Germans until 20 August on account of the fact that XV Corps commanded by General Haislip ▲ *237*, had been ordered to stop its advance.

LE-BOURG-SAINT-LÉONARD. *(Take the N26.)* The village was the scene of vicious combats between retreating Germans and the 90th Division advancing from the south. The crossroads in the centre changed hands four times in two days.

EXMES. *(Continue on the N26 as far as Haras du Pin and then take the D304 and D14 towards Exmes.)* As the road climbs there is a fantastic view to the left over the whole of the battlefield of the pocket. You can see the keep of the castle at Chambois

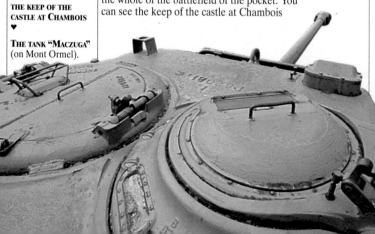

"HOWEVER, WHILE WE WERE WAITING IMPATIENTLY AT AVRANCHES FOR MONTY TO ARRIVE, THE ENEMY REOPENED THE BREACH."

OMAR BRADLEY

and the winding valley of the Dives which was the last escape route.

CHAMBOIS. *(To reach the town follow the D14 and then the D305 and D13.)* At Omeel in the heart of the Normandy horse-breeding country, the 2nd French Armoured Div. (Langlade Battle Group) took up their positions on 18 August from which they could rain down shells on the retreating Germans in support of the Poles fighting on Mont Ormel to the north. Imagine the noise of the battle and the swooping fighter-bombers ● 56, the whole scene (today very peaceful) on the plain below covered in smoke and the flames of burning tanks and ruined villages. In Chambois near the ruined keep of the mediaeval castle is a monument recording the historic meeting between Captain Waters of the 359th

Left, 90th Infantry Div. insignia. Below, US BC 341 traffic receiver ● 69. Below centre, US medical orderlies evacuating enemy wounded from an armoured ambulance of the 116th Pzd at Chambois on 21 August.

Infantry Regiment and Colonel Zgorzelsi, 10th Polish Dragoons, at 19.20 hours on 19 August. Waters was part of the 90th division that had fought its way northwards from Bourg-Saint-Léonard, taking 5,000 prisoners in the process.

MONT ORMEL. *(The D16.)* ▲ 242 As you leave Chambois you see ahead of you the long low ridge of Mont Ormel which was held by the Poles. As you start to climb up the ridge you are travelling the same direction as a German column that was wiped out by the Polish artillery at dawn on the 18th, but also where the Germans established their mortars to fire back into the Polish redoubt. On your left is the Mont-Ormel Monument together with a new

EISENHOWER ● *30, 104,* filming the battlefield with his camera. "Forty-eight hours after the closing of the gap I was conducted through it on foot, to encounter scenes that could only be described by Dante. It was literally possible to walk for hundreds of yards at a time, stepping on nothing but dead and decaying flesh."

TIGER TANK ● 62
On leaving Vimoutiers on the D979 and climbing up towards Gacé, one can see on the left beside the road a Tiger of the 2nd SS Panzerdivision.

Also worth seeing...
THE CAMEMBERT MUSEUM AT VIMOUTIERS

L'Aigle today.

GERMAN SOLDIER
Hitler's men fought to the bitter end with fanatic al courage.

museum devoted to the closing phase of the Battle of Normandy. From the terrace there is a view over the whole of the escape corridor, which explains why the Germans were so keen to eliminate the Poles from the ridge and the main road to Vimoutiers. (*Reach Vimoutiers via the D16 and the D26.*)

VIMOUTIERS

A TERRIBLE BATTLE. Continue towards Vimoutiers, driving parallel to the final escape route and crossing the line of attack mounted against the Polish redoubt from the north by the remnants of the 2nd SS Panzerkorps. Among the ordinary German soldiers there had been muttering that the SS were running away, but General Bittrich, who had extracted his corps on 17 August, had orders to hit the Poles from the north and keep the corridor open. All those who fought there at the time remember the terrible stench of death that hung over the area for weeks afterwards, as the ground was littered with the rotting bodies of men and horses. For four months the remaining villagers had to have clean water brought in by cart from outside.

THE MARTYRDOM OF A TOWN. Vimoutiers itself has been well reconstructed after those terrible events when the once proud crack divisions of Hitler's Army and SS struggled through its narrow streets, defeated and demoralized, constantly harried by Allied artillery and fighter-bombers.

L'AIGLE. (*Leave Vimoutiers via the D579 and at the Croix-Rouge crossroads take the D12.*) The Musée Juin-1944 displays a dozen historic scenes, from de Gaulle's broadcast on 18 June 1940 to the German retreat after the closing of the Falaise Pocket. The capture of the town on 22 August opened the way to the Seine for the Allied forces.

The Final Phase
Le Dénouement
The Closure of
the Falaise Pocket

Anthony Kemp

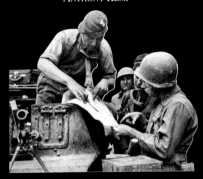

▲ THE FINAL PHASE
CAEN TO L'AIGLE

1 CAEN 2 SOLIERS 3 BOURGUÉBUS 4 CINTHEAUX CANADIAN CEMETERY 5 GRAINVILLE-LANGANNERIE POLISH CEMETERY 6 FALAISE 7 TRUN 8 CHAMBOIS 9 VIMOUTIERS 10 L'AIGLE

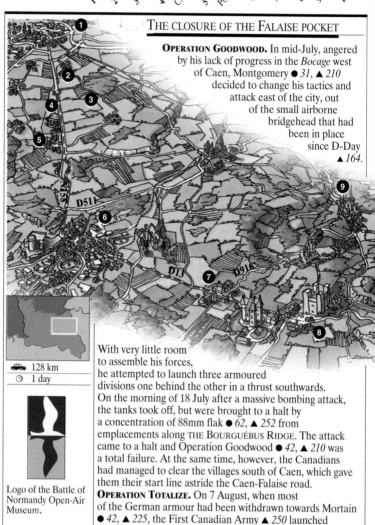

THE CLOSURE OF THE FALAISE POCKET

OPERATION GOODWOOD. In mid-July, angered by his lack of progress in the *Bocage* west of Caen, Montgomery ● *31*, ▲ *210* decided to change his tactics and attack east of the city, out of the small airborne bridgehead that had been in place since D-Day ▲ *164*.

🚗 128 km
🕐 1 day

Logo of the Battle of Normandy Open-Air Museum.

With very little room to assemble his forces, he attempted to launch three armoured divisions one behind the other in a thrust southwards. On the morning of 18 July after a massive bombing attack, the tanks took off, but were brought to a halt by a concentration of 88mm flak ● *62*, ▲ *252* from emplacements along THE BOURGUÉBUS RIDGE. The attack came to a halt and Operation Goodwood ● *42*, ▲ *210* was a total failure. At the same time, however, the Canadians had managed to clear the villages south of Caen, which gave them their start line astride the Caen-Falaise road.

OPERATION TOTALIZE. On 7 August, when most of the German armour had been withdrawn towards Mortain ● *42*, ▲ *225*, the First Canadian Army ▲ *250* launched Operation Totalize. After several thousand bombs had been dropped across the German defences, the Canadians set off at around midnight, their way lit by the beams of searchlights directed at the clouds. A further innovation was that many of the infantry were transported in Kangaroo armoured personnel carriers, which were older tanks with the turrets removed. Although rapid initial progress was made, Kurt Meyer ▲ *204* rallied the remnants of his 12th SS Panzerdivision ● *33*, ▲ *211*, and, using Tiger tanks ● *62*, ▲ *253*, managed to bring the advance to a halt halfway to Falaise.

OPERATION TRACTABLE. This started on 14 August with the 4th Canadian and

CAEN
2nd Can. I.D.
51st I.D.
Operation Totalize and Tractable
British Army
1st Pol. A.D.
4th Can. A.D.
Vimoutiers
13 Aug.
Falaise
15 Aug.
German Army
16 Aug.
US Army
13 Aug.

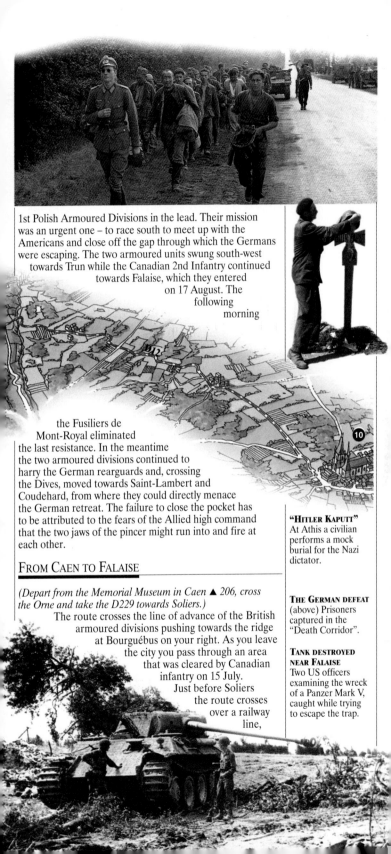

1st Polish Armoured Divisions in the lead. Their mission was an urgent one – to race south to meet up with the Americans and close off the gap through which the Germans were escaping. The two armoured units swung south-west towards Trun while the Canadian 2nd Infantry continued towards Falaise, which they entered on 17 August. The following morning the Fusiliers de Mont-Royal eliminated the last resistance. In the meantime the two armoured divisions continued to harry the German rearguards and, crossing the Dives, moved towards Saint-Lambert and Coudehard, from where they could directly menace the German retreat. The failure to close the pocket has to be attributed to the fears of the Allied high command that the two jaws of the pincer might run into and fire at each other.

FROM CAEN TO FALAISE

(Depart from the Memorial Museum in Caen ▲ 206, cross the Orne and take the D229 towards Soliers.)
The route crosses the line of advance of the British armoured divisions pushing towards the ridge at Bourguébus on your right. As you leave the city you pass through an area that was cleared by Canadian infantry on 15 July.
Just before Soliers the route crosses over a railway line,

"Hitler Kaputt"
At Athis a civilian performs a mock burial for the Nazi dictator.

The German defeat
(above) Prisoners captured in the "Death Corridor".

Tank destroyed near Falaise
Two US officers examining the wreck of a Panzer Mark V, caught while trying to escape the trap.

POLAND Brave fighters who had fought with the French during the First World War, the Canadians played an active part in the liberation in 1944. On D-Day a Canadian division assaulted Juno Beach and was soon built up into an army corps commanded by General Simmonds, keen to avenge the defeat at Dieppe. Another supporting unit later in the battle was the 1st Polish Armoured Division, feared by the Germans for their ferocity and audaciousness, of which they provided ample proof, notably in the battle on Mont Ormel.

THE 1ST POLISH ARMOURED DIVISION Its insignia bore the colours of all the component units.

MAJOR-GENERAL STANISLAW MACZEK Commander of the 1st Polish Armoured Division in the turret of his command tank.

Under the command of Major-General Maczek the first elements of the Polish Armoured Division landed at Arromanches and Courseulles on 30 July. Although they lacked combat experience, the men of the division received a rapid baptism of fire in Operation Totalize ● *42*, ▲ *248* as part of the First Canadian Army. The Poles doggedly fought their way down the Caen to Falaise road and then seized the height of Mont Ormel ▲ *242* which overlooked the German line of retreat towards Vimoutiers.

Polish soldiers.

THE CAPTURE OF CAEN

The Canadians were to hold the front around Caen. In late July the First Canadian Army commanded by General Crerar was formed. This helped the advance from Caen to Falaise which formed an arm of the pincer trapping the Germans.

THE CAPTURE OF CARPIQUET ▲ 245

The Canadians took part in the general offensive on 9 July, succeeding in dislodging the 12th SS Hitlerjugend Division from their positions around Carpiquet airfield, which enabled them to enter Caen from the west.

TOTALIZE ▲ 248

At the beginning of August the First Canadian Army, which included the Polish division, formed up to the south of Caen and launched a major attack down the main road towards Falaise. To avoid excessive cratering, the RAF dropped tons of fragmentation bombs on the German positions, to little avail. The Canadian advance was constantly slowed by successful German rearguard actions.

THE CANADIAN PRESS NEWS
PUBLISHED WEEKLY FOR THE CANADIAN FORCES OVERSEAS

CARPIQUET TAKEN

Veterans To Have Council

SWANSEA GETS SECOND

THE PRINCESS IRENE BRIGADE

Under the command of Lieutenant-Colonel de Ruyter van Steveninck, the Dutch brigade, which was formed in England in 1941, landed in Normandy shortly before the end of the campaign. Originally in the line to the east of Caen, it was attached to the Canadian Army for the advance to Falaise.

**RAF MOSQUITO
B IV ● 57**

Insignia of the
1st Polish Armoured
Division.

CANADIAN CEMETERY
Situated at Cintheaux
it has 2,959 graves.

POLISH CEMETERY
Situated in
the community
of Grainville-
Langannerie,
it contains 650 graves.

which
proved to
be a difficult
obstacle for
the leading
tanks of 11th
Armoured Division,
commanded by
General "Pip" Roberts.
To your left you can see
the steel-works at
Colombelles, on the towers of which the
Germans had an observation post, permitting
the surveillance of the entire battlefield of Goodwood ▲ 210,
as well as the control of all the operations on it. The Germans
had dug in their anti-tank guns in the villages below the ridge
which was held by elements of the 1st SS Panzerdivision,
the "Leibstandarte" and the 21st Panzer.

SOLIERS. Early on the morning of 18 July, 720 guns opened
up on Soliers and the surrounding villages, followed by
saturation bombing from 4,500 aircraft – the greatest aerial
bombardment ever carried out. Twelve 12-ton Tiger tanks
were upturned or buried and many German infantrymen
simply went mad. Yet enough guns survived to blunt the
advance by the 11th British Armoured Division and the
Guards who were behind them. That first day the British
lost 190 tanks, many to a well placed 88mm battery ▲ 196 in
CAGNY to the west of Soliers. Soliers itself, or what was left
of it, was captured when the attack was
renewed the following day, but on the
20th, Operation Goodwood was called
off, the hoped-for breakthrough towards
Falaise having failed.

BOURGUÉBUS RIDGE. *(Take the D230 up
to the village, then the D89 until you reach
the D229 up to the D41.)* The route
climbs up onto the ridge from where one
can have an excellent view of the whole
battlefield to the north. In fact, the British
armour failed to reach the ridge during
Operation Goodwood and had to settle
down in the villages below. In such
a position, the British armour was
subjected to a constant hail
of mortars as well as rockets from
the commanding heights.

CANADIAN CEMETERY AT CINTHEAUX*.
*(Follow the D41 to the N158 towards
Caen.)* The route crosses the
area fought over by
the Canadians in Operation
Spring which ran from 24 to 31 July, the aim being to clear
the villages south of Caen on either side of the main road,
to prepare a start line for a further advance towards
Falaise. In vicious and often hand-to-hand fighting with
the SS, the Canadians made little progress. *(A turning to
the right off the main road at La Jalousie leads to the
Canadian cemetery just before Cintheaux.)* It was in that area
on the night of 8 August that Michael Wittmann ▲ 211,

Insignia from left to right.
11th British Armoured
Division and the Guards
Armoured Division.

the German tank ace, was killed. He was credited with 138 "kills" during his short career.

POLISH CEMETERY AT URVILLE.
(Where the D43 crosses the N158.)
The route continues south to the large Polish cemetery on the right, just before Grainville-Langannerie.The stretch of road down which you have been driving was the route taken by the 4th Canadian Armoured Division which reached Grainville on 13 August, battling against a brilliant rearguard defence by the remnants of the 12th SS Panzer. It was from the positions on either side of the road that Operation Tractable was launched on 14 August. The Poles buried in this cemetery were all from the 1st Polish Armoured Division ▲ *211,* which had recently arrived in Normandy and had been assigned to serve with the Canadian Army.

FALAISE ♥. *(Remain on the N158 southwards.)* Falaise was the birthplace of William the Conqueror. Most of the buildings in the actual town, however, are relatively new as the old town was flattened by bombs and artillery. The Royal Air Force dropped a massive carpet of bombs on Potigny on the afternoon of 14 August. A considerable number of the inhabitants of the village were of Polish origin and they were particularly touched to be liberated by Polish troops on 15 August. The Canadian infantry fought their way down the road to enter the smoking ruins of Falaise on 17 August, while the armoured units on their left were struggling towards Trun. The final resistance in Falaise was by a fanatical group of fifty young grenadiers from the 12th SS who were holed up in the Girls' High School. In Falaise, there is a memorial and also a museum devoted to the history of August 1944 and it includes a display of several armoured vehicles.

SAINT-GERVAIS CHURCH
Today, after restoration, and in March 1945 when still in ruins.

Also worth seeing ...
FALAISE
The castle (11th to 14th cent.) of William the Conqueror
▲ *154, 197.*

GERMAN TIGER TANK
● *62,* ▲ *211*
The most powerful built during the war. Although not numerous in Normandy, Tiger units caused severe damage to Allied armour. Only air power could deal with them.

Thrown into a pointless counter-attack at Mortain, the German forces were unable to avoid the trap which the Allied chiefs of staff had planned for them on 8 August 1944. While the Canadians and General Maczek's Polish Armoured Division drove south towards Falaise, Bradley redirected XV Corps, which was part of Patton's Third US Army, northwards. In spite of spirited German resistance the vice slowly closed. While the Americans took Alençon and took up positions around Argentan, the Canadians, after four days of merciless fighting, entered Falaise on 17 August.

9 AUGUST
As the Canadians moved towards Falaise their route was blocked by the remnants of the 12th SS Panzerdivision. Galvanised by its young commander, Kurt "Panzer" Meyer, the Hitlerjugend division accounted for 60 Allied tanks.

FALAISE   TRUN

12 AUGUST
After having taken Alençon and then Argentan, the American corps moved in the direction of Bourg-Saint-Léonard and the Dives valley at Chambois.

14 AUGUST
Formidable Allied land forces and aircraft were poised to deal the death blow to the Seventh German Army, in headlong retreat.

SAINT-LAMBERT

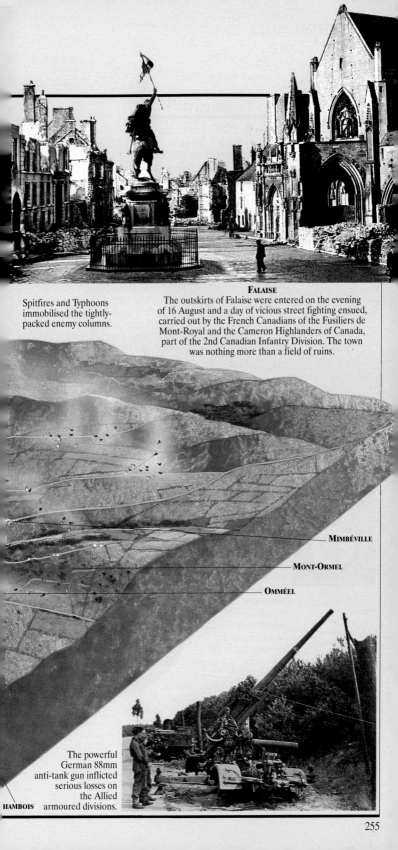

FALAISE

The outskirts of Falaise were entered on the evening of 16 August and a day of vicious street fighting ensued, carried out by the French Canadians of the Fusiliers de Mont-Royal and the Cameron Highlanders of Canada, part of the 2nd Canadian Infantry Division. The town was nothing more than a field of ruins.

Spitfires and Typhoons immobilised the tightly-packed enemy columns.

MIMBÉVILLE

MONT-ORMEL

OMMÉEL

The powerful German 88mm anti-tank gun inflicted serious losses on the Allied armoured divisions.

HAMBOIS

▲ THE FINAL PHASE
CAEN TO L'AIGLE

"THE DEFENCES AROUND TRUN PENETRATED"
A German newspaper issued in Brussels on 22 August exaggerated the important role played by the tanks of the 2nd Panzerdivision in keeping open an escape corridor for the fleeing Germans.

BRÜSSELER ZEITUNG
Der Sperriegel vor Trun gesprengt

Insignia of the 2nd Argyll and Sutherland Highlanders.

Also worth seeing ...
CHAMBOIS
The strange 16th-century château at Aubry-en-Exmes, built onto a 14th-century tower.

THE DEATH CORRIDOR
All around Chambois the Germans fled, abandoning weapons and vehicles under constant bombardment from aircraft and artillery. The bodies of animals and men added a note of horror to the chaos.

FROM FALAISE TO THE DIVES

(Follow the D63 to Trun and then the D13 towards Chambois.)
The route heads to the bridge on the Dives River through which the Germans escaped between 18 and 22 August. On the left the Polish 1st A.D. and 4th Canadian A.D. were on top of the Monts d'Éraines, sloping down to the Dives. The sky, full of Typhoons ● *57*, ▲ *226* and Spitfires ● *57* swooping down on the fleeing enemy, was blackened with smoke.

TRUN. The Canadian 4th Armoured columns reached Trun on 17 August, hot on the heels of the SS, while to their right British infantry were pushing the Germans into the net. A Polish column established itself on Mont Ormel ▲ *242*, right in their last line of retreat.

SAINT-LAMBERT-SUR-DIVES. Without the bridges at Trun, the Germans had to get to Saint-Lambert-sur-Dives. At the entrance to the village is a PLAQUE to Major Currie who won the Victoria Cross there.

CURRIE'S ATTEMPT TO CLOSE THE POCKET. On 18 August he led a battle group from the 4th Canadian A.D., consisting of 15 tanks and 130 men of the Argyll and Sutherland Highlanders of Canada, to close the Saint-Lambert bridges and to rejoin the Americans at Chambois. Entering the village the lead tank was destroyed and he withdrew onto the hill overlooking Saint-Lambert for the night. The following morning, Allied artillery opened fire on the village. Currie's men fought their way back into Saint-Lambert, but lost several more tanks and again had to withdraw. The following day, they beat off assaults from frantic German infantry until relieved.

A GERMAN GENERAL DIRECTED THE TRAFFIC. *(In the village, turn down the small lane on the right leading to the church and stop on the bridge over the Dives.)*
In the church tower, General von Luttwitz, commander of the 2nd Panzerdivision, directed the traffic. The stream was filled with bodies and abandoned equipment. Canadian tanks tried without success to close the last gap. Bodies piled up in the streets. At 22.30, the Canadians, having fought a way through, were again repelled.

CHAMBOIS. The Poles and the Americans finally met up to seal the Falaise-Chambois pocket on 19 August.
(The remainder of this itinerary from Chambois to L'Aigle is covered in the previous itinerary ▲ 245.)

PRACTICAL INFORMATION

Under a single command at the beginning of the Battle of Normandy, the Allied Units were regrouped from 12 August on into two armies, American and British.

BRITISH TWENTY-FIRST ARMY GROUP

Commanded by General Montgomery, it regrouped the Second British Army of General Dempsey and the First Canadian Army of General Crerar to which was attached the 1st Polish Armoured Division, corresponding in all to about 1,600,000 men before the formation of the Twelfth American Army Group.

THE BRITISH UNITS

ARMY CORPS : Corps H.Q. and its staff services (intelligence, signals, logistics, two defence companies, one reconnaissance regiment), making 50,000 men and 2,800 officers.

INFANTRY DIVISION
17,500 men including 780 officers and 1,600 vehicles, HQ of division (20 officers and 124 men), intelligence section, defence section, 3 infantry brigades of 3 battalions.

Infantry Brigade
120 officers and 2,850 men, GHQ (9 officers and 57 men), 3 battalions of 4 companies, 1 HQ company, 1 anti-tank battery , 1 signals company, 1 engineers company, 1 battalion of A.A.

Infantry Battalion
753 men and 33 officers, HQ of 60 men, 1 HQ company of 260 men, companies Able, Baker, Charlie, Dog of 5 officers and 119 men each.

Infantry Company
3 sections of 36 men and officers.

Infantry Section
36 men.

Service Division
Sections : administrations, signals, medical, engineers, anti-tanks and mortars. 90 transport vehicles.

ARMOURED DIVISION
13,943 men, 732 officers and 201 tanks.

Armoured Car Regiment
Composed of 67 Scout cars and 67 Brencarriers.

Armoured Reconnaissance Regiment
equipped with 76 tanks, 11 special tanks and 8 Scout cars.

Armoured Brigade
3 regiments and brigade HQ of 15 tanks and 3 armoured regiments of 72 tanks.

Motorised Infantry Battalion
Equipped with 80 half-tracks and Bren Carriers and composed of an infantry brigade of 3 regiments.

Independant Support Company
Equipped with heavy machine-guns and mortars.

Royal Artillery
2 Motorised Royal Artillery Field Regiments with 24 guns each, 1 A.A. of 54 guns, 1 anti-tank regiment of 48 17 pdr. guns.

AIRBORNE DIVISION
12,879 men including 780 officers.

Airborne Troops
2 brigades each composed of 3 battalions of 620 men.

Gliders
2 brigades each composed of 3 battalions of 650 men and 60 aircraft per brigade. The airborne divisional services, heavy weapons included Tetrarch tanks, of 6 tons, jeeps and anti-tank guns, trailers ....

Even after the formation of the two groups of Allied armies,
the British General Montgomery kept
the command of the troops
engaged in Battle for the liberation of France,
until the crossing of the Seine.

TWELFTH U.S ARMY GROUP
Formed on 12 August 1944, it was commanded by General Bradley.
It included the First Army commanded by General Hodges, and
the Third Army of Gen. Patton to which was linked the 2nd Armoured Division
of General Leclerc.

THE AMERICAN UNITS

STAFF : General Headquarter (HQ) 800 men and officers.
ARMY CORPS : HQ : 200 men and officers.
TROOPS : about 50,000 men.

INFANTRY DIVISION
(14,253 men) :
HQ (158 men),
3 infantry regiments
(9,354 men in all).

Infantry Regiment
1 HQ company,
1 maintenance company,
1 howitzer company,
1 anti-tank company,
3 infantry battalions.

Infantry Battalion
(871 men) :
1 HQ company, 1 heavy-
weapon company,
3 infantry companies.

Artillery Division
(2,160 men) :
1 battalion of "Mediums"
with 3 batteries
of 4 155-mm guns,
3 field with 3 batteries
of 4105 mm.

Service Division
(1,963 men) :
engineers, medical,
signals, reconnaissance,
ordnance, transport,
MP, band.

Other units
1 Regimental
Combat Team
(RCT: tank battalion and
infantry regiment),
1 chemical battalion,
1 motorised cavalry
squadron,
1 tank-destroyer battalion,
1 anti-aircraft battalion
(June).

ARMOURED DIVISION
(10,937 men) :
HQ (164 men) and
HQ company (138 men).

Infantry Battalions
3 battalions
of 1,000
men.

Armoured Battalions
3 battalions
of 729
men.

Cavalry
1 armoured squadron
of 935 men.

Signals
1 company
of 302 men.

Engineers
1 battalion
of 693 men.

Artillery
3 battalions (1,623 men).

Maintenance
1,373 men.

Equipment
501 half-tracks,
2,653 different vehicles,
186 medium Sherman
M4 A1
and A3 tanks,
77 light Stuart tanks,
54 motorised 105-mm
Priest guns,
455 M G cal. 50,
404 cal. 50,
2,803 PM cal. 45,
5,285 US M1 carbines,
2,063 M1 rifles.

AIRBORNE DIVISION
12,879 men
including 780 officers.

Airborne Regiment
1,800 men grouped into
3 battalions of airborne
soldiers, 1 company
of heavy weapons
and airborne regiment
services.

Airborne Battalion
550 parachutists
with collective weapons,
explosive material,
ammunitions
and medical material
per parachuted
package.

Armaments
4,961 autom. carbines
US M1, 6,169 semi-auto
M1 rifles, 300 FM B.A.R.,
763 Colt 45 pistols,
383 cal.-45 PM Thompson,
290 cal.-30 machine-guns,
150 cal.-50 machine-guns,
567 bazookas,
50 57-mm anti-tank guns,
81 60-mm mortars,
42 mortars 81 mm,
75 75-mm howitzers.

(14) Calvados (50) Manche (61) Orne : the asterisk indicates a site not included in the itineraries.

BATTLE OF NORMANDY CEMETERIES				
Site	Page	Graves	Situation	Access
AMERICAN				
Colleville/Saint-Laurent (14)	166	9 387	*From Arromanches to Grandcamp*	D 114
Saint-James (Montjoie-Saint-Martin) (50)	227	4 410	*From Avranches to Fougères*	D 230
BRITISH				
Banneville-Sannerville (14)	195	2 175	*From Caen to Troarn*	N 175
Bayeux (14)	158	4 142	*Bayeux-Ouest*	D 96
Brouay (14)	195	377	*From Caen to Bayeux*	D 94-D 217
Cambes-en-Plaine (14)	195	224	*From Caen to Courseulles*	D 79
Chouain (14)	195	40	*From Bayeux to Tilly-sur-Seulles*	D 187
Douvres-la-Délivrande (14)	134	1123	*From Caen to Luc-sur-Mer*	D 7
Fontenay-le-Pesnel (14)	211	520	*From Caen to Caumont-l'Éventé*	D 173a-D 139
Hermanville-sur-Mer (14)	132	986	*From Douvres-la-D. to Ouistreham*	D 35 et D 60b
Hottot-Longraye (14)	211	965	*From Caen to Caumont-l'Éventé*	D 9
Ranville (14)	127	2 151	*Near Pegasus Bridge (Colleville)*	D 224
Ryes (14)	143	979	*From Bayeux to Arromanches*	D 87
Saint-Manvieu/Norrey (14)	210	2 186	*From Caen to Caumont-l'Éventé*	D 9
Secqueville-en-Bessin (14)	195	117	*From Caen to Bayeux*	D 126
Tilly-sur-Seulles (14)	211	1 224	*From Caen to Balleroy*	D 13
Saint-Charles-de-Percy (14)	212	792	*Near Bény-Bocage*	D 290
Saint-Désir-de-Lisieux (14)	*	598	*West of Lisieux*	N 13-D 159
CANADIAN				
Bény-sur-Mer (14)	137	2 048	*Near Courseulles*	D 35
Cintheaux/Bretteville-s.-L. (14)	252	2 959	*From Caen to Falaise*	N 158 -D 23
FRENCH				
Radon-Le Gatey (61)	240		*North of Alençon*	D 26
POLISH				
Grainville-Langannerie (14)	252	650	*From Caen to Falaise*	N 158-D 131
GERMAN				
La Cambe (14)	174	21 400	*From Bayeux to Isigny*	N 13
Saint-Désir-de-Lisieux (14)	*	3 735	*West of Lisieux*	N 13-D 159
La Chapelle-en-Juger (50)	219	11 169	*From Saint-Lô to Coutances*	D 341
Orglandes (50)	217	10 152	*South of Valognes*	D 330
Huisnes-sur-Mer (50)	227	11 956	*East of Le Mont-Saint-Michel*	D 275

BATTLE OF NORMANDY MUSEUMS			
County	Museum	Page	Telephone
Alençon (61)	Musée Leclerc	240	02 33 26 27 26
Arromanches (14)	Musée du Débarquement	142	02 31 22 34 31
Arromanches (14)	Arromanches 360°	139	02 31 22 30 30
Avranches (50)	Musée de la Seconde Guerre mondiale	227	02 33 68 35 83
Bayeux (14)	Mémorial de la bataille de Normandie	158	02 31 92 93 41
Bayeux (14)	Musée mémorial du Général de Gaulle	162	02 31 92 45 55
Caen (14)	Le Mémorial. Un musée pour la Paix	206	02 31 06 06 44
Cherbourg (50)	Musée de la Libération	194	02 33 20 14 12
Commes (Port-en-Bessin) (14)	Musée des Épaves du Débarquement	152	02 31 21 17 06
Coudehard-Montormel (61)	Mémorial de Montormel	245	02 33 67 38 61
Douvres-la-Délivrande (14)	Musée du Radar	133	02 31 06 06 45
Falaise (14)	Musée Août-1944	253	02 31 90 37 19
Grandcamp-Maisy (14)	Musée des Rangers	174	02 31 92 33 51
L'Aigle (61)	Musée «Juin-1944»	246	02 33 24 19 44
Merville-Franceville (14)	Musée de la Batterie de Merville	124	02 31 24 21 83
Ouistreham (14)	Musée du Mur de l'Atlantique	130	02 31 97 28 69
Ouistreham (14)	Musée n°4 Commando	131	02 31 96 63 10
Quinéville (50)	Musée de la Liberté	189	02 33 21 52 20
Saint-Laurent-sur-Mer (14)	Musée Omaha 6 Juin 44	169	02 31 21 97 44
St-Martin-des-Besaces (14)	Musée de la Percée du Bocage	212	02 31 67 52 78
Sainte-Marie-du-Mont (50)	Musée du Débarquement (Utah Beach)	187	02 33 71 53 35
Sainte-Mère-Église (50)	Musée des Troupes aéroportées	185	02 33 41 41 35
Tilly-sur-Seulles (14)	Musée de la Bataille de Tilly	211	02 31 80 80 26
Ver-sur-Mer (14)	Musée America-Gold Beach	139	02 31 22 58 58

MAJOR AND SECONDARY SITES OF THE BATTLE OF NORMANDY[1]

Site	Page	Situation	Site	Page	Situation
MAJOR SITES					
ARROMANCHES, TABLE D'ORIENTATION (14)	141	Port-en-Bessin/Courseulles	MORTAIN, SITE DE LA CÔTE 314 (50)	227	Vire/Fougères
CRISBECQ, SITE DE LA BATTERIE (50)	188	West of Quinéville	POINTE DU HOC (14)	172	Grandcamp
LONGUES-SUR-MER, SITE DE LA BATTERIE (14)	143	West of Arromanches	SAINT-MARTIN-DE-VARREVILLE (50)	188	Utah Beach/Quinéville
			SAINT-LÔ (50)	176	
			UTAH BEACH (50)	187	North of Carentan
SECONDARY SITES					
Amfreville (14)	125	North-East Caen	Lébisey (14)	198	Caen-North
Argentan (61)	244	Falaise/Alençon	Lengronne (50)	222	Hambye/ Cérences
Aunay-sur-Odon (14)	212	Villers-B./Thury-H.	Lion-sur-Mer (14)	133	Ouistreham
Avranches (50)	227	Estuaire Sée	Marigny (50)	222	Coutances/St-Lô
Azeville (50)	189	Ste-Mère-Église/Montebourg	Méautis (50)	180	Carentan/Périers
Bénouville	127	Caen/Ouistreham	Le Mesnil-Tôve (50)	234	North Juvigny-le-T.
Bény-Bocage (14)	212	Vire/Villers-Bocage	Mont-Castre (50)	218	La Haye-du-Puits/Carentan
Bernières-sur-Mer (14)	135	St-Aubin/Ver-s/Mer	Montpinçon (14)	212	Thury-Harcourt/Aunay-sur-Odon
Bourg-Saint-Léonard (Le) (61)	244	Argentan/Nonant-le-Pin	Montebourg (50)	189	Valognes/Sainte-Mère-Église
Bourguébus (14)	252	South-East Caen	Néhou (50)	217	Saint-Sauveur-le-Vicomte
Bretteville-l'Orgueilleuse (14)	210	Bayeux/Caen	Le Neufbourg (50)	227	Mortain/Sourdeval
Bréville (14)	125	North-East Caen	Périers (50)	219	Lessay/Carentan
Briouze (61)	234	Flers/Argentan	Plessis-Lastelle (50)	219	Valognes/Périers
Carentan (50)	180	Isigny/Périers	Pont de Tourmauville (14)	210	Cheux/Évrecy
Carpiquet (14)	204	West Caen	Pont du Taureau (14)	212	North of Vire
Carrefour des Closeaux (50)	227	Saint-Hilaire-du-Harcouët/Mortain	Pontaubault (50)	227	Estuaire Sélune
Caumont-l'Éventé (14)	212	Caen/Torigni-sur-Vire	Port-en-Bessin (14)	152	Omaha Beach/Arromanches
Chambois (61)	245	Trun/Le Bourg-Saint-Léonard	Ranville (14)	127	South-east of Caen
Chérencé-le-Roussel (50)	234	Brécey/Sourdeval	Roncey (50)	222	Coutances/Hambye
Cheux (14)	210	Bretteville-l'Orgueilleuse/Villers-Bocage	Rouvres	*	Caen/Falaise
Colleville-Montgomery (14)	132	West Ouistreham	Saint-Aubin-sur-Mer (14)	134	Bernières-sur-Mer/Langrune
Colleville-sur-Mer (14)	166	Vierville/Port-en-Bessin	Saint-Barthélemy (50)	234	Sourdeval /Mortain
Cote 112 (14)	210	South Évrecy	Saint-Clair-sur-l'Elle (50)	176	Isigny/Saint-Lô
Courseulles-sur-Mer (14)	135	Arromanches/Bernières-sur-Mer	Saint-Côme-du-Mont (50)	181	Carentan/Sainte-Mère-Église
Coutances (50)	222	West Saint-Lô	Saint-Georges-des-Groseilliers (61)	234	Flers/Condé-sur-Noireau
Crépon	140	South Ver-sur-Mer	Saint-Hilaire-du-Harcouët (50)	227	Avranches/Domfront
Croix de Médavy (61)	240	Argentan/Sées	Saint-Jean-de-Daye (50)	178	Carentan/Saint-Lô
Écouché (61)	241	Argentan/Briouze	Saint-Lambert-sur-Dives (61)	256	Trun/Chambois
Évrecy (14)	211	Aunay-sur-Odon	Saint-Laurent-sur-Mer (14)	168	Le Ruquet/Omaha Beach
Exmes (61)	244	Argentan/Gacé	Saint-Manvieu (14)	210	Caen-West
Falaise	253	Falaise	Soliers (14)	252	Caen-South-East
Flers (61)	234	Condé-sur-Noireau/La Ferté-Macé	Sourdeval (50)	234	Mortain/Vire
Fontenay-le-Pesnel (14)	211	Caen/Caumont-l'Éventé	Tinchebray (61)	234	Sourdeval/Flers
Graye-sur-Mer (14)	136	West Courseulles	Tribehou (50)	179	Carentan/Marigny
Hermanville/Mer (14)	132	West Ouistreham	Trun (61)	256	Falaise/Argentan
Hottot-les-Bagues (14)	211	Caen/Caumont-l'Éventé	Valognes (50)	192	Cherbourg/Sainte-Mère-Église
Isigny-sur-Mer (14)	175	Bayeux/Carentan	Vierville/Mer (14)	170	Omaha Beach
Juvigny-le-Tertre (50)	234	Le Mesnil-Tôve/Saint-Hilaire-du-Harcouët	Villers-Bocage (14)	211	Caen/Saint-Martin-des-Besaces
La Haye-du-Puits (50)	218	Lessay/Saint-Sauveur-le-Vicomte	Vimoutiers (61)	246	Livarot/Gacé
Langrune-sur-Mer	134	St-Aubin-sur-Mer	Vire (14)	212	Villers-B./Mortain

1. Sites of the Battle of Normandy Open-Air Museum marked with the logo

City names are followed by their postcode.
The numbers and letters (eg **D5**)
refer to the map on the front endpaper.

CALVADOS			
BALLEROY	14490	TO 02 33 21 60 61	D5
CHÂTEAU-MUSÉE DE BALLEROY	Open Mar. 15–June 30 & Sep. 1–Oct. 15 : Mon.,Wed.-Sun. 9-12am, 2-6pm		
BAYEUX	14400	TO 02 31 51 28 28	E5
CATHÉDRALE NOTRE-DAME	Open July–Aug. : daily 9am-7pm		▲ 159
MUSÉE BARON-GÉRARD ☎ 02 31 92 14 21	Open June 1–Sep. 15 : daily 9am-7pm ; Sep. 16–May 31 : daily 10-12.30am, 2-6pm		▲ 159
TAPISSERIE DE LA REINE MATHILDE ☎ 02 31 51 25 50	Open daily : May–Aug. : 9am-7pm ; Mar. 15–Apr. 30 & Sep. 1–Oct. 17 : 9am-6.30pm ; Oct.–Mar. 14 : 9.30-12.30am, 2-6pm		▲ 159
BÉNOUVILLE	14970		F5
CHÂTEAU ☎ 02 31 95 53 23	Open July 1–Sep.15 : Mon., Wed.-Sun. 2-6pm		▲ 127
BONNEBOSQ	14340		
MANOIR DU CHAMP-VERSAN ☎ 02 31 65 11 07	Open Easter –June 30 & Sep. : Wed.-Sun. 2.30-6pm ; July–Aug. : Tue.-Sun. 2.30-6pm		
CAEN	14000	TO 02 31 27 14 14	F5
ABBAYE-AUX-DAMES ☎ 02 31 06 98 98	Open daily. Guided tours at 2.30pm and 4pm		▲ 199
ABBAYE-AUX-HOMMES ☎ 02 31 30 42 81	Open daily. Guided tours at 9.30am, 11am, 2.30pm and 4pm		▲ 202
ÉGLISE N.-D. DE LA GLORIETTE	Open daily. Closed 12am-2pm		▲ 203
ÉGLISE SAINT-GEORGES	Closed to public, except during concerts		▲ 200
ÉGLISE SAINT-JULIEN	Open during temporary exhibitions only		▲ 199
ÉGLISE SAINT-PIERRE	Open daily. Closed 12am-2pm		▲ 201
ÉGLISE SAINT-SAUVEUR	Open daily. Closed 12am-2pm		▲ 201
MUSÉE DES BEAUX-ARTS ☎ 02 31 25 28 63	Open Mon., Wed.-Sun. 10am-6pm Closed on public hols		▲ 199
MUSÉE DE LA POSTE ☎ 02 31 50 12 20	Open Sep. 16–June 14 : Tue.-Sat. 1.30-5.30pm ; June 15–Sep. 15 : Tue.-Sat. 10-12am, 2-6pm		▲ 201
CAUMONT-L'ÉVENTÉ	14240	TH 02 31 77 50 29	D6
SOUTERROSCOPE Mine d'ardoise ☎ 02 31 71 15 15	Open July–Aug. : daily 10am-7pm ; May–June & Sep. : Mon.-Fri. 10am-5pm, Sat.-Sun. & public hols 10am-7pm; Oct.–Apr. : Tue.-Fri. 10am-5pm, Sat.-Sun. & public hols 10am-6pm		
CANAPVILLE	14800		
MANOIR DES ÉVÊQUES ☎ 02 31 65 24 75	Open June 15–Aug. 31: Mon., Wed.-Sun. 2-6pm ; Apr. 1–mid-June & Sep.–Oct. : Sat.-Sun. & public hols 2-6pm		
CLÉCY	14570	TO 02 31 22 44 00	
MUSÉE DU CHEMIN DE FER MINIATURE ☎ 02 31 69 07 13	Open July–Aug. : daily 10-12am, 2-6.30pm ; Easter–June & Sep. : daily 10-12am, 2-6pm ; Oct.–Nov. : Sun. 2-7pm ; Mar.–Easter : Sun. 2-5.30; closed Dec.–Feb.		
COLOMBIÈRES	14710		
CHÂTEAU FÉODAL ☎ 02 31 22 51 65	Open July–Aug. : Mon., Wed.-Sun. 2.30-6pm ; Sep. : Sat.-Sun. 2.30-6pm		
CREULLY	14480		
CHÂTEAU FORT ☎ 02 31 80 18 65	Open July–Aug. : Tue.-Fri. 10-12am, 3-6pm Low season : by appointment		▲ 137
CRÈVECŒUR-EN-AUGE	14340	TO 02 31 63 72 43	
CHÂTEAU ET MUSÉE DE L'ARCHITECTURE NORMANDE ☎ 02 31 63 02 45	Open July–Aug. : daily 11am-7pm ; Mar. 27-June 30 & Sep. : Mon., Wed.-Sun. 11am-6pm		
FALAISE	14700	TO 02 31 90 17 26	F7
CHÂTEAU FÉODAL ☎ 02 31 41 61 44	Open Apr.–Sep. : Mon.-Fri. 9.30am-4.30pm, Sat.-Sun. 9.30am-5.30pm; Oct.–Mar. : Mon.-Tue., Thur.-Fri. 9.30am-4.30pm, Sat.-Sun. 9.30am-5.30pm		▲ 253

TELEPHONE NUMBERS :
TH : town hall
TO : tourist office

ÉGLISE SAINT-GERVAIS	*Open daily*	▲ 253
MUSÉE DES AUTOMATES ☎ 02 31 90 02 43	*Open Apr.–Sep. : daily 10-12.30am, 1.30-6pm ; Oct. 1-Jan.14 & Feb.16–Mar. 31 : Sat.-Sun., public and school hols 10-12.30am, 1.30-6pm*	
FONTAINE-HENRY	**14610**	
CHÂTEAU ☎ 02 31 80 00 42	*Open Easter–June 15 & Sep. 16–Nov. 2 : Sat.-Sun. & public hols 2.30-6.30pm ; June16–Sep. 15 : Mon., Wed.-Sun. 2.30-6.30pm*	
HONFLEUR	**14600** TO 02 31 89 23 30	**H4**
MUSÉE EUGÈNE-BOUDIN ☎ 02 31 89 54 00	*Open Mar. 15–Sep. 30 : Mon., Wed.-Sun. 10-12am, 2-6pm ; Oct. 1–Mar. 14 : Mon., Wed.-Fri. 14.30-5pm, Sat.-Sun. 10-12am, 2.30-5pm. Closed Jan. 1– Feb. 14 & public hols*	
JUAYE-MONDAYE	**14250**	
ABBAYE DE MONDAYE ☎ 02 31 92 58 11	*Open June–Sep. : guided tours Mon.-Sat. at 11am, 3pm, 4pm, Sun. at 3pm, 4pm, 5.30pm ; Oct.–May : Sun. & public hols at 3pm, 4pm, 5.30pm*	
LION-SUR-MER	**14780** TH 02 31 36 12 00	**F5**
ÉGLISE	*Open daily*	▲ 132
LISIEUX	**14100** TO 02 31 62 35 22	**H6**
BASILIQUE SAINTE-THÉRÈSE ☎ 02 31 48 55 08	*Open May–Oct. : daily 8.30am-8pm ; Nov.–Apr. : daily 9am-6.30pm*	
LONGUES-SUR-MER	**14400** TH 02 31 21 78 22	**E5**
ABBAYE DE SAINTE-MARIE	*Open Thur. 10am-6pm ; other days : by appointment*	
MÉZIDON-CANON	**14270**	
CHÂTEAU DE CANON ☎ 02 31 20 05 07	*Open July–Sep. : Mon., Wed.-Sun. 11am-7pm ; Easter–June : Sat.-Sun. & public hols 2-6pm*	
OUISTREHAM	**14150** TO 02 31 97 18 63	**F5**
ÉGLISE SAINT-SAMSON	*Open daily*	▲ 130
PONTÉCOULANT	**14110**	
MUSÉE DÉPARTEMENTAL ☎ 02 31 69 62 54	*Open Apr. 16–Sep. 30 : Mon., Wed.-Sun. 10-12am, 2.30-7pm ; Nov. 2–15 : Mon., Wed.-Sun. 10-12am, 2.30-4.30pm ; Nov. 16– Apr. 15 : Wed.-Sun. 2.30-16.30pm. Closed Oct.*	
PONT-L'ÉVÊQUE	**14130** TO 02 31 64 12 77	
MUSÉE DU CALVADOS ET DES MÉTIERS ☎ 02 31 64 12 87	*Open July–Aug.: daily 10am-6.30pm ; Apr.–June & Sep.–Oct. : daily 10-12.30am, 2.30-6.30pm*	
SAINT-GERMAYN-DE-LIVET	**14100**	
CHÂTEAU ☎ 02 31 31 00 03	*Guided tours. Open Apr.–Sep. : Mon., Wed.-Sun. 10-12am, 2-7pm ; Oct.15–Nov. 30 & Feb.–Mar. : Mon., Wed.-Sun. 10-12am, 2-5pm*	
SAINT-PIERRE-SUR-DIVES	**14170** TO 02 31 20 97 90	**G6**
ÉGLISE ABBATIALE	*Open daily 9am-6pm. Guided tours June 15– Sep. 15 : Tue. at 5pm, Thur. at 11am*	
THURY-HARCOURT	**14220** TO 02 31 79 70 45	**E6**
CHÂTEAU ☎ 02 31 79 65 41	*Open May–Sep. : daily 2-6.30pm ; Apr. & Oct. : Sun. & public hols 2.30-6.30pm*	
TOUR-EN-BESSIN	**14400**	
CHÂTEAU DE VAULAVILLE ☎ 02 31 92 52 62	*Open July 1–Sep. 15 : Thur.-Tue. 2.30-6.30pm ; May–June & Sep. 15–Oct. 31 : Sat.-Sun. 2.30-6.30pm*	
VENDEUVRE	**14170**	
CHÂTEAU -MUSÉE INTERNATIONAL MOBILIER MINIATURE ☎ 02 31 40 93 83	*Open May–Sep. : daily 10am-6pm ; Mar.–Apr. & Oct. 1–Nov. 11 : Sun. & public hols 2-6pm ; All Saint's Day & Easter' school hols : daily 2-6pm*	

VIRE	14500	TO 02 31 68 00 05	D7
ÉGLISE NOTRE-DAME	Open daily		▲ 212

MANCHE			

AVRANCHES	50300	TO 02 33 58 00 22	B8
MANUSCRITS DU MONT-SAINT-MICHEL ☎ 02 33 68 33 18	Open daily. July–Aug. : 10am-6pm ; June & Sep. : 10-12am, 2-6pm. Guided tours by appointment		
MUSÉE MUNICIPAL ☎ 02 33 58 25 15	Open June–Sep. : daily 9.30-12am, 2-6pm ; Easter–May : Mon., Wed.-Sun. 9.30-12 am, 2-6pm		
TRÉSOR DE LA BASILIQUE ST-GERVAIS ☎ 02 33 89 29 40	Open July–Aug.: daily 9.30-12am, 2-6pm ; Easter–May, June & Sep. : Mon., Wed.-Sat. 9.30-12am, 2-6pm, Sun. 2-6pm		

BRICQUEBEC	50260	TH 02 33 87 22 50	B4
MUSÉE ARCHÉOLOGIQUE ET D'ETHNOLOGIE	Within the castle's walls. Open June 15–Aug. 31 : Mon., Wed.-Sun. 10-12am, 2-6pm		

CARENTAN	50500	TO 02 33 71 23 50	C5
ÉGLISE NOTRE-DAME	Open daily		▲ 180

CERISY-LA-FORÊT	50680		
ABBAYE SAINT-VIGOR ☎ 02 33 56 11 48	Abbey church : open Easter–Nov. 15 : daily 9am–6.30pm ; priest chapel, law room, museum : Easter–Sep. : daily 10.30-12.30am, 2.30-6.30pm ; Oct. 1–Nov. 15 : Sat.-Sun. & public hols 10.30-12am, 2.30-6pm		

CHERBOURG	50100	TH 02 33 87 88 89	C3
MUSÉE D'ETHNOGRAPHIE, D'HISTOIRE NATURELLE ET D'ARCHÉOLOGIE ☎ 02 33 23 02 23	Open Tue.-Sun. 10-12am, 2-6pm		
MUSÉE THOMAS-HENRY ☎ 02 33 23 02 23	Paintings by Millet Open Tue.-Sun. 10-12am, 2-6pm		

COUTANCES	50200	TO 02 33 19 08 10	B6
CATHÉDRALE NOTRE-DAME ☎ 02 33 45 17 79	Open daily 9am-7pm Guided tours by appointment		▲ 222
MUSÉE QUESNEL-MORINIÈRE ☎ 02 33 45 11 92	Open July 1–Sep. 15 : Mon., Wed.-Sun. 10-12am, 2-6pm ; Sep. 16–June 30 : Mon.-Sat. 10-12am, 2-7pm, Sun. 10-12am. Closed on public hols		

CROSVILLE-SUR-DOUVE	50360		
CHÂTEAU ☎ 02 33 41 67 25	Open Easter–Oct. 1 : daily 2-6pm Temporary exhibitions and cultural events		

GRANVILLE	50400	TO 02 33 91 30 03	B7
MUSÉE ANACRÉON ☎ 02 33 51 02 94	Open July–Sep. : Mon., Wed.-Sun. 10-12am, 2-6pm ; Apr. 3–May 2 : Wed., Sat.-Sun. 2-6pm		

GRATOT	50200		
CHÂTEAU ☎ 02 33 45 18 49 /02 31 27 97 40	Open daily		

HAMBYE	50450		C6
ABBAYE ☎ 02 33 61 76 92	Abbey : open Feb. 1–Dec. 15 : daily 10-12am, 2-6pm ; convent buildings : May 1–Oct. 15 : daily 10-12am, 2-6pm		

ÎLE TATIHOU	50550		C3
MUSÉE MARITIME ☎ 02 33 23 19 92	Open Easter–Sep. : daily 10-12.30am, 2-5pm ; Oct.-Apr. : Sat.-Sun. 10-12.30am, 2-5pm		

LA LUCERNE-D'OUTREMER	50200		
ABBAYE DE L'ORDRE DE PRÉMONTRÉ ☎ 02 33 48 83 56	Open Apr.–Déc. : daily 10-12am, 2-6.30pm ; Feb.–Mar. : Mon., Wed.-Sun. 10-12am, 2-5.30pm		

LESSAY	50430		
ABBATIALE SAINTE-TRINITÉ ☎ 02 33 46 46 18	Open daily ; July 15–Aug. 31 : guided tours 10-12am, 2.30-6.30pm		

MARTINVAST	50690	
DOMAINE DE BEAUREPAIRE ☎ 02 33 87 20 80	*Garden : open Apr.–Sep. : daily 8-12am, 2-6pm ; Oct.–Mar. : Mon.-Fri., Sun. 8-12am, 2-6pm Château : open «Journées du Patrimoine»*	
MONT-SAINT-MICHEL	50170	TO 02 33 60 14 30 **B8**
ABBAYE ☎ 02 33 60 14 14	*Open May–Sep. : daily 9.30am-5.30pm ; Oct.– Apr. : daily 9.30am-4.30pm. Closed public hols*	
LOGIS TIPHAINE ☎ 02 33 60 23 34	*Du Guesclin's house. Open daily. June–Sep. : 9am- 7pm ; Oct. 1–Nov. 15 & Feb.–May : 9am-6pm*	
MUSÉE HISTORIQUE ☎ 02 33 60 14 09	*Open daily 9am-6pm (5pm during low season) ; closed Jan.*	
MUSÉE MARITIME ☎ 02 33 60 14 09	*Open daily 9am-6pm (5pm during low season) ; closed Jan.*	
MORTAIN	50140	**D8**
ABBAYE BLANCHE ☎ 02 33 79 47 47	*Open June 15 –Oct. 1 : Mon., Wed.-Sat. 9.30-12am, 2.30-5pm, Sun. 2.30-5pm*	
PIROU	50770	
CHÂTEAU ☎ 02 33 46 34 71	*Open Feb. school hols.–Dec. 31: daily 10-12am, 2-6.30pm (5.30 in winter). Closed Tue. in low season*	
SAINTE-MÈRE-ÉGLISE	50480	TH 02 33 41 31 18 **C4**
ÉGLISE	*Open daily*	
SAINT-LÔ	50000	TO 02 33 77 60 35 **C6**
HARAS NATIONAL ☎ 02 33 55 29 09	*Guided tours. Open June–Sep. : every afternoon Group visits by appointment*	
MUSÉE MUNICIPAL DES BEAUX-ARTS ☎ 02 33 72 52 55	*Open Mon., Wed.-Sun. 10-12am, 2-6pm*	
SAINT-SAUVEUR-LE-VICOMTE	50390	TO 02 33 21 50 44 **B4**
ABBAYE SAINTE-MARIE-MADELEINE ☎ 02 33 21 63 20	*Open daily 10-12am, 2-6pm Group visits by appointment*	
FORTERESSE ☎ 02 33 41 60 28	*Guided tours by appointment with the TO*	
MUSÉE BARBEY-D'AUREVILLY ☎ 02 33 41 65 18	*Open May 15–Sep. 15 : Mon., Wed.-Sun. 10-12am, 3-6pm ; Sep.16–May. 14 : Sat.-Sun. 3-6pm*	
TORIGNI-SUR-VIRE	50160	
CHÂTEAU ☎ 02 33 56 71 44	*Open July–Aug. : daily 2.30-6pm ; June 15–30 & Sep. 1–15 : Sat.-Sun. 2.30-6pm*	
TOURLAVILLE	50110	
CHÂTEAU ☎ 02 33 93 58 02	*Château : guided tours June–Aug. : daily 2-6pm. Garden : free access daily*	
URVILLE-NACQUEVILLE	50700	
CHÂTEAU ☎ 02 33 03 27 89	*Open Easter–Sep. 30 : Mon., Wed.-Thur., Sat.-Sun. guided tours at 2pm, 3pm, 4pm and 5pm*	
VAINS	50300	
MANOIR ☎ 02 33 58 24 46	*On the coastal road between Avranches and Jullouville. Open July 1–Sep. 15 : Mon.-Fri. 3-6pm*	
VALOGNES	50700	TO 02 33 40 11 55 **B4**
HÔTEL DE BEAUMONT ☎ 02 33 40 12 30	*Open July 1–Sep. 15 : Mon., Wed.-Sun. 2.30- 6.30pm, Tue. 10.30-12am ; open Easter week.-end*	▲ 192
HÔTEL DE GRANDVAL-CALIGNY	*Guided tours by appointment with the TO*	▲ 192

ORNE

ALENÇON	61000	TO 02 33 26 11 36 **G9**
ÉGLISE NOTRE-DAME	*Open daily 8.30-12am, 2-5.30pm*	▲ 240
MAISON NATALE DE SAINTE-THÉRÈSE ☎ 02 33 26 09 87	*Open June–Sep. : 9-12am, 2-6pm ; Oct.–May (except Jan.) : Mon., Wed.-Sun. 9.30-12am, 2.30-5pm*	▲ 240
MUSÉE DES BEAUX-ARTS **ET DE LA DENTELLE** ☎ 02 33 26 27 26	*Open July–Aug. : daily 10-12am, 2-6pm ; Sep.–June : Tue.-Sun. 10-12am, 2-6pm*	▲ 240

AUBE	61270	
Musée de la Comtesse de Ségur ☎ 02 33 24 60 09	Open June 12–Sep. 26 : Mon., Wed.-Sun. 2-6pm	
AUBRY-EN-EXMES	61160　　　　　TH 02 33 36 70 53	
Château	Closed to public	▲ 256
BOURG-SAINT-LÉONARD	61310	
Château ☎ 02 33 36 68 68	Open July–Aug. : daily 2-6pm ; May–June & Sep.–Oct. : Sat.-Sun. 2-6pm	
CARROUGES	61320　　　　TO 02 33 27 40 62　F8	
Château ☎ 02 33 27 20 32	Open June 16 –Aug. 31 : daily 9.30-12am, 2-6pm ; Apr. 1–June 15 & Sep. : daily 10-12am, 2-6pm ; Oct.–Mar. : daily 10-12am, 2-4.30pm	▲ 234
CROUTTES	61120	
Prieuré Saint-Michel ☎ 02 33 39 15 15	Open July–Aug. : Mon., Wed.-Sun. 2-7pm ; May–June & Sep. : Sat.-Sun. & public hols 2-6pm	
FLERS	61100　　　　TO 02 33 65 06 75　E7	
Musée du Bocage normand ☎ 02 33 64 66 49	Open Apr. 4 –Oct. 17 : Mon., Wed.-Sun. 10-12am, 2-6pm	▲ 234
GACÉ	61230　　　　TO 02 33 35 50 24　H7	
Musée de la Dame aux camélias	Open June–Aug. : Tue.-Sun. 2-6pm	
L'AIGLE	61360　　　　TO 02 33 24 12 40　I7	
Musée d'Archéologie	Open Mon.-Sat. 9.30-12.30am, 2.30-6.30pm	
LA FERTÉ-MACÉ	61600　　　　TO 02 33 37 10 97　F8	
Musée du Jouet ☎ 02 33 37 04 08	Open July–Aug. : daily 3-6pm ; Apr.–June & Sep.–Oct. : Sat.-Sun. & public hols 3-6pm	
LONLAY-L'ABBAYE	61700	
Abbaye bénédictine ☎ 02 33 38 53 97	Open Apr.–Sep. : daily 8.30am-7pm ; Oct.–Mar. : daily 9am-6pm	
MÉDAVY	61570	
Château ☎ 02 33 35 34 54	Open July 14–Sep. 14 : daily 10-12am, 2-6pm	
MORTRÉE	61570	
Château d'Ô ☎ 02 33 35 34 69	Open July–Aug. : daily 10.30-12am, 2.30-6pm ; Apr.–June & Sep. : Mon., Wed.-Sun. 2.30-6pm ; Oct.–Mar. : Mon., Wed.-Sun. 2.30-5pm	▲ 240
SAINT-CHRISTOPHE-LE-JAJOLET	61570	
Château de Sassy ☎ 02 33 35 36 90	Open Apr. 1–Nov. 1 : daily 3-6pm	▲ 241
SÉES	61500　　　　TO 02 33 28 74 79　G8	
Cathédrale	Open daily. Illuminations Sat.-Sun. & public hols	▲ 241
SOLIGNY-LA-TRAPPE	61380　　　　TH 02 33 34 50 29	
Abbaye Notre-Dame-de-la-Trappe ☎ 02 33 84 17 00	Closed to visitors. Attending the church offices may be possible. Monastic products on sale and exhibition : daily 10-12am, 2.30-6pm	
VILLERS-EN-OUCHE	61550	
Château ☎ 02 33 34 90 30	Open Apr. 4–Sep. 15 : daily 2-6pm	
VIMOUTIERS	61120　　　　TO 02 33 39 30 29　G7	
Musée du Camembert	Open Apr.–Oct. : Mon. 2-6pm, Tue.-Sat. 9-12am, 2-6pm, Sun. & public hols 10-12am, 2-6pm ; Nov.–Mar. : Mon. 2-5.30pm, Tue.-Sat. 10-12am, 2-5.30	▲ 246

ANNEXES

◆ TABLE OF ILLUSTRATIONS

◆ Table of illustrations

◆ Table of illustrations

LA ROUTE DU CIDRE

GENERAL
◆ HISTORY ◆

◆ ARNOLD-FORSTER (M.) :
The World at War.
Collins, 1973.
◆ BRYANT (A.) :
The Turn of the Tide.
Collins, 1959.
◆ HAMILTON (N.) :
*Monty, Master of the
Battle Feild.*
Hamish Hamilton, 1983.
◆ LAMB (R.) :
*Montgomery in Europe,
1943-1945.*
Buchan and Enright,
1983.
◆ LIDDELL HART (CAPTAIN
B.) : *The Other Side of
the Hill.* Cassel,
1951. (ed.)
The Rommel Papers.
Collins, 1953.
◆ OVERY (R.-J.) :
The Air War 1939-1945.
Stein and Day,
New York, 1981.
◆ RITGEN (H.) :
*Die Geschichte
der Panzer Lehr
Division im Westen,
1944-1945.*
Motorbuch Verlag,
Stuttgart, 1979.
◆ SHULMAN (M.) :
Defeat in the West.
Secker and Warburg,
1947.
◆ STACEY (COLONEL C.-P.) :
*The Canadian Army,
1939-1945.*
The King's Printer,
Ottawa, 1948.
◆ WILMOT (C.) :
*The Struggle for
Europe.* Collins, 1952.

◆ MEMOIRS ◆

◆ BRADLEY (GENERAL O.) :
A Soldier's Story. Holt,
New York, 1951.
◆ COLLINS (GENERAL
J.-L.) : *Lightning Joe.*
Baton Rouge, 1979.
◆ CHURCHILL (W. S.) : *The
Second World War.* 6
vols. Cassell,
1948-51.
◆ DE GUINGAND
(GENERAL SIR F.) :
Operation Victory.
London, 1947.
◆ EISENHOWER (GENERAL
D.-D) :
Crusade in Europe.
Heinemann, 1948.
◆ GUDARIAN (GENERAL
H.) : *Panzer Leader.*
Michael Joseph, 1952.
◆ HORROCKS (GENERAL
SIR B.) :
Corps Commander.
London, 1977.
◆ MONTGOMERY FEILD
(MARSHAL VISCOUNT) :
Memoirs.
Fontana, 1960.

◆ PATTON (GEN. G.-S.) :
War as I knew it.
Houghton Mifflin,
Boston, 1947.
◆ SPEIDEL (GENERAL H.) :
*We Defended
Normandy,*
London, 1951.

D-DAY
◆ PREPARATION ◆

◆ DUNCAN (N.-W.) :
*79th Armoured Division:
Hobo's Funnies,*
London, 1972.
◆ FOOT (M.-R.-D.) :
SOE in France.
H.M.S.O. 1966.
◆ HASWELL (J.) :
*The Intelligence
and Deception of
the D-Day Landings.*
London, 1979.
◆ HINSLEY (F.-H.) :
*British Intelligence in
the Second World War.
Vol. 2.* H.M.S.O. 1981.
◆ HOYT (E.-P.) :
*The Secret Battle of
Slapton Sands.*
Military Heritage Press.
USA, 1985.
◆ KEMP (A.) :
Southhampton at War.
Ensign, Southampton,
1989 and 1995.
*South Hampshire and
the D-Day Landings.*
Milestone Press,
Horndean, 1984.
◆ MORGAN (GENERAL SIR
F.) : *Overture to
Overlord.* Hodder and
Stoughton, 1950.
◆ RUBY (M-F.) :
Section SOE.
Leo Cooper, 1988.
◆ STAGG (J.-M.) :
Forcast for Overlord.
London, 1971.

◆ D-DAY ◆

◆ BERTIN (P.) :
*Ce jour-là
en Normandie.*
Ouest France,
Rennes, 1994.
◆ CAMILLY (J.) :
*6 Juin 1944,
le débarquement.*
Cherche-Midi Editeur,
Paris, 1993.
◆ CARELL (P.) :
*Invasion, they're
coming.*
Harrap, 1962.
◆ COMPAGNON (J.) :
*6 juin 1944.
Débarquement en
Normandie;
victoire stratégique.*
Ouest France,
Rennes, 1984.
◆ CROOKENDEN (N.) :
Drop Zone Normandy.
Ian Allen, 1976.

◆ HOWARTH (D.) :
The Dawn of D-Day.
London, 1959.
◆ JEFFERSON (A.) :
The Guns of Merville.
John Murray, 1987.
◆ JUTRAS (P.) :
*Saint-Mère-Eglise
dans la nuit du 5 au 6.*
Heimdal, Bayeux, 1976.
◆ NELLANDS (R.) AND
DE NORMAN (R.) :
*D-Day 1944.
Voices for Normandy.*
Weidenfeld and
Nicholson, 1993.
◆ KEMP (A.) :
Pegasus Bridge.
Memorial/Ouest France,
Caen, 1995.
◆ PERRAULT (G.) :
*Le Grand Jour :
Le livre anniversaire
du débarquement.*
Lattes, Paris, 1994.
◆ RAGACHE (G.) :
*Le Jour J: 6 juin 1944:
le débarquement.*
Seuil, Pairs, 1984.
◆ RYAN (C.) :
The Longest Day.
Simon and Schuster,
New York, 1959.
◆ TANTER (J.) : *Jour J
en Normandie.*
Charles Corlet,
Conde/Noireau, 1982.
◆ TUTE (W.), COSTELLO
(J.) AND HUGHES (T.) :
D-Day. Sidgwick
and Jackson, 1974.
◆ WARNER (P.) :
The D-Day Landings.
London, 1980.

BATTLE
OF NORMANDY
◆ GENERAL ◆

◆ BADSLEY (S.) :
Normandy 1944.
Campaign Series
No. 1. Osprey, 1990.
◆ BELFEILD (E.)
AND ESSAME (H.) :
*The Battle for
Normandy.*
Leo Cooper, 1975.
◆ BERBAGE (G.) :
*Invasion Journal
Pictorial.* Heimdal,
Bayeux, 1991.
◆ BLUMENSON (M.) :
Breakout and Pursuit.
Dept. of the Army,
Washington, 1962.
◆ D'ESTE (C.) :
Decision in Normandy.
Collins, 1983.
◆ ELLIS (GENERAL L.-F.) :
*Victory in the West.
Vol 1. : The Battle
of Normandy.*
H.M.S.O. 1966.
◆ FLORENTIN (E.) :
Stalingrad en Normandie.
Presses de la Cité.
Paris, 1981.
◆ GALE (GENERAL SIR R.) :
With the 6th Airborne

Division in Normandy.
London, 1948.
◆ HASTINGS (M.) :
*Overlord: D-Day
and the Battle for
Normandy.*
Simon and Schuster,
New York, 1985.
◆ HOW (J.-J.) :
*Normandy : The British
Break-out.* London,
1981.
◆ JACKSON (W.G.F.) :
*Overlord: Normandy
1944.* London, 1978.
◆ KEEGAN (J.) :
*Six Armies in
Normandy.*
Viking, New York,1982.
◆ KEMP (A.) :
*D-Day. The Normandy
Landings
and the Liberation
of Europe.*
Thames and Hudson,
1994.
◆ LANE (R.) :
*The Rangers at the
Point du Hoc.* Heimdal,
Bayeux, 1980.
◆ LEMONNIER (A.-G.) :
*Les Cent Jours
de Normandie.*
France Empire,
Paris, 1961.
◆ LUCAS (J.) AND BARKER
(J.) : *The Killing Ground.*
London, 1978.
◆ McKEE (A.) :
Caen: Anvil of Victory.
London, 1965.
◆ MAULE (H.-G.) :
Caen. London, 1976.
◆ OSE (D.) :
*Entscheidung
im Westen 1944.*
D.V.A. Stuttgart, 1982.
◆ PIEKALKIEWICZ (J.) :
*Invasion: Frankreich
1944.*
Sudwest Verlag Munich,
1979.
◆ QUETEL (C.) :
A Memorial for Peace.
Editions du Regard,
Caen, 1993.
◆ RUGE (F.) :
Rommel in Normandy.
San Raphael,
California, 1979.
◆ STACEY (COLONEL C.-
P.) : *Canada's Battle
in Normandy.*
King's Printer, Ottawa,
1946.

SPECIAL
◆ FORCES ◆

◆ FUNK (A.) :
*Hidden Ally.
The French Resistance,
Special Operations,
and the Landing
in France, 1944.*
Greenwood. Westport,
Connecticut, 1992.
◆ KEMP (A.) :
*The SAS at War,
1941-1945.*

◆ Bibliography

John Murray, 1991.
◆ HASTINGS (M.) :
Das Reich. Michael
Joseph, 1981.

EYE WITNESS
◆ ACCOUNTS ◆

◆HICKEY (MONSIGNOR
M.) : *The Scarlet
Dawn.*
Unipress, Canada,
1980.
◆Jary, Sydney.
18 Platoon.
Sydney Jary Ltd.
Surrey, 1987.
◆ LOVAT (LORD) :
March Past.
Weidenfeld and

Nicholson, 1979.
◆ LUCK (H. VON) :
Panzer Commander.
Praeger,
New York, 1989.
◆ McCONAHEY (W. M.)
: *Battalion Surgeon.*
Priv pub. Rochester,
Minnesota, 1966.

ATLANTIC
◆ WALL ◆

◆ DESQUESNES (R.) :
Le Mur de l'Atlantique.
Heimdal, 1976.
◆ GAMELIN (P.) :
*Les Blockhaus
de l'illusoire.*
Daniel et Cie. Paris,

1984.
◆ PARTRIDGE (C.) :
Hitler's Atlantic Wall.
D.I. Publications,
Guernsey, 1976.
◆ WILT (A.F.) : *The
Atlantic Wall: Hitler's
Defences in the West.*
Ann Arbor, Michigan,
1993.
◆ WIRTZ (A.) :
*Témoins du Mur de
l'Atlantique.*
(Text also in Dutch).
Heimdal, 1944.

◆ GUIDE BOOKS ◆

◆ BENAMOU (J.-P.) :
Normandy 1944,

*an illustrated field
guide.*
Heimdal, Bayeux,
1944.
◆ FLORENTIN (F.)
AND ROUSSEL (P.) :
*Le Guide des plages
du débarquement
et les champs de
bataille de
Normandie.* Presses
de la Cité, Paris,
1984.

All the above
published in London
unless otherwise
stated.

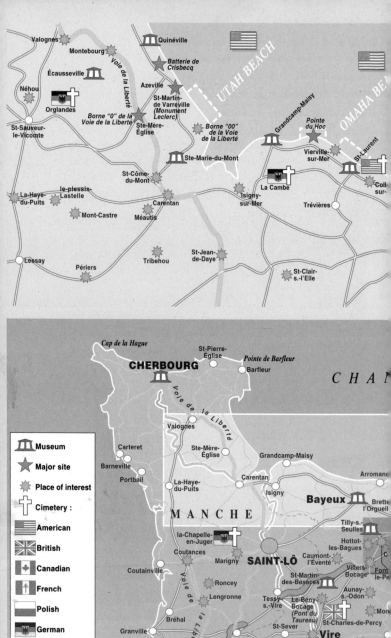

UTAH BEACH

OMAHA BEACH

Valognes
Montebourg
Quinéville
Batterie de Crisbecq
Écausseville
Azeville
Néhou
St-Martin-de-Varreville (Monument Leclerc)
Orglandes
Borne "0" de la Voie de la Liberté
St-Sauveur-le-Vicomte
Ste-Mère-Église
Borne "00" de la Voie de la Liberté
Grandcamp-Maisy
Pointe du Hoc
Vierville-sur-Mer
St-Laurent
Ste-Marie-du-Mont
Colleville-sur
St-Côme-du-Mont
La Cambe
La-Haye-du-Puits
le-plessis-Lastelle
Carentan
Isigny-sur-Mer
Trévières
Mont-Castre
Méautis
Lessay
Périers
Tribehou
St-Jean-de-Daye
St-Clair-s.-l'Elle

Cap de la Hague
St-Pierre-Église
Pointe de Barfleur
CHERBOURG
Barfleur
Voie de la Liberté
CHANNEL
Valognes
Ste-Mère-Église
Carteret
Grandcamp-Maisy
Barneville
Carentan
Portbail
La-Haye-du-Puits
Isigny
Bayeux
Arromanches
Brette l'Orgueil
MANCHE
la-Chapelle-en-Juger
Tilly-s.-Seulles
Coutances
Hottot-les-Bagues
Coutainville
Marigny
Caumont-l'Éventé
SAINT-LÔ
Villers-Bocage
Font le-Pe
Roncey
St-Martin-des-Besaces
Lengronne
Tessy-s.-Vire
Aunay-s.-Odon
Bréhal
Le-Bény-Bocage (Pont du Taureau)
Mon
St-Charles-de-Percy
Granville
St-Sever
Vire
Villedieu-les-Poêles
Cherencé-le-Roussel
Tinchebray
Mont-Saint-Michel
Avranches
Sourdeval
le-Mesnil-Tôve
St-Barthélemy
Fler
le Neufbourg
Juvigny-le-Tertre
Ossuaire du Mont d'Huisnes
Pontaubault (Pont)
Mortain
Domfront
Carrefour des Closeaux
St-Hilaire-du-Harcouët
St-James
Ambrières-les-Vallées
Fougères

Legend

🏛 Museum

⭐ Major site

✴ Place of interest

✝ Cimetery :

🇺🇸 American

🇬🇧 British

🍁 Canadian

✝ French

🇵🇱 Polish

German

Normandy landing site protected by the Conservatoire du Littoral

A Normandie-Terre-Liberté signpost is found at each historic site of the Battle of Normandy Open-Air Museum (the sites are indicated by a star on this map).